# Multidisciplinary Perspectives on Family Violence

Edited by Renate C.A. Klein

ROUTLEDGE
London and New York

First published 1998
by Routledge
11 New Fetter Lane, London EC4P 4EE

Simultaneously published in the USA and Canada
by Routledge
29 West 35th Street, New York, NY 10001



Typeset in Palatino by Routledge
Printed and bound in Great Britain by MPG Books Ltd, Bodmin



*British Library Cataloguing in Publication Data*
A catalogue record for this book is available from the British Library

*Library of Congress Cataloguing in Publication Data*
Multidisciplinary perspectives on family violence / [edited by] Renate C.A. Klein.
p. cm.
Includes bibliographical references and index.
1. Family violence – Research. 2. Family violence – Cross-cultural studies. I. Klein, Renate, 1959– .
HV6626.M85 1998
362.82'92–dc21 97-30855
CIP

ISBN 0–415–15844–3 (hbk)
ISBN 0–415–15845–1 (pbk)

# Contents

# Tables

# Contributors

**Ileana Arias** Department of Psychology, University of Georgia, USA

**Rebekah Bradley** Department of Psychology, University of South Carolina, USA

**M. Angeles Cerezo** Department of Psychology, University of Valencia, Spain

**Rosaleen Croghan** Department of Psychology, Open University, UK

**Keith Davis** Department of Psychology, University of South Carolina, USA

**Frank D. Fincham** School of Psychology, University of Wales, United Kingdom

**Carol Hagemann-White** Department of Educational and Cultural Sciences, University of Osnabrück, Germany

**Renate C.A. Klein** Department of Human Development and Family Studies, University of Maine, USA

**Anna Kwiatkowska** Department of Psychology, University of Warsaw at Bialystok, Poland

**Didier Le Gall** Department of Sociology, University of Caen-Basse Normandie, France

**Sylvia Mastenbroek** Private Psychotherapy Practice, Amsterdam, The Netherlands

**Dorothy Miell** Department of Psychology, Open University, UK

**K. Daniel O'Leary** Department of Psychology, The University at Stony Brook, USA

**Renée Römkens** Faculty of Social Sciences, University of Utrecht, The Netherlands

**Bo Wagner Sørensen** Department of Anthropology, University of Copenhagen, Denmark

**Mara Theodossopoulou** School of Philosophy, University of Athens, Greece

**Vana Theodossopoulou-Papalois** The London School of Economics, University of London, UK

Chapter 1

# Conflict and violence in the family

## Cross-disciplinary issues

*Renate C.A. Klein*

Renate Klein teaches family conflict and domestic violence at the University of Maine. Her work on conflict in close relationships is widely published. She is founder and coordinator of the European Research Network on Family Conflict and Domestic Violence.

*I received my doctoral degree in psychology from the University of Marburg, Germany. My current research focuses on couple conflict, especially on the role of informal third parties such as friends and family and on couples' perceptions of how legitimate their conflicting interests and demands are.*

*Research on family conflict and domestic violence has developed rapidly over the last two decades, in some countries more so than in others, and has become very specialized within the conceptual and methodological bounds of different disciplines. In this chapter I would like to draw the reader's attention to a number of interesting conceptual questions that cut across disciplinary and national boundaries and have the potential to generate interdisciplinary research on family conflict and domestic violence, which may deepen our understanding of this important topic.*

### ABOUT THIS BOOK

In the spring of 1995, I began to interest social scientists in Europe and the USA in an interdisciplinary symposium on family conflict and domestic violence. The only thing we knew about each other at that point was that we were open to "diversity" and curious to see how scholars from neighboring disciplines and countries approach the study of conflict and violence in personal relationships. In the course of one year, a loose network of researchers formed on the Internet, some of whom met in person in the summer of 1996 in Banff, Canada, for a full day workshop at the biennual meeting of the International Society for the Study of Personal Relationships (ISSPR). In the meantime, ISSPR had encouraged the idea of publishing a book based on the Canada symposium and became its sponsor.

The purpose of this book is to cross disciplinary and national boundaries by bringing together scholars from different cultural, intellectual, and disciplinary backgrounds. The book does not provide an entirely comprehensive overview of interdisciplinary or international work on family conflict and domestic violence, the field is much too broad for that purpose. However, the book is representative and testifies to the diversity of research approaches in this field and, at the same time, highlights converging ideas, complementary findings, and exciting common ground.

## OVERVIEW

While each chapter is a self-contained unit, the book as a whole offers a "tour" of some of the challenging terrain of relationship territory. As a tour map for this terrain, this introduction highlights the following chapters, their internal character and collective contribution. The introduction also points out themes that are shared across disciplines and the questions they raise about conflict and violence in the family.

This book takes you on a trek through an imaginary neighborhood, where we visit "nuclear" families, hear from the extended family and look at the wider community in which families and relationships exist. We witness struggles for power, safety and integrity, and the never-ending quest of explaining why those we love do sometimes hurt us. As for appropriate gear, the reader needs intellectual curiosity and conceptual stamina, but no specialized knowledge of any particular discipline.

Each chapter is preceded by a short biographical paragraph which describes the author's academic background and the particular vantage point from which he or she observes conflict and violence in the family. As there are many ways of observing relationships, and many things to see, these introductions may help understand each author's academic ancestry and angle of vision.

Part I, *Dyadic Dilemmata*, concerns the dynamics of abusive interpersonal relationships and individuals' attempts to cope with abuse.

In Chapter 2 we find ourselves in an imaginary kitchen or living room sneaking a view behind closed doors and observing parent–child confrontations first hand. M. Angeles Cerezo (University of Valencia, Spain) describes sequential analyses of coercive parent–child interactions in abusive and nonabusive families. Her work focuses on common parent–child confrontations and their potential to escalate into child abuse. While most families experience minor forms of coercive episodes, in some families they escalate into physical abuse. For instance, micro-level analyses of such episodes indicate that, in abusive parent–child dyads, a coercive behavior is more likely to invoke a consistent but negative response from either interaction partner, thus creating a predictable social environment, albeit at a very high price.

In Chapter 3 we have settled down in the living room and listen to how mothers account for the difference between their expectations of ideal family life and their actual experiences of it. Rosaleen Croghan and Dorothy Miell (both at the Open University, UK) introduce us to women who are experiencing the stress of first-time mothering with no support from their partners as well as to women who have experienced abuse as children or adults. We hear how these women try to explain the obvious discrepancies between ideal and real family life, and how cultural notions of appropriate gender roles supply this interpretive activity with its central arguments.

Chapter 4 focuses on a related dyadic dilemma: physical abuse of teenage girls by their boyfriends. Renée Römkens (University of Utrecht) and Sylvia Mastenbroek (psychotherapist in private practice, Amsterdam) provide an overview of recent surveys on dating violence and present findings of an in-depth interview study with teenage girls who reflect on past abusive relationships. The issues the young women raise illustrate the ambivalence of meanings in dating relationships and the importance of drawing fine lines, such as deciding whether the boy's behavior is attentive or controlling, whether his strength, imagined or real, is reassuring or dangerous, and which of the woman's own mixed feelings should have priority (e.g. feeling hurt versus being in love).

Part II, *Extended Family*, goes beyond the nuclear family and intimate dyadic relationships. To stay with the initial metaphor, we are now leaving the family home for a stroll through the neighborhood where we meet members of the extended family.

In Chapter 5 we hear more from teenagers. Didier Le Gall (University of Caen, France) presents findings from an extensive interview study with young men and women in their late teens. As they become more and more aware of disagreements and tensions in their families, their notions of the ideal family change, and this awareness, even though painful, is part of their transition to adult life. Le Gall takes a wide perspective and touches on issues such as "camps" and "alliances" in the extended family, the resurrection of old sibling conflicts at the entry into adult life, and class-related patterns of conflict expression and management.

In Chapter 6 we enter the living room of another nuclear family and witness how they discuss a problem that arose in another branch of the extended family. Using a participant–observer approach Vana Theodossopoulou-Papalois (London School of Economics, UK) and Mara Theodossopoulou (University of Athens, Greece) document a real-life conflict-resolution discussion in a Greek family. The immediate discussants of this case are mother, father, and their grown daughter who discuss a problem that arose when the mother's sister and her husband took a loan from the mother's parents but didn't pay it back. The mother has become the extended family's designated mediator and has to develop an intervention strategy. Theodossopoulou-Papalois and Theodossopoulou focus on how mother, father and daughter interpret the conflict in terms of the Greek notion of *philotimo* ("love of honor"). Thus, conflict explanations, this time by third parties, arise from each party's unique interpretation of a shared psychocultural concept.

Part III, *Cultures and Communities*, concerns traditions, gender stereotypes, and beliefs about violence against women in the community. In Chapter 7 Anna Kwiatkowska (University of Warsaw at Bialystok, Poland) argues that cultural, religious and political traditions inform gender stereotypes, which in turn are related to beliefs about family violence. She describes female and male gender stereotypes in a sample of Polish teachers and examines the extent to which such stereotypes predict beliefs about family violence.

In Chapter 8 Bo Wagner Sørensen (University of Copenhagen, Denmark) extends the analysis of cultural understandings beyond his own country of origin in his field work on Greenland. Sørensen illustrates the part that cultural interpretations play in explanations for wife beating and how they can be adapted for different "purposes." For instance, such explanations change when his informants shift their focus from specific cases of wife beating to wife beating in general. They also change when a nationalist agenda (i.e. Greenlandic sovereignty *vis-à-vis* former colonial power Denmark) overshadows concern for women's rights; similar influences on explanations for violence against women also appear in Anna Kwiatkowska's analysis.

In Chapter 9 Carol Hagemann-White (University of Osnabrück, Germany) concludes Part III with an essay on the feminist movement in Germany and its action to prevent violence against women. She integrates feminist analyses with an examination of violence as a relational phenomenon and, informed by feminist practice and keen insight, transcends both approaches placing violence against women in the wider community in which families and personal relationships are embedded. Her conclusions emphasize the need to create, and breathe life into, a "symbolic community" of women *and* men who reject violence against women and live an ethic of mutual respect; a community that offers the solidarity, support, and moral clarity in which healing and justice are possible for all victims of violence.

Our trek of the neighborhood ends here and we can reflect on what we have seen along the way as, in Part IV, have Frank Fincham (University of Wales, United Kingdom), Rebekah Bradley and Keith Davis (University of South Carolina, USA), Ileana Arias (University of Georgia, USA) and Daniel O'Leary (The University at Stony Brook), who share their impressions of the journey in four final commentaries.

## CROSS-DISCIPLINARY ISSUES

### Interests, interpretations, and power

Chapters 2 to 9 focus on "contested events" in family and personal relationships such as mother–child confrontations, men's lack of participation in child care, or boys coercing their girlfriends into having sex. The term "contested events" is used to emphasize that different characteristics of interpersonal conflicts can be contested. In the present collection of articles, three such characteristics stand out: interests, interpretations, and power. These features may co-occur but are conceptually and experientially distinct.

A common contested event in Römkens and Mastenbroek's study is sex in teenage dating relationships that can be used to illustrate the differences between interests, interpretations, and power. The notion of *contested interests* refers to conflicts of interest and the incompatible, or seemingly incompatible aspirations and demands of the conflict parties, in this case whether or not to have sex (Klein 1995; Margolin 1988; Rubin *et al.* 1994). The notion of *contested interpretations* refers to the ambiguity in interpreting interpersonal contested events. For instance, does the boyfriend's insistence on having sex indicate love and affection or self-concern and disrespect? *Contested power* refers to the struggle for interpersonal dominance and control: Is the boy going to coerce his girlfriend into having sex?; how much force does he use?; and how much resistance can she muster? Cerezo's studies provide another example: Mother–child confrontations can arise from conflicts of interest (e.g. when to go to bed), are subject to different interpretations (e.g. child noncompliance means aggression versus noncompliance means autonomy), and can escalate into power struggles (e.g. who will have the upper hand). From this perspective, both examples suggest that contested events are prone to turn abusive only when the contest for power takes precedence over the contest of interest and interpretation—an argument central to feminist analyses of violence against women.

The remainder of this introductory chapter offers some thoughts on how interests, interpretations, and power may be related. The interplay of interests, interpretations, and power suggests several interesting cross-disciplinary research questions about the relationship between interpretation and power, the relationship between conflict and violence, the role of sociocultural beliefs and local communities, and their effects on individual identity.

In the dating example, both girl and boy may struggle to interpret their feelings and desires and explore the meaning of love and sex, intimacy and respect. This "interpretive activity" (Ross 1993) is an important, perhaps essential, part of development and maturation. The situation changes as soon as the boy tries to coerce his girlfriend into sexual activity. This coercion constitutes the abuse, not the confusion of interpretations. Furthermore, the very use of force is apt to prevent both girl and boy from developing a clearer understanding of love and intimacy as it does not allow for the time, safety, and freedom necessary to figure out complicated interpersonal events.

While contested choices may be the stuff of confrontation and disagreement, uncontested choices can also be telling. For instance, whereas mothers' decisions to leave an abusive partner were contested by their daughters, fathers' decisions to leave their families were not (see Croghan and Miell); whereas the anthropologist wanted the police to intervene during a fight, the locals did not (see Sørensen).

**Relationship between interpretation and power**

Do partners, as we have argued, interpret their interactions within a context of power and utilize their power in ways suggested by their interpretations (Klein and Johnson 1997)? Apparently, "self-limiting" and "self-liberating" interpretations of the same behavior are possible. For example, Römkens and Mastenbroek suggest that adolescent girls gained power once they reinterpreted their boyfriends' controlling behavior as unwelcome and abusive. By implication, interpreting the boy's controlling behavior as a sign of love limited the girl's personal power. In other situations, lack of power limits the interpretations that a partner can entertain convincingly, such as in the accounts of the women interviewed by Croghan and Miell who were struggling to convince themselves that they were having egalitarian relationships while they were unable to obtain the kind of support from their partner that would have been an indication of equality.

The process of interpreting interpersonal events—of "making meaning" (Duck 1994) requires time and space: the time to reflect and reconsider, to talk with the Other and to talk with third parties; and the personal space where an individual can safely think and experiment with meanings and revise them if they are not convincing. This includes the personal space to draw and revise interpersonal boundaries (e.g. How much do I trust this person? What kind of sexual contact do I want and what kind do I not want?). For two individuals to engage in these complex and potentially time-consuming activities, they need to give themselves and each other the necessary time and personal space. If the boy forces his girlfriend to have sex he not only violates her space and interferes with her interpretive activity, he also passes up the opportunity to develop his own understanding of interpersonal events as he does not take the time to reconsider his motives and actions.

Thus, using coercion to exercise power over another individual seems to impair both partners' ability to interpret and understand contested events. In this regard it is interesting to consider a developmental psychologist's view of children's conflict strategies. Shantz (1993) classifies such strategies according to the "degree to which strategies appear to require the use of social knowledge of others' psychological functioning, that is, from minimal knowledge being needed to flee or *use force* to maximal knowledge to reason and compromise" (p. 190, emphasis mine).

**Relationship between conflict and violence**

Political scientist Marc Ross is among the many social scientists who have argued that conflict is "interpretive activity" (Ross 1993; see also Mather and Yngvesson 1981; Morley 1992). Three examples illustrate the notion of interpretive activity, one from anthropology, one from developmental psychology, and one from feminist analyses of wife beating. From a comparative analysis of different societies Ross (1993) concluded that the evolution of conflict depends on how societies interpret and construct interpersonal or intergroup problems such as the acquisition of scarce resources. Apparently, similar interpretive activity occurs on the playground. Research on childhood aggression indicates that boys who are considered aggressive by their peers more often interpret accidental collisions of the playground as deliberate aggression from others against which they feel the need to defend themselves (Lochman and Dodge 1994). This view of aggressive responses to interpersonal encounters is strikingly similar to feminist analyses of wife beating, which emphasize how abusive men interpret and construe their female partner's behavior as hostile and provocative regardless of what their partner is actually doing (Dobash and Dobash 1979). Analyses of batterers' motivations also indicate that batterers actively construe their victims as the appropriate targets for their aggression independent of the victims' actions (Corson 1989; Dutton 1995).

Conflict indicates that family members or relationship partners contest each other's choices and interpretations. From the above analysis of interpretation and power it follows that, although conflict and violence can co-occur, conflict-management does not necessarily require any form of violence. In contrast, the use of force to "resolve" conflict is apt to stifle interpretation and thus prevent more advanced understandings of the actors and their relationships. The fact that many conflicts involve violence does not mean that violence is necessary to resolve them. It rather indicates that those who use violence either cannot think of a better strategy or believe violence to be the method of choice.

In addition, the co-occurrence of conflict and violence can be due to the fact that there is a conflict of interest as well as a struggle for dominance and control. While the conflict of interest could be resolved peacefully, the struggle for dominance thrives on the use of coercion. Although violent attacks in the family may appear to be out-of-control events, feminists have argued convincingly that male violence against women is not an indication of loss of control but rather a means of establishing control (e.g. Horsfall 1991; Yllö 1993). Violence indicates that one family member is ready to back up his or her bid for influence with pure force, even at the expense of the other's safety and integrity. More recently, social psychologists Tedeschi and Felson (1994) suggested that aggression and violence be understood as coercive processes that reflect the aggressor's deliberate decision (a) to use force against the victim and, more specifically, (b) the decision to punish the victim for perceived transgressions or to retaliate against perceived wrongdoing. Both the feminist and the social psychological argument have at least two important implications for conflict and violence in the family. First, they highlight that the use of force is a matter of choice within the individual's control, not outside of it. Second, they imply that the aggressor interprets or construes family events as though they required the use of force. This perspective concurs with Sørensen's arguments that men beat their wives "in order to" coerce or punish them rather than "because of" alcohol intoxication or loss of control.

### Sociocultural beliefs

Sociocultural beliefs such as gender stereotypes (Kwiatkowska), notions of the ideal family (Croghan and Miell, Le Gall), or values (Theodossopoulou-Papalois and Theodossopoulou) can guide the interpretation of contested events. For instance, Croghan and Miell describe how beliefs about appropriate gender roles (e.g. with regard to child care responsibilities) influence the "interpretive repertoires" of women whose experiences are at odds with available cultural models. Theodossopoulou-Papalois and Theodossopoulou argue that the value of "philotimo" influences conflict-management in an informal family setting. Much of the work presented in this volume suggests that sociocultural beliefs have implications for community as well as individual identity. Such beliefs can be applied to the individual case but are general enough to appeal to different individuals and give meaning to different case stories. In other words, while they can be used to interpret individual life experiences that are unique and concrete, sociocultural beliefs link such separate experiences on a more abstract level of shared symbolism and meaning.

However, all individual experiences do not fit the proscriptions of cultural beliefs, regardless of how widely they are shared. Instead, experience and belief can provide contradictory messages. Examples of such contradictions are the experience of conflict or abuse and the cultural model of "ideal family"; the experience of coerced sex and the cultural model of romantic love; the experience of breach of trust and the notion of "philotimo"; the presence of violence against women and national images of a peaceful society. Contradictions between experience and beliefs could arise also when the model is negative and the individual experience is positive. For example, in a couple who have switched traditional gender roles, the husband may enjoy caring for the newborn baby while his colleagues consider his decision to quit his job as incomprehensible and "unmanly."

Many examples in this volume contrast women's actual experiences with available sociocultural beliefs "for women," but it is doubtful that only women experience these contradictions. For men, they may occur differently or in different arenas; for instance, the actual experience of alienated work or unemployment and the abstract notion of being the provider, or the actual experience of fear, pain, and injury and the abstract notion of being a hero. Indeed, there are critical debates of sociocultural beliefs about men such as emerging images of "gentle masculinity" in Spain (Hagemann-White, personal communication) as well as those branches of the men's movement in the USA that are interested in transforming traditional male gender stereotypes into images of masculinity that integrate strength and tenderness (Kimmel 1995).

**Local communities**

Another interesting theme arising from this book is the emphasis on local communities ("symbolic communities" in Hagemann-White, "circles" in Le Gall). Both concepts include the individuals who make up a community or social network and the sociocultural beliefs which these individuals sustain (e.g. their attitudes toward women, their notions of decent family life, their ideas about appropriate conflict-management). The notion of local community is interesting because it breaks down the seemingly uniform and impersonal concept of culture into a variety of "local" models that are filled with life by groups of identifiable individuals. Thus, it becomes necessary to be more specific about the nature of local models, and the coexistence of different, perhaps contradictory, beliefs. That is what Kwiatkowska argues when she points out how contradictory gender stereotypes can flourish in one "culture."

Also, it becomes necessary to be more specific about how local communities reach consensus about local cultural models and how they imbue them with legitimacy and clout. The family discussion observed by Theodossopoulou-Papalois and Theodossopoulou could be an example of the interaction processes involved in the emergence of the "local" forms of a general sociocultural concept (i.e. philotimo). In this context also belong the processes of taking side with some branches of the family and distancing oneself from others that Le Gall describes. On the level of the community, Hagemann-White describes how separation from mainstream (male) culture facilitated the emergence of local (female) communities that, in such seclusion, could nurture solidarity for victims of male violence into a strong ethic of respect for the safety and integrity of women.

The contradictions within existing cultural models are apparent in yet another way. Sørensen describes how different local communities (e.g. Greenlandic politicians, anthropologists, women's rights activists) use different templates to explain wife beating depending on their political agenda. He points out that one community can try to generalize its cultural models to others, reminiscent of cultural hegemony.

Obviously, family, social networks, and communities give life to sociocultural beliefs and are the agents of their maintenance and change. There are some interesting parallels in the extent to which contested events are understood as extended family or community affairs and the predominant sociocultural beliefs expressed in the language used to describe such events. For example, Lederach (1991) illustrates how "family conflict" is phrased in a Latin American fishing community. No one uses the term "conflict," let alone "fight." Instead, a son describes how he can "connect" with his father but not with his mother because she is "shut" and "won't let him in." The community talk about how to get to the mother who is considered the central "trunk" of the family tree: the way to the trunk leads through the right "branches." Hence, in order to communicate with his mother the son will start talking to those of his brothers who can connect with her. The son's conflict with his mother is played out not directly but through intermediaries who are engaged in a collective effort to use those interpersonal ties that provide open lines of communication and mutual influence.

This is a conception of contested family events that is less confrontational than the "fight" so commonly used in the USA, a conception that involves other family members besides the "opponents" and does not invoke underlying sociocultural beliefs about winning and losing but rather beliefs about intricate webs, careful disentanglement, and the changing currents of interpersonal affection.

The quality and cross-cultural variability of sociocultural beliefs underlying conflict language and conflict management is not addressed systematically in US family studies. In the neighboring field of negotiation the predominant conceptualization of interpersonal conflict has, for decades, been based on notions of self-interested bargainers who are trying to maximize their gains (cf. Kramer and Messick 1995; Morley 1992). Although this is a legitimate conceptualization of conflict, obvious intercultural differences in bargaining and negotiation (Kimmel 1994) make it necessary to analyze conflict language and conceptualization. Such a "problematization" (Foucault 1976) of concepts is likely to shed more light on how our theoretical, empirical, and pragmatic approaches to conflict are related to underlying sociocultural beliefs and values.

Besides conflict language and symbolism the fishing community example underscores the involvement of informal third parties (e.g. other family members or friends; Klein and Milardo 1993) in what could be construed, or "mistaken," as dyadic conflict between mother and son. Psychological approaches, emphasizing individual cognition and behavior, have underestimated the significance of "others," whereas sociological approaches are more apt to bear such social forces in mind (e.g. Le Gall, Hagemann-White, this volume). Third parties are apt to influence contested events in the family in many ways that go beyond acting as mediators or go-betweens (Kressel and Pruitt 1989). Feedback and support, judgment and interference, or simple disinterest from others in extended family, social network, or community can tip the scales in the contest of interests, interpretations, and power (Baumgartner 1993; Klein and Milardo 1995; Black and Baumgartner 1993).

**Identity**

Last, but not least, contested social events have implications for individual identity. Le Gall explicitly links the experience of conflict and the ensuing reinterpretation of sociocultural notions (e.g. ideal family) to individual growth and maturation. Similarly, Croghan and Miell emphasize the implications for identity of contradictions between experience and sociocultural beliefs. Such contradictions provide the impetus to develop more complex forms of identity that are able to integrate conflicting "data." Hence, the contest of interests and interpretations holds the potential for individual growth. In contrast, the contest of power, or more precisely the use of violence and coercion, is likely to impede individual growth. Extreme violence and abuse threaten to annihilate the identity of the victim and corrupt that of the perpetrator (Seifert 1996). When the use of force engenders feelings of strength, power, and safety in the aggressor that are experienced concurrently with the victim's fear, pain, and vulnerability, we are looking at an experience that lends itself to the conclusion that a "strong" Self requires a "weak" Other. Thus, violence is apt to mesh the identities of victim and perpetrator, defining the strength of the latter through the defeat of the former and thus preventing the development of independent identities for both.

The contest of interests, interpretations, and power raises many questions about the complex relationships between conflict and violence, sociocultural beliefs, community and identity. Trekking through the strenuous terrain of family conflict and domestic violence, the reader will encounter both detailed maps of well-charted territory and surprising vistas of unexplored space.

## ACKNOWLEDGEMENTS

Many thanks to Bob Milardo, Gary Schilmoeller and Marc Baranowski in the Department of Human Development and Family Studies for comments on an earlier draft and to Eloise Kleban in the University of Maine Computing Center who expertly (and patiently) would open chapter files for me that I could not read.

## BIBLIOGRAPHY

Baumgartner, M.P. (1993) "Violent networks: The origins and management of domestic conflict," in R.B. Felson and J.T. Tedeschi (eds) *Aggression and violence*, Washington: American Psychological Association.

Black, D. and Baumgartner, M.P. (1993) "Toward a theory of the third party," in D. Black (ed.) *The social structure of right and wrong*, San Diego: Academic Press.

Corson, J.A. (1989) *Stress, self-concept, and violence*, New York: AMS Press.

Dobash, R.E. and Dobash, R. (1979) *Violence against wives*, New York: Free Press.

Duck, S. (1994) *Meaningful relationships*, Thousand Oaks, CA: Sage.

Dutton, D.G. (1995) *The batterer: A psychological profile*, New York: Basic Books.

Foucault, M. (1976) *Histoire de la sexualité, Vol. 1: La volonté de savoir*, Paris: Gallimard.

Horsfall, J. (1991) *The presence of the past: Male violence in the family*, North Sydney: Allen & Unwin.

Kimmel, P.R. (1994) "Cultural perspectives on international negotiations," *Journal of Social Issues* 50: 179–196.

Kimmel, M.S. (1995) *Manhood in America: A cultural history*, Berkeley: University of California Press.

Klein, R.C.A. (1995). "Integrative Konfliktlösung in engen Paarbeziehungen" [Integrative conflict resolution in close relationships], report to the German Research Foundation.

Klein, R.C.A. and Johnson, M.P. (1997) "Strategies of couple conflict," in S. Duck, K. Dindia, W. Ickes, R. Milardo, R. Mills and B. Sarason (eds) *Handbook of personal relationships* (2nd edn), Chichester: Wiley.

Klein, R.C.A. and Milardo, R.M. (1993) "Third-party influences on the management of personal relationships," in S. Duck (ed.) *Social context and relationships*, Newbury Park, CA: Sage.

—— (1995) "The social context of pair conflict: Origin and function of informal third parties," paper presented at the 1995 conference of the International Network on Personal Relationships, Williamsburg, Virginia.

Kramer, R.M. and Messick, D.M. (eds) (1995) *Negotiation as a social process*, Thousand Oaks, CA: Sage.

Kressel, K. and Pruitt, D.G. (1989) *Mediation research*, San Francisco: Jossey-Bass.

Lederach, J.P. (1991) "Of nets, nails, and problems: The folk language of conflict resolution in a Central American setting," in K. Avruch, P.W. Black and J.A. Scimecca (eds) *Conflict-resolution: Cross-cultural perspectives*, Westport, CT: Greenwood.

Lochman, J.E. and Dodge, K.A. (1994) "Social-cognitive processes of severely violent, moderately aggressive, and nonaggressive boys," *Journal of Consulting and Clinical Psychology* 62: 366–374.

Margolin, G. (1988) "Marital conflict is not marital conflict is not marital conflict,"

in R. De V. Peters *et al.* (eds) *Social learning and systems approaches to marriage and the family*, New York: Brunner/Mazel.
Mather, L. and Yngvesson, B. (1981) "Language, audience, and the transformation of disputes," *Law and Society Review* 15: 775–821.
Morley, I.E. (1992) "Intra-organizational bargaining," in J.F. Hartley and G.M. Stephenson (eds) *Employment relations*, Cambridge, MA: Helm.
Ross, M.H. (1993) *The culture of conflict*, New Haven: Yale University Press.
Rubin, J.Z., Pruitt, D.G. and Kim, S.H. (1994) *Social conflict: Escalation, stalemate, and settlement* (2nd edn), New York: McGraw-Hill.
Seifert, R. (1996) "The second front: The logic of sexual violence in wars," *Women's Studies International Forum* 19: 35–43.
Shantz, C.U. (1993) "Children's conflicts: Representations and lessons learned," in R.R. Cocking and K.A. Renninger (eds) *The development and meaning of psychological distance*, Hillsdale, NJ: Erlbaum.
Tedeschi, J.T. and Felson, R.B. (1994) *Violence, aggression, and coercive action*, Washington, DC: American Psychological Association.
Yllö, K.A. (1993) "Through a feminist lens: Gender, power, and violence," in R.J. Gelles and D.R. Loseke (eds) *Current controversies on family violence*, Newbury Park, CA: Sage.

# Part I

# Dyadic dilemmata

Chapter 2

# Parent–child conflict, coercive family interaction, and physical child abuse

*M. Angeles Cerezo*

M. Angeles Cerezo is Professor of Psychology at the University of Valencia, Spain, and the director of the Aggression and Family Research Unit. She received her degree in psychology at the University of Valencia and her doctorate in psychology at the University of Madrid. She also received the National Best Academic Achievement Award presented by H.M. Juan Carlos I, King of Spain. As a Fulbright Scholar she received her post-doctoral research training at the Child Behavior Institute with Robert G. Wahler at the University of Tennessee, USA.

*As a scientist dedicated to the study of the behavior and psychological functioning of human beings, it is a challenge to understand the keys of violence, particularly between parents and children. In order to provide effective prevention and treatment strategies we need to understand the factors involved in conflict and violence cycles, verbal or physical, that characterize the lives of some families.*

*As a citizen, I am concerned about the multiple faces of violence in our societies. As a mother, I am interested in family life and its problems because the family is the primary school where the next generation of men and women is growing up right before our eyes.*

*Violence and parent–child conflict is by definition an interactional issue and to understand this issue one needs not only a macrolevel approach but also a microanalysis focused on the ongoing social exchanges that crystallize into automatic routines. Particular interaction patterns play an important role as the immediate context of physical assault, and the study of these phenomena requires observational methodology. Advances in this particular area of knowledge help design treatment strategies based on changing the relationship through changing the interactional patterns. I believe both macrolevel and microlevel factors need to be addressed. I also believe that the relationship between these macro- and microlevels needs to be further theorized in psychology. Observational research offers a unique and rich picture of parent–child interaction that complements other pieces of information provided by other methodological approaches. In other words, as I usually say to my psychology students, there are two broad ways of approaching people: "to look," or "to ask"—so far, my main focus of research has been based on "looking."*

*I would like the reader to take home three thoughts from this chapter. First, that a fundamental key for understanding physical child abuse is found in parent–child interaction processes, which are more complex than looking at just the parent or just the child. Some results indicate that the interaction processes should be considered in a broader window than just the adjacent pairs of sequences, such as in the case of the notion of unpredictability. Second, from a developmental perspective, the negative interactional experiences that are involved in a dysfunctional parent–child relationship affect the optimal development of the child's competencies. Third, from a macrolevel approach, there are factors that contextualize the family interaction and affect the micro cosmos of the ongoing interaction. Consequently, we need to integrate both levels of approaches to understand violence in the parent–child relationship.*[1]

"For the children and their special world that can help grown-ups grow so much."

In the family violence field, abusive parenting represents not only a major area but also its harshest facet because abusive parenting implies children's suffering within the very context that is expected to affectively support and protect them. Children who are victims of their parents' chronic aggression, besides being physically threatened and harmed, are under severe psychological stress due to their affective bond with, and their physical dependency on, the perpetrator.

Physical child abuse involves severe interactional disturbances in the family. The family, which may be considered as a relational matrix, is the place where the child has to accomplish his or her socialization and developmental processes, and the primary caregiver, through appropriate parenting, has to provide the child with the physical and psychological support needed to go through these processes. From this perspective, child maltreatment represents an extreme form of dysfunctional parenting that threatens and affects the development of the child's competence in its sociocognitive, emotional and behavioral domains (Cerezo 1995; Cerezo and Frias 1994; Wolfe 1987).

A more detailed look at parenting practices leads us to consider them not in terms of a dichotomous or bipolar category (i.e. good vs bad practices) but rather in terms of a continuum of competence, where competent practices represent one extreme end and incompetent or inappropriate practices the other. Competent practices are displayed by appropriately resolving child-rearing conflicts, and by positive, affective interactions that help children accomplish their developmental milestones. Incompetent practices are reflected in inappropriate parental skills to resolve child-rearing conflicts, and inadequate care and affection for the child (Ammerman 1990; Cerezo 1992; Cicchetti and Rizley 1981; Wolfe 1987). This view of parenting practices allows us to consider child abuse in terms of the *degree* to which parents use negative, inappropriate child-rearing and control strategies with the child (Wolfe 1987) and to destroy the conventional myth that inappropriate practices do not coexist with some appropriate care in violent families (Gelles and Cornell 1990).

The interactional nature of the processes involved in child abuse has been considered since the late 1970s (Ammerman and Hersen 1990; Parke and Collmer 1975; Reid *et al.* 1982; Wolfe 1985, 1987). From an interactional approach, the interpersonal setting between the parenting adult and the child is underscored as the immediate context of abuse. Consequently, confrontations arising from common child-rearing problems—and the parental functioning required to cope with these problems—directly affect the likelihood of abuse. Abused children living in adverse family contexts, in turn, are more likely to develop psychological disorders that put limited parenting skills further to the test, thus highlighting the interactional nature of family processes (Kadushin 1981; Parke and Collmer 1975; Vasta and Copitch 1981).

The interactive nature of the processes involved in child abuse leads us to focus on the detailed study of family interactions that may be considered as the microsocial level of family relationships (Cerezo 1997). Observational strategies provide a fine-grained analysis of the stream of social exchanges; these strategies are particularly helpful in families characterized by conflict and violence. In fact, some studies reveal that up to 60 percent of physically abusive episodes take place in the context of a conflict which escalates into assault (Gil 1970). Not only are inadequate parenting strategies overt in the context of conflict but so are the reciprocal influences between parent and child.

Within the past fifteen years, child maltreatment researchers have made an effort to develop comprehensive theories of the etiology of physical child abuse (Azar 1991; Tzeng *et al.* 1991). However, there is a need to focus on the "critical causes" of child abuse that provide explanations of its origins and lead to its prevention (Crittenden and Ainsworth 1989). The interactive processes and patterns through which the complex social phenomena of conflict and parental violence against children are sustained and experienced, constitute critical factors that point out prevention and treatment strategies.

The present chapter examines relevant interactive patterns that initiate or maintain child abuse in the context of the family process. On the one hand, this micro-level view is completed by analyzing the role of the child's negative interactional experiences within family in the development of the child's competence; on the other it is completed by providing a broader focus on the setting factors that contextualize the abusive parenting. Some critical questions are discussed, and the connecting points between the interactive patterns and the broader picture of family life are also addressed.

## PARENT–CHILD COERCIVE INTERACTION PATTERNS

Research conducted by Patterson and his associates at the Oregon Social Learning Center (OSLC) about coercive family processes has shed light on the daily interactional patterns of aggressive families (Patterson 1976, 1982; Patterson and Reid 1970). Although this group's research interest has mainly focused on the development of child antisocial behavior, their findings on dysfunctional parenting processes are also applied to families where children are physically abused (Reid *et al.* 1981, 1982). Patterson (1982) reported a study in which three samples of normal, socially aggressive, and abused children were compared on the likelihood of parental aversive consequences for the child's deviant behavior. The abusive parents were more punitive than parents from the other two samples. Both mothers and fathers of abused children were significantly more likely to react aversively to coercive child behavior than parents of normal children. Interestingly, the differences between parents of abused children and socially aggressive children were not significant. These findings highlight parental socialization practices as a link between research on antisocial children and research on child physical abuse. The findings also highlight the coercive process as a parent–child relationship dysfunction associated with unfortunate outcomes for the child who is at risk of being abused and of developing a maladaptive interpersonal style.

### Theoretical background

One basic premise of coercion theory holds that the number and length of parent–child confrontations are increased by poor parenting skills in coping with *common* child-rearing problems. In fact, Patterson underscores as a key assumption that "the analyses of processes comprised of innocuous, garden-variety of aversive events will lead to an understanding of physical violence among family members" (Patterson 1982: 155). According to Patterson (1982), child beatings are thought to be the outcome of processes that have been set in motion for some time. In these processes the dyad moved or "escalated" from the exchange of low amplitude (i.e. minor) aversive events to "the higher amplitude aggressive behaviors which characterized child abuse" (p. 13). This process of changing intensity over time ("escalation") results from extended aversive interchanges, in which anger and hostile attributions play an important role; the development and maintenance of escalation is assumed to be supported by negative reinforcement operations that increase the likelihood of high amplitude responses in future confrontations (Snyder 1991). It should be pointed out that the negative reinforcement arrangements proposed in coercion theory are embedded in social interaction and present important differences from the reinforcement processes studied in the laboratory (Patterson 1982), first, because in social interaction the components in the negative reinforcement arrangements are connected in a probabilistic sense, and, second, because in social interaction the partial changes in the stimuli context contrast with the present/absent condition of the aversive stimulus in the laboratory. Thus, the subject who is behaving aversively and stops his or her behavior after being counterattacked does not leave the situation, it is only that the situation changes.

Coercive behaviors do indeed "pay off" on a short-term basis. However, in the long run, the problem escalates and the coercive process increases the intensity and frequency of parent–child confrontations. Patterson (1982) termed this lack of agreement between the short-term and long-term effects "the reinforcement trap."

## Empirical findings

### *Escalation process*

Some mother–child interactive sequences involving poor parental skills have been used as an operational index of the hypothesized escalation phenomenon in highly coercive families. Thus, to the extent that escalation is operating in these dysfunctional families, we can expect that aversive adult behavior, such as disapproval or reprimand, accelerates the child's aversive response instead of stopping his or her behavior. In other words, the parental response fails to terminate the child's deviant behavior when the child's reaction to this parental response is again aversive. To examine this sequential pattern empirically, Reid *et al.* (1981) conducted an interesting study in which distressed abusive, distressed nonabusive, and nondistressed families were compared. The findings showed that the children were likely to further escalate aversive parental responses and consequently demonstrated the parental lack of skills in handling discipline confrontations. The distressed abusive mothers failed to terminate 53 percent of child aversive sequences, their distressed nonabusive counterparts failed in nearly 35 percent of instances and the nondistressed group failed in only 14 percent. All between-group comparisons were statistically significant. These findings with self-reported cases of abuse were later also supported with documented cases of abuse (Reid cited in Lorber *et al.* 1984).

The hypothesized escalation process, and the abuse as its endpoint, indicates that extended sequences of aversive interactions are more frequent in abusive families, and that the frequency of coercion covaries with its intensity. Results reported by Lorber *et al.* (1984) supported the first hypothesis; compared to distressed nonabusive families and nonproblem families, mothers and children in the abuse group displayed a significantly higher frequency of extended aversive sequences (longer than 18 seconds). In support of the second hypothesis Reid *et al.* (1981) also reported significant correlations in the range from 0.40 to 0.70 between the Total Aversive Behavior score and the Hitting score. Thus, to the extent that the mother increased her coerciveness, the child was at greater risk of physical discipline.

*Parental skills*

Lorber *et al.* (1984) developed a parenting skills index defined as the inappropriateness of a mother's response to her child's behavior in extended sequences of aversive interaction. By considering both pro-social and aversive child behaviors preceding the onset of extended aversive sequence, Lorber and his colleagues distinguished between "unprovoked" and "provoked" aversive maternal responses. They found that abusive mothers were involved with their children in a significantly greater proportion of inappropriateness, or "unprovoked" extended aversive exchanges, than were the distressed nonabusive mothers. Once the abusive mothers were entrapped in these sequences, they also displayed very few skills for effectively stopping the coercive inter-change.

Instructional episodes and discipline represent a major proportion of the parental socialization practices. Consequently, the lack of child-management skills of highly coercive families is particularly overt in command/compliance episodes or disciplinary situations when the parents try to elicit child compliance. Thus, more than 60 percent of abusive incidents registered by the protective services agencies occurred in the context of parental disciplinary action (Gil 1970). When this type of episodes was studied, abusive mothers were found to respond to child noncompliance with more repeated isolated commands and to accom-pany more of them with power-assertive control strategies than with positive oriented strategies. Moreover, these mothers responded as often with power-assertive tactics as with positive responses to their child's compliance, which differs from the nonabusive mothers who respond to their child's compliant behavior with some positive reaction but never with a power-assertive response (Oldershaw *et al.* 1986).

Parental discipline tactics for child transgressions in general, including noncompliance, were studied by Trickett and Kuczynski (1986). The abusive parents were found to use more and more severe forms of physical punishment as disciplinary techniques than did the controls, who used more reasoning and requests. Moreover, when the analyses were focused on the parental consequences considering the different types of child transgression (initial noncompliance, high arousal disruptive behavior, conventional social transgression and moral transgression), results showed that the abusive parents used punishment as a predominant strategy for all of them while nonabusive parents were more flexible in their ability to adapt the control strategy to the kind of child transgression. The nonabusive parents primarily used reasoning as a strategical choice to deal with a child violating norms and values, which are considered transgressions with a long-term effect on the child's functioning.

The sequential approach to the study of instructional coercive episodes provides a complementary perspective about the hypothesized processes of negative reinforcement operations in the mother–child exchanges. Related to this line of thinking, an interesting conceptualization of instructional episodes of Patterson's coercive process is represented by "the maternal compliance hypothesis" (Wahler and Dumas 1986; Wahler *et al.* 1984). In essence, a compliance episode was defined as an interactive sequence where the mother's instructional behavior generates a setting in which the child's oppositional and aversive behavior is successful in terminating the mother's demand; thus, the mother, by her compliant behavior to the child's opposition, escapes from the aversive situation.

The sequential patterning of compliance episodes and the child's aversive behavior was examined in detail by Wahler *et al.* (1990). In their study of distressed but nonabusive dyads they tracked the occurrence of maternal compliance episodes in the stream of the family interactional behavior, and also they tracked the instances of child's deviant behavior out of those maternal compliance episodes. As expected, child aversive behavior functioned to increase the probability of subsequent maternal compliance episodes. In other words, mothers were more likely to yield to their child's opposition within instructional sequences *after* the occurrence of the child's deviant behavior than *before* it. This sequential pattern was also found in abusive dyads (Cerezo and D'Ocon 1995a; D'Ocon 1994). In D'Ocon's (1994) study a nonabusive nonclinical group was included for comparison purposes. The expected sequential relationship between the child's aversive behavior and the maternal compliance episodes was also found in the nonabusive group. However, there were statistically significant differences between abusive and nonabusive dyad that pointed out quantitative rather than qualitative differences between these groups (D'Ocon 1994).

## Additional considerations

Patterson's coercive process model and the main predictions derived from it have found empirical support in abusive families and have greatly contributed to the placement of child physical abuse in the context of parental socialization practices (Cerezo 1997). Although the coercion model and its components have received some criticisms which stimulate scientific debate (Gardner 1989; Knutson 1982; Robinson and Jacobson 1987), it is clearly one of the most valuable programmatic contributions to the field of family violence. An added value of the contribution *per se* is the opening of new perspectives of knowledge in the field and the development of therapeutic strategies for the treatment of family violence and the development of childhood disorders.

Escalation stands out among the various aspects of the coercion model and the hypothesized related processes which have stimulated research. One of the most intriguing phenomena in coercive interaction among dysfunctional families is the short-term impact of aversive consequence as the accelerator of the child's ongoing coercive behavior. The significant accelerating effect that the abusive mother's punishment has on the ongoing child deviant behavior (Patterson 1982; Reid *et al.* 1981) raises the question of why these children are more likely to react aversively than their nonabused counterparts. Research regarding the role of indiscriminate or arbitrary maternal aversive behavior may provide an answer to this question.

# MATERNAL INDISCRIMINATE INTERACTIVE PATTERNS

## Theoretical background

Indiscriminate parenting is an interesting complex notion that is almost as old as Psychology. Since the last century, different theoretical approaches have adduced that indiscriminate or inconsistent socialization negatively affects a child's psychological functioning (Higgins 1966). Indiscriminate parenting can be conceptualized in different ways. First, inconsistency may be *inter*parental, with one parent responding positively to a child's action and the other negatively, or *intra*parental, with one parent responding positively to a given child's behavior at one time and negatively at another; also, after a certain period of time the parent may change his or her pattern—for instance the mother may be positive during the first six months of her baby's life and may then become apathetic, displaying inconsistency which could be termed "temporal." Second, if instead of directing our attention towards the agent, the nature of his or her conduct is considered, indiscriminate parenting can consist in responding with positive behavior regardless of the child's conduct or, contrarily, responding indiscriminately with aversive behaviors. Finally, inconsistent parenting is present when the form of a communication or message is inconsistent with its content.

The notion of inconsistent socialization as parenting practice leads to the consideration of the process from the child's view. When the child receives erratic maternal attention, his or her social interactional context is marked by uncertainty or unpredictability (Cerezo and D'Ocon 1995a). Unpredictability itself can be very aversive, as has been well documented in laboratory studies (for a review, see D'Ocon 1994; Biglan *et al.* 1990). For instance, signaled shock conditions are preferred over unsignaled ones, even when the intensity is higher in the signaled condition (i.e. Badía *et al.* 1973, 1979; Biederman and Furedy 1976). Therefore, it may be assumed that escaping from unpredictable contexts will be rewarding. Because the child's coercive behaviors are those responses that are most likely to elicit aversive though predictable parental responses, this kind of child behavior will be instrumental in escaping from unpredictable contexts and obtaining brief respites of predictable social exchanges: an extended highly coercive parent–child exchange. Interestingly, some classic research points out that the likelihood of aggressive behavior is increased by noncontingent aversive stimulation (Ulrich and Azrin 1962). If, instead of escapable, the shock is inescapable—that is, the subject lacks control over the aversive events—important effects (emotional and cognitive deficits) are expected and learned helplessness is developed, as has been extensively documented by Seligman and his associates (Seligman 1975; Abramson *et al.* 1978) .

This review offers a dense panorama that assists in the placement of recent efforts. It also contrasts the great number of possibilities that remain to be studied, with the specific and limited facet of inconsistency that is currently being studied: i.e. the maternal inconsistent response to child's behavior, operationalized in terms of particular interactive child–mother sequences, which exemplifies maternal reactions that are not attuned, in content or valence, to what her child does or says.

## Empirical findings

The majority of the research carried out by Wahler and his associates at the University of Tennessee has been devoted to translating the notion of maternal inconsistency into observable interactive sequences in multi-stressed families characterized by highly coercive interaction (Cerezo *et al.* 1986; Dumas and Wahler 1985; Wahler and Dumas 1986; Wahler *et al.* 1984).

According to the predictability hypothesis proposed by Wahler and Dumas (1986), the escalation phenomenon that takes place in coercive exchanges is rewarding because the child's aversive behavior is functional in attaining a more predictable maternal response. The hypothesis was initially formulated in correlational terms and found empirical support. However, the exact sequential association between child coercive behaviors and mother indiscriminate attention could not be examined.

The important question regarding whether maternal indiscriminate episodes are more likely before than after child coercive behavior was tested in Wahler *et al.*'s study (1990) by sequential analysis strategies and by using a revised version of the coding system which allowed the use of real-time code (Cerezo *et al.* 1986; Cerezo 1991). In their study with distressed nonabusive mothers, sequential analyses showed a higher conditional probability for indiscriminate episodes *before* a child's coercive behavior, while this value decreased dramatically *after* a child's coercive behavior. Thus, the child's behavior was functional in reducing the probability of indiscriminate episodes. These relationships were also found in a study with child-abusive mothers and their children (Cerezo and D'Ocon 1995a; D'Ocon 1994).

These sequential studies (D'Ocon 1994; Wahler *et al.* 1990) were aimed at examining not only the predictability hypothesis and the compliance hypothesis, a conceptualization of coercive process for instructional episodes, but also the sequential relationship between these two episodes. In this sense, Wahler *et al.* (1990) found that given a compliance episode—that is, a mother's acquiescence to her child's refusal to obey—the likelihood of a following indiscriminate episode was significantly higher than expected. The findings were replicated by D'Ocon (1994) who reported a similar pattern of relationship. The comparison analyses between the precedent lag and the subsequent lag to the compliance episode showed a significant increase of the likelihood of a maternal indiscriminate episode (Cerezo and D'Ocon 1995a).

In contrast to Wahler *et al.*'s (1990) study, D'Ocon (1994) included a comparison group of nonabusive mothers in her study. The sequential relationship between indiscriminate mothering and child coercive behavior obtained in the abusive dyads was also found in the nonabusive dyads, which suggested that the differences between abusive and nonabusive groups were more quantitative than qualitative. However, in nonabusive dyads compliance and indiscriminate episodes were not related at all, suggesting a qualitative difference between the abuse and nonabuse groups. At this point, it is suggested that there may be an unknown threshold for a given mother–child dyad, beyond which, compliance and indiscriminate episodes begin to occur on a contingent basis (Cerezo and D'Ocon 1995a). The present findings are suggestive, and many further studies are needed to reach more definitive conclusions. The main obstacles in this regard are methodological. On the one hand, the interaction is by definition dynamic and occurs over time, therefore analytical instruments need to reflect the ongoing nature of interaction. On the other hand, some of the relevant interactive sequences are low-rate events, which restricts the number of options to analyze these sequences statistically.

The consideration of the nature of a child's antecedent behavior provides a further step in the study of the role of inconsistent socialization. Based on earlier work on maternal inconsistency indices (Cerezo 1992), Cerezo and D'Ocon (1995b) examined maternal inconsistent responses to a child's prosocial (positive or neutral) and maternal inconsistent responses to a child's deviant behavior. In almost two hundred hours of observation, child–mother pair behavior instances were tracked along the stream of behavior in two fifteen-dyad groups, abusive and nonabusive. For each dyad, two scores were computed in terms of the proportion of inappropriate maternal responses relative to the mother's total responses toward the child's behavior, either prosocial or deviant. These ratios were considered as indices of the mother's mistakes in dealing with prosocial or deviant child behavior. A lower ratio indicated fewer mistakes and more discriminate maternal behavior. As expected, in response to the child's prosocial behavior the abusive mothers had a significantly higher ratio of inconsistent responses than the nonabusive mothers. However, in response to negative child behavior the abused mothers displayed a low ratio of inconsistent responses that was similar to that of nonclinical mothers. These findings were supported in an extension of the previous study with twenty-five abusive and twenty-five nonabusive dyads (Cerezo and D'Ocon, forthcoming).

In sum, these studies suggested that abusive mothers could be distinguished from nonabusive mothers on the basis of their indiscriminate behavior in response to the child's prosocial behaviors. Recently this factor has been found to be a relevant predictor of the abusive vs. nonabusive status of a group of dyads (Cerezo *et al.* 1996).

### *Social continuity*

Wahler's (1994) theoretical contribution may be considered as a further step in this line of inquiry. He argued that the notion of social continuity provides a comprehensive framework to interpret the relationship between coercive behavior and inconsistent parenting and the child's entrapment in the coercive process. Social continuity implies that the parent sets the stage for cooperative transactions with the infant/child by detecting and anticipating his or her interests and needs. These transactions are cooperative in the sense that, regardless of who leads, both individuals attend carefully to one another and they act in ways that support the cooperative enterprise. As a result, predictable or synchronous patterns of social exchange with the parent provide the child with social connection. Wahler's arguments point to these predictable or synchronous cooperative exchanges as an indicator of social continuity. In contrast, insensitive "out of synch" care hampers the establishment of social continuity and leads the child to develop disruptive behaviors in an attempt to "create" synchronous interactions. Thus, the child learns to generate synchronicity through coercion by which painful but highly predictable aversive matchups replace unpredictable exchanges. In fact, the child will work toward any sort of predictable connection with the caregiver, even if this connection is aversive and temporary.

The few findings available, as well as common experience, tell us that sometimes nonclinical mothers are arbitrary or inconsistent with their children and also sometimes these children "win" in a confrontation. That is to say, these patterns as such, may, with lower intensity and frequency, appear in mother–child interactions regardless of whether the dyads are clinically coercive or not. Therefore, an important research question that remains to be addressed is: Beyond which point, for a given parent–child dyad, is the occurrence of indiscriminate or compliant episodes no longer occasional, but rather the sign of a serious deterioration of social continuity?

Wahler's (1994) contribution points out conceptual links among findings in social learning, developmental psychology, and child developmental psychopathology. Particularly consistent with Wahler's approach is the research about "synchrony," a property of mother–infant interactions, that summarizes the degree to which a mother's reactions to her child's responses are "relevant" or "appropriate" (Isabella *et al.* 1989; Field *et al.* 1989; Lester *et al.* 1985) and the related area of attachment, where maternal sensitivity in early mother–child interaction is highlighted as a precursor of a child's secure attachment (Ainsworth *et al.* 1978).

In attachment research, Crittenden's studies about child abuse are particularly relevant (Crittenden and Ainsworth 1989). Maltreating mothers tend to be insensitive toward their children and they fail in attuning their behavior to their children's rhythms and needs (Crittenden 1981, 1988; Lyons-Ruth *et al.* 1987). There is no synchrony in the interaction. Longitudinal studies have shown that children with a history of maternal insensitive care are more likely to develop an insecure attachment (Ainsworth *et al.* 1978; Cantero 1996; Crittenden and Ainsworth 1989).

In a longitudinal study by our group, Cantero (1996) reported interesting findings about sequential relationships in mother–child interactions during the first year of life that differentiated securely attached children from insecurely attached children. When a baby acted upset, uncomfortable, or irritable the likelihood of maternal attention and sensitive responses increased significantly for mothers in the securely attached group, whereas the mothers of children who later developed insecure attachment showed no change. In other words, it seemed that the difficult behavior of securely attached babies was functional in getting increased maternal attention attuned to their needs and discomfort, whereas this behavior was not functional among the children who later developed insecure attachment. Although these findings need to be replicated, they suggest that some indices of the deterioration of social continuity can be developed to trace the origins and meanings of parent–child coercive processes in the socialization context.

## THE CHILDREN AND THEIR NEGATIVE INTERACTIONAL EXPERIENCES

Research indicates that dysfunctional parenting practices play a role in the development of child psychological disorders (Jacob 1987). Child physical abuse is an outcome of extreme dysfunctional parenting. Therefore, it is hardly surprising that abused children are at high risk of developing behavioral problems and psychological disorders (Burgess and Richardson 1984; Cerezo 1995; Cicchetti and Olsen 1990).

Studies of infants and preschool children consistently show that abused toddlers are more likely to develop insecure attachment (Youngblade and Belsky 1990). Some studies reported that abused toddlers tend to be delayed or impaired in their affective reactions in self-recognition tasks (Schneider-Rosen and Cicchetti 1991; Lewis and Brooks-Gunn 1979) and that abused preschool children are more likely to show deficits in social relationships with their peers (Main and George 1985).

Physically abused school-aged children present a significantly greater number of behavioral problems than nonabused children according to parents' reports (D'Ocon *et al.* 1996; Kravic 1987; Wolfe and Mosk 1983), and also according to teachers' reports (Erickson *et al.* 1989; Hoffman-Plotkin and Twentyman 1984; de Paúl and Arruabarrena 1995). Particularly relevant are the findings from a randomly selected community sample reported by Dodge *et al.* (1995). Their longitudinal study shows that the experience of intentional physical harm within the first five years of life was associated with a fourfold increase of risk for externalizing conduct problems in Grades 3 and 4.

Likewise, direct observation of children's behavior at home reveals that abused children display a higher rate of deviant behavior than nonabused children (Cerezo 1997). The studies carried out in the Aggression and Family Research Unit consistently found that average rates of child deviant behavior ranged from 0.34 to 0.43 among abused groups (Cerezo 1992; Cerezo and D'Ocon 1995b), a higher value than in nonabused groups. In a recent observational study (Cerezo *et al.* 1996) the "child deviant interactional behavior," which included aversive demands, neutral or negative oppositional behavior, and physical or verbal aversive social approaches, was found to be the most important predictor of status (abusive vs. nonabusive group) membership; this predictor accounted for 28 percent of the variance and the discriminant function correctly classified 74.5 percent of the subjects. These findings are supported by other studies that found abused children to be more oppositional and less compliant (Oldershaw *et al.* 1986) and displaying higher rates of aggressive behavior than their nonabused peers (Bousha and Twentyman 1984; Patterson 1982). In fact, abused children's conduct resembles the behavior displayed by children who are referred for conduct disorders (Lorber *et al.* 1984; Reid *et al.* 1981; Whipple and Webster-Stratton 1991) and Patterson (1986) pointed out that the lack of social survival skills in different relevant areas found in abused children resembled those of their conduct-disordered peers who develop antisocial behavior.

Likewise, a number of studies, both retrospective and prospective, have found a link between early, severe physical child abuse and later delinquent and violent behavior (Lewis *et al.* 1989; McCord 1987). Moreover, Patterson (1986) tested a model that showed strong correlation between harsh and inconsistent parental discipline and the development of child antisocial behavior. In addition to the behavioral facet, the abused children's functioning shows deficits in emotional and cognitive areas. Thus, children who have been victims of physical and emotional abuse show a higher level of depressive symptomatology and depressogenic attributional style than their nonabused peers and report lower self-esteem (Cerezo and Frias 1994; Fantuzzo 1990; Kazdin *et al.* 1985).

In sum, the extreme dysfunctional practices of physically abusive parenting can leave their mark in different domains of child competency. Of course, these marks and their manifestations will depend on the child's developmental stage, and the chronicity and severeness of the dysfunctional interactions. Generally, given that development proceeds by the integration of earlier competencies into later modes of functioning, an early disturbance in functioning may develop into larger disturbances at a later stage (Cicchetti 1989).

## Theoretical approaches

From the child's point of view, abusive parenting occurs in interactional experiences, and in this regard, and despite stemming from different orientations, coercion theory and attachment theory share a common denominator. Both theories agree that the quality of the child's interactional experiences affects the development of his or her competence but they differ in the routes or processes by which the interactional experiences influence the child's functioning. Coercion theory mainly focuses on the reinforcement arrangements that take place in the rapid flow of social exchanges, whereas attachment theory proposes that interactional experiences lead the child to develop internal representations or models of his or her relationship with the caregiver.

Coercion theory, focusing on microprocesses in family interaction, emphasizes the reinforcement operations that take place in fast social exchanges where the interaction partners inadvertently become enmeshed in streams of interaction routines. Thus, parental failures in family management skills set the basis for training the child in coercive behaviors and prevent the child from having critical learning experiences (Patterson 1982).

According to attachment theory (Bowlby 1969, 1973), repeated experiences with his or her primary caregiver lead the infant to develop expectations about the caregiver's future behavior. These expectations are the basis for the infant's development of internal representational models of caregiver and self. Attachment researchers assume that these internal working models "underlie consistent patterns of behavior, [although] neither the model nor the resultant pattern is assumed to be consciously available to the individual" (Crittenden 1992: 330).

Consistently responsive and sensitive care will lead the infant to develop a representational model of the caregiver as accessible and predictable, and a model of self as competent in eliciting the caregiver's response and worthy of it. Consequently, the child will develop a secure attachment. On the contrary, if the parent has been hostile and rejecting, the child's representational model will reflect the expectations of unpredictable maternal care and the self as unworthy and ineffective in getting her sensitive care and the child will develop insecure attachment (Ainsworth *et al.* 1978; Crittenden and Ainsworth 1989).

Because the attachment behavioral system competes with other important systems—namely, the exploratory system with regards to the physical environment, and the affiliative system with regards to the social environment—insecure attachment affects the child's options to explore the immediate physical and social environment. The behavior of a child with insecure or anxious attachment is primarily focused on maintaining proximity to an untrustful figure and this prevents the child from exploring the social or physical environment (Crittenden and Ainsworth 1989).

Therefore, attachment theory points out that the child's previous experience is encoded as an internal representational model about others, self and social relationships, and this affects the ways that the child copes with mother, others and the environment (Crittenden 1992). Consequently, a higher likelihood of difficult social relationships may be expected among those children with an insecure attachment history than among their securely attached counterparts. The social information processing may provide a more detailed picture of the global deficits hypothesized by attachment theory. Thus, findings have been reported that show that children with a history of anxious attachment are more likely to display hostile attributions and perceptual bias than children with a history of secure attachment (Elicker *et al.* 1992).

Regardless of explanatory mechanisms that may explain how the negative interactive experiences involved in abusive parenting affect the child's development of competencies, research points out the relevant role of inadequate response-contingent stimulation that physically abused children experience in their primary social matrix. We believe that interactional studies of physically abused children and their caregivers, in the family context, will help identify the critical factors that, keeping a parsimonious approach to these phenomena, point toward effective treatment and prevention strategies.

## THE CONTEXTUAL FACTORS IN MOTHER–CHILD INTERACTION

An important question from the findings about mother–child interactive patterns and relationship is: Why do the mothers show insensitive care, or indiscriminate behavior with their children? The search for an answer to this question leads us to focus on the context of the interaction—that is, adverse setting factors that impinge on the family and affect the microcosm of the ongoing interaction and the general tone of the relationship. Although an analysis of these factors is beyond the scope of this chapter, some findings that put the interactional issues in perspective will be addressed.

A pattern of aversive social contact within the community and a lack of supportive interchanges with friends characterize the "insular" mothers (Wahler 1980). Isolation from positive and supportive social contacts affects maternal care behavior. Thus, mothers were more aversive and indiscriminate with their children on days in which the mothers reported coercive exchanges with others in their community (Dumas and Wahler 1985; Wahler 1980; Wahler and Graves 1983). The influences of insularity on maternal indiscriminate behavior seem to be mediated through attentional deficits (Wahler and Afton 1980). In addition, mothers who report aversive social contacts with other adults also report other sources of problems such as socioeconomic disadvantage and emotional distress. Cerezo and Pons (1996) found that maternal indiscriminate response to child prosocial behavior was predicted by a three-variable model which accounted for 59 percent of the variance. The best predictor was socioeconomic disadvantage, followed by the mother's report of depressive mood, and the child's conduct problems reported by the mother.

Related to maternal attentional deficit, it has been hypothesized that an adverse ecosystem may also contribute to mothering behavior through the mother's perceptual bias. Sansbury and Wahler (1990) reported that the mother's global report of her child's behavior and the poor quality of her ecosystem more likely predicted the maternal indiscriminate response to her child's behavior. The mother's global report seemed to reflect her perceptual bias about her child's behavior. In this way, Cerezo and Pons (1996) used the externalizing score of the Child Behavior Checklist (CBC.E; Achenbach and Edelbrok 1983) as a maternal judgement of the child's problems that requires her to aggregate her perception of the child over a certain period of time. In their study, the best predictor of the CBC.E score was the mother's own aversive child-directed behavior, displayed over five hours of observation, followed by the average quality of the mother's community contacts.

Parental perception of a child's problem is related to attributions and expectations as well as parental knowledge of the child's development, needs, and skills (Azar *et al.* 1984). Parents punished what they see as "deviant"; in this sense, parental perception is an important factor which affects the parental behavior. Thus, if a mother is overinclusive and global—that is, if she perceives part of her child's neutral or even positive behaviors as deviant and uses vague and general descriptors of her child's behavior—she will have problems providing an appropriate monitoring of her child's behavior (Wahler and Sansbury 1990).

As an integrating framework for the deficits found in abusive parents, Milner (1993) proposed a social information-processing analysis of parenting behavior. From this comprehensive perspective, the influence of stressors on parenting behavior will be mediated by deficits in one or more of the sequential steps in responding to children's social cues (see also Hillson and Kuiper 1994).

Milner (1993) cited research that, though not conducted to test the model directly, supported the information-processing model as a plausible way to organize the findings about abusive parents' cognitions and their relations to each other. Interestingly, this author suggested that, compared to nonabusers, physical abusers "engage in more automatic processing of child-related data in ambiguous and stressful situations" (p. 278). Because automatic processing can be initiated without the parent's awareness, in these situations the perception of the child's behavior will lead directly to the parental response.

In sum, we have reviewed empirical findings which show that contextual factors affect the microcosm of the ongoing mother–child interaction. From the social-interactional approach, those adverse factors affect the family interaction by decreasing the parental competency (either temporarily or permanently) and by increasing the risk of confrontations. A decreased parental competence and frequent confrontations with the child are related to a higher likelihood of abusive episodes (Reid 1983). Assuming, as a macro-level of analysis, the influences of contextual factors on parent–child interaction, it remains an important research question of whether these influences are either directly related to parenting activities or are exerted through mediational processes, such as social information processing. Currently this is a debatable issue for further theorizing.

## CONCLUSIONS

Understanding interaction processes requires a microsocial approach. This approach is supported by relevant empirical findings, accumulated in the last three decades, that have shed light on family interaction in highly coercive families (Patterson 1982). Likewise, clinically and experimentally, improvement in family management skills has shown to reduce coercive exchanges (Reid 1985; Wahler *et al.* 1993). In spite of these promising outcomes, it could be suggested that other dysfunctional patterns, in addition to the coercive and inconsistency patterns, may be operating in physically abusive families. Based on clinical impressions regarding the treatment of abusive families, Patterson (1982: 159) wrote that "there may be *several* progressions leading to violence in families, in addition to the hypothesized escalation process."

In addition to micro-level analysis, a macro-level approach is needed to consider appropriately the complex social phenomenon of physical child abuse. As Dishion *et al.* (1995) argue, both levels of analysis—micro and macro, with their respective strengths and weaknesses—are necessary to understand family interaction processes and their role in child developmental competencies. Consequently, integrating both levels of analyses in the design of empirical research will open up new and interesting perspectives in the study of family violence.

## NOTE

1 The preparation of this chapter was partly supported by a research grant from Plan Nacional de Investigación, DGICYT, Project PS94–0192.

## BIBLIOGRAPHY

Abramson, L.Y., Seligman, M.E.P. and Teasdale, J.D. (1978) "Learned helplessness in human and reformulation," *Journal of Abnormal Psychology* 87: 49–74.

Achenbach, T.M. and Edelbrock, C. (1983) *Manual for the Child Behavior Checklist and Revised Child Behavior Profile*, Burlington, VT: University of Vermont Press.

Ainsworth, M.D.S., Blehar, M.C., Waters, E. and Wall, S. (1978) *Patterns of attachment: A psychological study of Stranger Situation*, Hillsdale, NJ: Lawrence Erlbaum.

Ammerman, R.T. (1990) "Etiological models of child maltreatment: A behavioral perspective," *Behavior Modification* 14: 230–254.

Ammerman, R.T. and Hersen, M. (1990) "Research in child abuse and neglect," in R.T. Ammerman and M. Hersen (eds) *Children at risk: An evaluation of factors contributing to child abuse and neglect*, New York: Plenum Press.

Azar, S.T. (1991) "Models of child abuse: A metatheoretical analysis," *Criminal Justice and Behavior* 18: 30–46.

Azar, S.T., Robinson, D.R., Hekimian, E. and Twentyman, C.T. (1984) "Unrealistic expectations and problem solving ability in maltreating and comparison mothers," *Journal of Consulting and Clinical Psychology* 52: 687–691.

Badía, P., Harsh, J. and Abbott, B. (1979) "Choosing between predictable and unpredictable shock condition: Data and theory," *Psychological Bulletin* 86: 1107–1131.

Badía, P., Coker, C. and Harsh, J. (1973) "Choice of higher density signaled shock over lower density unsignaled shock," *Journal of Experimental Analysis of Behavior* 20: 27–55.

Biederman, G.B. and Furedy, J. (1976) "The preference for signaled shock phenomenon," *Bulletin of the Psychonomic Society* 7: 129–132.

Belsky, J. (1993) "Etiology of child maltreatment: A developmental-ecological analysis," *Psychological Bulletin* 114: 413–434.

Biglan, A., Lewin, L. and Hops, H. (1990) "A contextual approach to the problem of aversive practices in families," in G.R. Patterson (ed.) *Depression and aggression in family interaction*, Hillsdale, NJ: Lawrence Erlbaum.

Bousha, D.M. and Twentyman, C.T. (1984) "Mother–child interactional style in abuse, neglect, and control groups: Naturalistic observation in the home," *Journal of Abnormal Psychology* 93: 106–114.

Bowlby, J. (1969) *Attachment and Loss. Vol. 1: Attachment*, New York: Basic Books.

—— (1973) *Attachment and Loss. Vol. 2: Separation*, New York: Basic Books.

Burgess, R.L. and Richardson, R.A. (1984) "Coercive interpersonal contingencies as a determinants of child abuse: Implications for treatment and prevention," in R.F. Dangel and R.A. Polster (eds) *Parent Training*, New York: Guilford Press.

Cantero, M.J. (1996) "Patrones interaccionales madre–hijo y conducta de apego en la prevención del desarrollo de conductas coercitivas infantiles. Un estudio longitudinal" [Mother–child interactive patterns and attachment behavior in the prevention of child coercive behavior. A longitudinal study], unpublished Ph.D. thesis, University of Valencia.

Cerezo, M.A. (1991) *Interacciones familiares: un sistema de evaluación observacional.* [Family Interaction: An instrument for observational assessment], Madrid: Mepsa.

—— (1992) *Programa de asistencia psicológica a familias con problemas de relación y abuso infantil.* [The psychological program for families with relational problems and child abuse], Generalitat Valenciana: Regional Government Press.

—— (1995) "El Impacto psicológico del maltrato: Primera infancia y edad escolar" [Psychological impact of maltreatment: infancy and school-aged children], *Infancia y Aprendizaje* 71: 135–157.

—— (1997) "Abusive family interaction: A review," *Aggression and Violent Behavior: A review journal* 2: 215–240.

Cerezo, M.A. and D'Ocon, A. (1995a) "The predictability hypotheses in coercive

mother–child interactions: Sequential analyses of abusive Spanish mothers," paper presented at the 29th Annual Conference for the Advancement of the Behavior Therapy, Washington, DC.
—— (1995b) "Maternal inconsistent socialization: An interactional pattern in maltreated children," *Child Abuse Review* 4: 14–31.
—— (forthcoming) "Las pautas de socialización inconsistente con niños maltratados: Una perspectiva interactiva desde la metodología observacional" [Socialization patterns in maltreated children: An interactive view from the observational methodology], in M.T. Anguera (ed.) *Metodología Observacional en la investigación psicológica. Estudios empíricos*, Barcelona: PPU.
Cerezo, M.A. and Frias, D. (1994) "Emotional and cognitive adjustment in maltreated children," *Child Abuse and Neglect* 18: 923–932
Cerezo, M.A. and Pons, G. (1996) "Ecosystem adversity as setting factor in mother's judgments of child behavior and indiscriminate mothering," *European Journal of Psychological Assessment* 12: 103–111
Cerezo, M.A., D'Ocon, A. and Dolz, L. (1996) "Mother–child interaction patterns in abusive families vs. nonabusive families: An observational study," *Child Abuse and Neglect* 20: 573–587.
Cerezo, M.A., Keesler, T.Y., Dunn, E.Y. and Wahler, R.G. (1986) *Standardized observation codes: SOC III.* Unpublished document of the Child Behavior Institute, University of Tennessee.
Cicchetti, D. (1989) "How research on child maltreatment has informed the study of child development: Perspectives from developmental psychopathology," in D. Cicchetti and V. Carlson (eds) *Child Maltreatment*, New York: Cambridge University Press.
Cicchetti, D. and Olsen, K. (1990) "The developmental psychopathology of child maltreatment," in M.R. Lewis and S.M. Miller (eds) *Handbook of developmental psychopathology*, New York: Plenum Press.
Cicchetti, D. and Rizley, R. (1981) "Developmental perspectives on the etiology, intergenerational transmission and sequelae of child maltreatment," *New Direction for Child Development* 11: 31–55.
Crittenden, P. (1981) "Abusing, neglecting, problematic and adequate dyads: Differentiating by patterns of interaction," *Merrill-Palmer Quarterly* 27: 201–218.
—— (1988) "Relationship at risk," in J. Belsky and T. Nezworski (eds) *Clinical implications of attachment*, Hillsdale, NJ: Lawrence Erlbaum.
—— (1992) "Children's strategies for coping with adverse home environments: An interpretation using attachment theory," *Child Abuse and Neglect* 16: 329–344.
Crittenden, P. and Ainsworth, M.D.S. (1989) "Child maltreatment and attachment theory," in D. Cicchetti and V. Carlson (eds) *Child maltreatment*, New York: Cambridge University Press.
D'Ocon, A. (1994) "Factores en el mantenimiento de las relaciones coercitivas madre–hijo en familias con problemas de abuso infantil" [Factors in the maintenance of mother–child coercive interaction of abusive families], unpublished Ph.D. thesis, University of Valencia.
D'Ocon, A. Dolz, L., Pons-Salvador, G. and Cerezo, M.A. (1996) "Behavioral problems among victims of parental maltreatment: a comparative study between maltreated and control children," paper presented at the XIth International Congress on Child Abuse and Neglect, Dublin.
Dodge, K.A., Pettit, G.S., Bates, J.E. and Valente, E. (1995) "Social information

processing patterns partially mediate the effect of early physical abuse on later conduct problems," *Journal of Abnormal Psychology* 104: 632–643.

de Paúl, J. and Arruabarrena, I. (1995) "Behavior problems in school-aged physically abused and neglected children in Spain," *Child Abuse and Neglect* 19: 409–418.

Dishion, T.J., French, D.C. and Patterson, G.R. (1995) "The development and ecology of antisocial behavior," in D. Cicchetti and Donald J. Cohen (eds) *Developmental Psychopathology Vol 2: Risk, disorder, and adaptation*, New York: Wiley.

Dumas, J.E. and Wahler, R. G. (1985) "Indiscriminate mothering as a contextual factor in aggressive-oppositional child behavior: Damned if you do, damned if you don't," *Journal of Abnormal Child Psychopathology* 13: 1–17.

Elicker, J., Englund, M. and Sroufe, L.A. (1992) "Predicting peer competence and peer relationships in childhood from early parent–child relationship," in R.D. Parke and G.W. Ladd (eds) *Family–peers relationships: Models of linkage*, Hillsdale, NJ: Lawrence Erlbaum.

Erickson, M., Egeland, B. and Pianta, R. (1989) "The effects of maltreatment on the development of young children," in D. Cicchetti and V. Carlson (eds) *Child Maltreatment*, New York: Cambridge University Press.

Fantuzzo, J.W. (1990) "Behavioral treatment of the victims of child abuse and neglect," *Behavior Modification* 14: 316–339.

Field, T., Healy, B. and LeBlanc, W. (1989) "Sharing and synchrony of behavior states and heart rate in nondepressed vs. depressed mother–infant interactions," *Infant Behavior and Development* 12: 357–376.

Gardner, F.M. (1989) "Inconsistent parenting: Is there evidence for a link with children's conduct problems?," *Journal of Abnormal Child Psychology* 17: 223–233.

Gelles, R.J. and Cornell, C.P. (1990) *Intimate violence in families*, Newbury Park, CA: Sage.

Gil, D.G. (1970) *Violence against children: Physical child abuse in the United States*, Cambridge, MA: Harvard University Press.

Higgins, J. (1966) "Inconsistent socialization," *Psychological Reports* 23: 303–336.

Hillson, J.M.C. and Kuiper, N.A. (1994) "A stress and coping model of child maltreatment," *Clinical Psychology Review* 14: 261–285.

Hoffman-Plotkin, D. and Twentyman, C.T. (1984) "A multimodal assessment of behavioral and cognitive deficits in abused and neglected preschoolers," *Child Development* 55: 794–802.

Isabella, R.A., Belsky, J. and von Eye, A. (1989) "Origins of infant–mother attachment: An examination of interactional synchrony during the infant's first year," *Developmental Psychology* 25: 12–21.

Jacob, T. (ed.) (1987) *Family interaction and psychopathology*, New York: Plenum Press.

Kadushin, A. (1981) "Child abuse as an interactional event," in A. Kadushin (ed.) *Child Abuse*, New York: Columbia University Press .

Knutson, J.F. (1982) "Perspective on Chapter 7," in G.R. Patterson (ed.) *Coercive family process*, Eugene, OR: Castalia.

Kazdin, A.E., Moser, J., Colbus, D. and Bell, R. (1985) "Depressive symptoms among physically abused and psychiatrically disturbed children," *Journal of Abnormal Psychology* 94: 298–307.

Kravic, J.N. (1987) "Behavior problems and social competence of clinic-referred abused children," *Journal of Family Violence* 2: 11–120.

Lester, B., Hoffman, J. and Brazelton, T.B. (1985) "The rhythmic structure of

mother–infant interaction in term and pre-term infants," *Child Development* 56: 15–27.
Lewis, M. and Brooks-Gunn, J. (1979) *Social cognition and the acquisition of self*, New York: Plenum Press.
Lewis, D.O., Mallouh, C. and Webb, V. (1989) "Child abuse, delinquency and violent criminality," in D. Cicchetti and V. Carlson (eds) *Child Maltreatment* New York: Cambridge University Press.
Lorber, R., Felton, D. and Reid, J. B. (1984) "A social learning approach to the reduction of coercive processes in child abusive families: A molecular analysis," *Advances of Behavior Research and Therapy* 6: 29–45.
Lyons-Ruth, K., Connell, D. B., Zoll, D. and Stahl, J. (1987) "Infants at social risk: Relations among infant maltreatment, maternal behavior and infant attachment behavior," *Developmental Psychology* 23: 223–232.
Main, M. and George, C. (1985) "Responses of abused and disadvantaged toddler to distress in agemates: A study in the day-care setting," *Developmental Psychology* 21: 407–412.
Milner, J.S. (1993) "Social information processing and physical child abuse," *Clinical Psychology Review* 13: 275–294.
McCord, J. (1987) "Instigation and insulation: How families affect antisocial aggression," in D. Olweus, J. Block and M. Radke-Yarrow (eds) *Development of antisocial and prosocial behavior: Research, theory and issues*, New York: Academic Press.
Oldershaw, L., Walters, G. and Hall, D. K. (1986) "Control strategies and noncompliance in abusive mother–child dyads: An observational study," *Child Development* 57: 722–732.
Parke, R.D. and Collmer, C.W. (1975) "Child abuse: An interdisciplinary analysis," in E. M. Hetherington (ed.) *Review of Child Development Research* (vol. 5), Chicago: The University of Chicago Press.
Patterson, G.R. (1976) "The aggressive child: Victim and architect of a coercive system," in L.A. Hamerlynck, L.C. Handy and E.J. Mash (eds) *Behavior modification and families: Theory and research* (vol.1), New York: Brunner/Mazel.
—— (1982) *Coercive family process*, Eugene, OR: Castalia.
—— (1986) "Maternal rejection: Determinant or product for deviant child behavior," in W. Hartup and Z. Rubin (eds) *Relationships and development*, Hillsdale, NJ: Lawrence Erlbaum.
Patterson, G.R. and Reid, J.B. (1970) "Reciprocity and coercion: Two facets of social systems," in C. Neuringer and J.L. Michael (eds) *Behavior modification in clinical psychology*, New York: Appleton.
Reid, J. (1983) "Social interactional pattern in families of abused and nonabused children," in C.Z. Waxler, M. Cummings and R. Iannotti (eds) *Altruism and aggression: Biological and social origins*, New York: Cambridge University Press.
—— (1985) "Behavioral approaches to intervention and assessment with child-abusive families," in P. Bornstein and A. Kazdin (eds) *Handbook of clinical behavior therapy with children*, preprint.
Reid, J.B., Patterson, G.R. and Loeber, R. (1982) "The abused child; victim, instigator or innocent bystander?," in D.J. Bernstein (ed.) *Response structure and organization*, Lincoln, NE: University of Nebraska Press.
Reid, J.B., Taplin, P.S. and Lorber, R. (1981) "A social interactional approach to the treatment of abusive families," in R.B. Stuart (ed.) *Violent behavior: Social learning approaches to prediction, management and treatment*, New York: Brunner/Mazel.
Robinson, E.A. and Jacobson, N.S. (1987) "Social learning theory and family

psychopathology: A Kantian model in behaviorism?," in T. Jacob (ed.) *Family interaction and psychopathology*, New York: Plenum Press.

Sansbury, L.L. and Wahler, R.G. (1990) "Pathways to maladaptive parenting with mothers and their conduct disordered children," in N. Singh and T. Landrum (eds) *Special issues in behavior modification, social behavior of children and adolescents*, preprint.

Seligman, M.E.P. (1975) *Helplessness*, New York: Freeman.

Schneider-Rosen, K. and Cicchetti, D. (1991) "Early self-knowledge and emotional development: Visual self-recognition and effective reactions to mirror self-images in maltreated and nonmaltreated toddlers," *Developmental Psychology* 27: 471–478.

Snyder, J. (1991) "Discipline as a mediator of the impact of maternal stress and mood on child conduct problems," *Development and Psychopathology* 3: 263–276.

Trickett, P.K. and Kuczynski, L. (1986) "Children's misbehaviors and parental discipline strategies in abusive and nonabusive families," *Developmental Psychology* 22: 115–123.

Tzeng, O.C.S., Jackson, J.W. and Carlson, H.C. (1991) *Theories of child abuse and neglect*, New York: Praeger.

Ulrich, R.E. and Azrin, N.H. (1962) "Reflexive fighting in response to aversive stimulation," *Journal of the Experimental Analysis of Behavior* 5: 511–520.

Vasta, R. and Copitch, P. (1981) "Simulating conditions of child abuse in the laboratory," *Child Development* 52: 164–170.

Wahler, R.G. (1980) "The insular mother: Her problems in parent–child treatment," *Journal of Applied Behavior Analysis* 13: 207–219.

—— (1994) "Child conduct problem: Disorders in conduct or social continuity?," *Journal of Child and Family Studies* 3: 143–156.

Wahler, R.G. and Afton, A.D. (1980) "Attentional processes in insular and non-insular mothers," *Child Behavior Therapy* 2: 25–41.

Wahler, R.G. and Dumas, J. (1986) "Maintenance factors in coercive mother–child interaction: Predictability and compliance hypotheses," *Journal of Applied Behavior Analysis* 19: 13–22.

Wahler, R.G. and Graves, M.G. (1983) "Setting events in social networks: Ally or enemy in child behavior therapy?," *Behavior Therapy* 14: 19–36.

Wahler, R.G. and Sansbury, L.E. (1990) "The monitoring skills of troubled mothers: The problems in defining child deviance," *Journal of Abnormal Child Psychology* 18: 577–589.

Wahler, R.G., Cartor, P.G., Fleichman, J. and Lambert, W. (1993) "The impact of the synthesis teaching and parent training with mothers of conduct disorder children," *Journal of Abnormal Child Psychology* 21: 425–440.

Wahler, R.G., Williams, A. and Cerezo, M A. (1990) "The compliance and predictability hypotheses: Sequential and correlational analyses of coercive mother–child interactions," *Behavioral Assessment* 12: 391–407.

Wahler, R.G., Rogers, D., Collins, B. and Dumas, J.E. (1984) "Maintenance factors in abusive mother–child interactions: The compliance and the uncertainty hypotheses," paper presented at the 18th Annual Convention of the Association for the Advancement of Behavior Therapy, Philadelphia.

Whipple, E.E. and Webster-Stratton, C. (1991) "The role of parental stress in physically abusive families," *Child Abuse and Neglect* 15: 279–291.

Wolfe, D.A.(1985) "Abusive parents: An empirical review," *Psychological Bulletin* 97: 462–482.

—— (1987) *Child abuse: Implications for child development and psychopathology*, Beverly Hills, CA: Sage
Wolfe, D.A. and Mosk, M.D. (1983) "Behavioral comparisons of children from abusive and distressed families," *Journal of Consulting and Clinical Psychology* 51: 702–708.
Youngblade, L.M. and Belsky, J. (1990) "Social and emotional consequences of child maltreatment," in T. Ammerman and M. Hersen (eds) *Children at risk*, New York: Plenum Press.

Chapter 3

# Making sense of family conflict

## Influences on account making

*Rosaleen Croghan and Dorothy Miell*

Rosaleen Croghan has a background in social work, social policy and psychology. She is currently employed as a research Fellow at the Open University. Dorothy Miell is a Senior Lecturer at the Open University and is a social psychologist. The research reviewed in this chapter reflects both researchers' long-term interest in the connections between social and ideological conditions and subjectivity. Both are particularly interested in the way in which women's experience is circumscribed and molded by the wider social and political context, and the way in which women challenge these expectations and effect change.

*This chapter reviews two studies from a research program that has looked at the way in which family conflict is construed by women who are attempting to come to terms with either childhood abuse and disruption or maternal stress. These studies raise issues about the way in which representations of "normal" family life have their roots in wider social processes, and how the personal history and experiences of individuals interact to produce different forms of subjectivity. The focus in the analysis is on the interpretative repertoires that women draw on in coming to terms with family conflict and maternal stress, and their ability to create new meanings within existing frameworks. The research uses semi-structured interview data and a method of analysis which combines a focus on language use with an understanding of the wider context in which accounts are produced.*[1]

### INTRODUCTION

Feminist critiques of the family suggest that there are powerful assumptions around family life that have real effects on the way in which family conflict is understood (Caplan 1981, 1985; Hollway 1984; Nice 1992). One such assumption is that the family is a "private haven," set apart from the wider society, and an arena for the provision of mutual support and the realization of individual potential. As a result, conflict experienced within this setting is likely to pose a major accounting problem for the individual. Feminist critiques also suggest that gender role expectations form the pivotal axis around which family identity is constructed, and that, because of this, family conflict needs to be understood as embedded in the expectations surrounding women's roles within the family. Making sense of family conflict, and in particular the attribution of responsibility for that conflict, is thus likely to be an intensely personal experience which is rooted in the expectations and values of the cultural milieu in which such conflict occurs. It is this tension between family conflict as a personal experience and as a social construction that we wish to explore.

Developments in social constructionism, in discourse analysis, and in feminism have focused attention on the way in which subjectivity is formed by social relationships which are themselves constructed by wider social processes (Chodorow 1978; Fraser 1992; Gergen 1991; Weedon 1987). Such approaches offer an insight into the way in which the meaning that individuals ascribe to their personal history and experience is mediated through socially constructed representations of reality. Rhetorical psychologists and discourse analysts have drawn attention to variability and contradiction in discourse and to the difficulties associated with assuming that social representations are assigned to specific fixed groups or that they mean the same to each individual (Potter and Wetherell 1987; Shotter 1993; Wetherell 1995; Wetherell and Potter 1992). This has dictated a shift in focus from the employment of shared representations to their construction in everyday speech and the ability of account makers to construct new categories in the face of changing information or situations.

One of the main tensions that is explored in recent studies of the discursive construction of close relationships is that which arises between personal autonomy and the power of social representations to construct subjectivity (Burman 1990, 1992; Gill 1995). This tension between individual autonomy and social representations is central to the present study which examines the way in which women account for family conflict within the discursive framework surrounding family life and, in particular, the expectations surrounding appropriate gender roles. We are concerned with both the constitution of meaning and the sanctioning of modes of conduct (Giddens 1979) and with the process through which particular versions of events become admissible or inadmissible. Discourse is viewed as both constitutive and regulative—that is, both as a cultural resource and as a personal creation. We are therefore concerned with the creation of meaning which takes place against a background of powerful social representations. We are interested in the process through which such representations are reflected and challenged in discourse and the way in which individuals construct and position themselves in relation to views of "normal" family life and gender roles.

## THE STUDIES

Two studies are presented that looked at women's subjective appraisal of family life and the sense they make of stress and conflicts in close relationships. Both studies share certain features although each had a different subject group and research topic. Both were qualitative semi-structured interview studies in which those interviewed were encouraged to explore their feelings about family relationships. Both looked at the women's subjective understanding of family conflict examining the extent and nature of common interpretative repertoires and the conditions and context in which these were challenged, and made links between the women's subjective understanding and their position in wider social processes and hierarchies.

The studies looked at specific areas of stress and conflict and at women's appraisal of that conflict. Study One looked at conflict arising from stress in first-time mothering, whereas Study Two looked at the way in which the women came to terms with childhood abuse and disruption. Both were carried out by the same female interviewer and for both studies the major sampling consideration was that interviews should cover the full range of participants' experience and background in order to provide as much diversity as possible. For Study One, twenty-five first time heterosexual mothers with children aged between 3 months and 12 months were interviewed. These interviews focused on the women's interpretations of their close relationships, their expectations of themselves as mothers and of their social network (particularly their sexual partner) and how far these expectations were fulfilled. In order to ensure that a broad range of current stress was represented, about 50 percent of these mothers were recruited from among women who had suffered childhood disruption and who were living currently in circumstances of high social stress. For the second study, fifty-three adult women aged between 19 and 36 were interviewed, all of whom had experienced severe childhood disruption in their family relationships and all of whom had been separated from natural parents before the age of 16 and placed in substitute families or in institutional care.

The interview covered the women's childhood and current experiences and invited them to explore their feelings about their early family relationships and their current relationships. The interviewer used specific probes to elicit responses. However, the interview style was informed by a commitment to explore the women's own perspective and not to impose categories on the data at too early a stage. Following feminist theorists who have questioned the nature of value-free research, particularly in qualitative research, the interview was seen as a specific interaction between interviewer and subject that was likely to elicit a particular context-bound response (Wilkinson 1988). The researchers were acutely aware that the accounts were likely to reflect the expectations and inferences that the women held about acceptable discourse and the values held by the interviewer. The research involved a discussion of painful and sometimes hitherto undisclosed personal information. It was therefore an important ethical and methodological consideration of this study that the interviewer should explicitly dissociate herself from an "expert" view that measured the women against an arbitrary standard of excellence either as mothers or as individuals. To this end the interviewer disclosed her own experience where appropriate and made it clear that there was no hidden agenda to sort "good" from "bad" mothers, or "normal" from "abnormal" families.

In both studies, personal accounts of family conflict were understood as constructed within a culturally organized framework that prescribes women's identity and the nature of family life. However, the account maker is likely to have a complex relationship with ideas of the "normal" family which may be treated both as a cultural resource and as a vehicle for the construction of meaning which fulfills different purposes in different situations. Thus, while it is possible to identify common themes in the construction of family life, we do not suggest that all these women constructed family life in an identical way, but only that it is possible to identify common features in these accounts and to relate these to wider social processes and representations of the family.

## ANALYSIS

The interviews from both studies were audiotaped and analyzed using techniques derived from discourse analysis and feminist qualitative methodology (Griffin 1990; Oakley 1981; Wilkinson 1981). We looked at the interpretative repertoires that the women used in describing their family relationships (Potter and Wetherell 1987) and examined the uses and functions of these repertoires, the influences upon them, and the ways in which the women took issue and debated with them.

The accounts were first analyzed to generate broad categories that reflected both the women's preoccupations and our particular focus. The preliminary coding organized material around the research themes and identified and characterized the interpretative repertoires that the women drew on in constructing their accounts. For the next stage of the analysis an interpretative scheme was developed which enabled us to capture some of the regularities and common patterns within and across accounts. The initial coding centered on the women's subjective appraisal of conflict and the construction of "normal" family life. This allowed us to identify some of the cultural narratives on which the women drew in describing the problematic aspects of family life and the extent to which they differed both as individuals and as groups. These shared interpretative schemes were related to common assumptions about gender roles and family life and the ascription of responsibility for family conflict and failure. Finally, we looked for variation within subgroups of women—for example, among women who had disrupted and nondisrupted backgrounds, or between those who had low or high levels of current social stress, in order to compare variations between individuals and to hypothesize some of the reasons for this variation. Particular attention was paid to contradiction within the accounts and to the tensions and dilemmas that appeared to arise when women drew on discourses of "normal" family life that were themselves contradictory.

In these studies, the analysis of discourse was grounded in a parallel appraisal of the women's socioeconomic conditions and their position in power and status hierarchies and of the very real pressures and tensions that may come from stress and disadvantage. In each of the studies, the women's subjective appraisal of events was set against a complementary analysis of their social conditions; for example, poor housing or the impact of living on a low income. The final stage of the analysis involved an assessment of key factors in the women's experience that were likely to have influenced their perceptions of family conflict, and the implications of these interpretative repertoires for the women's lives, in particular the tensions that might arise between this interpretative framework and the women's social situation.

## FAMILY CONFLICT AND THE DISCOURSE OF THE "NORMAL" FAMILY

Although these studies covered different research topics, both were concerned with the subjective interpretation of family relationships. This allowed us to link the personal accounts in each study to shared representations of "normal" family life. In particular, it allowed us to focus on the way in which the women positioned themselves in relation to their understanding of women's roles and responsibilities within the family, and to make links between this and the way in which family conflict was interpreted.

Family conflict is likely to be a common feature of the adjustment process in the postnatal period, particularly because of shifts in the balance of power between new mothers and fathers (La Rossa and La Rossa 1981; Pleck 1982, 1985). In the first study we looked at women's accounts of stress and support following the birth of their first child. In addition to the interviews, the women were asked to complete time-use diaries. These showed that there were marked inequalities in the division of labor between men and women in parenting and domestic work. The way that mothers accounted for this was then considered.

It became clear that, for these women, the meanings they ascribed to stress and support were mediated through an understanding of what family relationships ought to be and through the expectations that they held of others and of themselves. These were in turn closely linked to a traditional understanding of gender relationships and roles. For example, there were marked differences between the expectations surrounding the roles of men and women. All these accounts were characterized by high expectations of maternal responsibility and effort and lower expectations of paternal involvement.

Thus, although there were variations in the level of participation that the women expected from men, there was always a significant gap between the contributions of men and women to the work of parenting. This proved to be a key issue in the interpretation of family conflict. The women's sense of responsibility as mothers limited their expectation of other support, particularly from their male partner, and obviated their sense of grievance at the long hours they worked and their unequal share in the burdens of parenthood. Because the women saw themselves as primarily responsible for parenting, paternal involvement was constructed as an optional gift rather than as a right. Mothers who were in stable cohabitations identified their sexual partner as both the main and preferred source of support despite this lack of involvement, distancing themselves from other relationships (for example, with friends or in-laws).

However, although the women were aware of inequality, they found it difficult to assign blame to noncooperative partners because of their adherence to powerful discourses of maternal responsibility. The women appeared to be employing two conflicting discourses here which have been identified by many previous researchers as cornerstones in the construction of family life (Barrett 1980; Barrett and MacIntosh 1982; Brannen and Wilson 1983; Graham 1983). On the one hand, they drew on discourses that emphasized the importance of motherhood and women's responsibility for the maintenance of the emotional tenor of the family while, on the other, they drew on discourses that emphasized the reciprocal nature of heterosexual relationships and the importance of the companionate marriage. For example, they appeared to accept primary responsibility for parenting whatever the stress they experienced. They also accepted responsibility for inducting the spouse into the parental role and preparing him for his responsibilities.

Caught between these two conflicting constructions of their experience that ruled that both their experiences of acute stress and their demands for support were inadmissible, the women were presented with the task of explaining their stress without calling into question the central relationship with their partner. Thus the women in heterosexual relationships tended to minimize conflict, explaining their partner's non-involvement as due to difficulties in personal adjustment, or by reconstructing the notion of support to exclude practical help and to cover only emotional support. In this way spouses who did not participate in child care and domestic work could still be presented as "supportive." The following extracts in which two women attempt to account for their partners' minimal involvement in child care illustrate both these strategies. When lack of support was compounded by the mother's extra commitment to paid work and a lack of available resources to buy in alternative domestic help, the notion of the heterosexual relationship as supportive became particularly strained.

ENID I think he feels it more than me, because I just get used to it. It's not that he's not willing to, I think he's just, he's one of these distractible people, he's always kind of off somewhere else. Uh, not that he's neglectful, but I think, like, Leo's nappy needs changing now, and I'll go and do that, whereas he'll just kind of not realize till the last minute. That makes him sound awful, but he's not.

FIONA I think he gets more tired. The effects of tiredness during the day time have more effect on him than they do on me. Even though he doesn't get woken up so much, because he sleeps through when she wakes up.

This dilemma was particularly acute for those who, like Kim (below), worked full time in relatively low paid, unrewarding occupations and were still expected to carry out all the domestic chores. However, the women's sense of powerlessness appeared to arise not simply from their economic circumstances but from their commitment to and their disappointment in a relationship that was defined in terms of mutual support. The violation of these expectations was in itself another form of stress. It was in order to avoid violating these notions of support, that are so central to the meaning of the relationship and to the woman's status as an equal partner, that the women strove to redefine the notion of support. In the following accounts, for example, the partner's contribution is presented as optional, and any resentment as illegitimate.

KIM I went to the doctors, and it was the best thing I ever did. He gave me some tranquillizers which did help, which he said would help me with the anger. I felt so angry.

RESEARCHER Who did you feel angry with?

KIM Mainly with myself and with everything.

PAULA I did talk to him about it all and he's a really lovely bloke, very understanding. Even when I said that I was really angry with him, he was so kind, he is ever such a kind and lovely bloke.

RESEARCHER You were angry with Ben? (partner)

PAULA No, I didn't get angry with Ben, just with him (the baby). Well I just get angry with me really.

Women in highly stressed situations simply appeared to work harder at fitting their experience into the prescribed framework, rather than calling it into question. They speculated at length on their partners' motivations, and brought in a range of mitigating factors to explain their behaviors. Most common among these was the use of the implicit assumption that men were unprepared for parenting and had to be inducted into the task, and that the mother as primary carer should mediate between father and child and induct him into his role. The construction of mothering as non-work or as not equivalent to paid work also came into play frequently, although this explanation became particularly strained for women who were themselves in full-time employment. All these resources appeared to have one end in view, that is to regain equilibrium in the relationship and to minimize conflict. Not to do so would be to put the relationship in jeopardy, since an open acknowledgement that the relationship was unequal and that the male partner was actively choosing to perpetuate that inequality would have changed the status of the relationship from mutually supportive to confrontational. Few women were prepared to do this, and those who did found themselves in a state of combined resentment and dependence from which it was difficult to extricate themselves.

A few of the women were both overtly feminist and were married to men who considered themselves to be "new men," that is, to share ideals of equal partnership and parenting. This provided the women with an added lever, and these women were more likely to be confrontational and to demand equal support, although even for these women there was a strong sense that ultimately they would not put the relationship at risk.

GEORGIA He'll do things if I ask him or nag him, and he'd like to believe that he does half, like to think he does half. . . . When Karl does things for him (baby), like not the washing because he doesn't do that, but if Karl gives him a bath or gets his food ready, I'll tend to say, "thanks for doing that." We've talked about it a lot because Karl doesn't say thank you to me when I do things, and I do feel if I say thank you, maybe he'll do it more often. Praise him. It's kind of subtle, managing men.

Women who were *currently* in relationships that they described as exploitative or abusive did not employ the discourse of mutuality and were often at a loss to account for their choice of partner, or the benefits if any to be gained from staying in the relationship. However, these mothers were still engaged in constructing a rationale for their partner's behavior. There was a marked difference between women's accounts of current and of previous relationships. The women tended to underplay the responsibility of current partners by describing violence as a personality trait, or as a response to lack of control induced by drink or drugs rather than as an act of will, or by presenting themselves as contributing to the violence.

RESEARCHER Does Des hit you then?
DI Yes. Not so much at the moment. It's because I can wind him up to a state.

In contrast, abusive *former* partners were most often presented as fully responsible for their actions. All but one of the women who had been abused and who were not currently in a heterosexual relationship presented the last relationship as exceptional. These women looked forward to forming a "normal" relationship with a supportive man. Only one woman who had been in a series of abusive relationships called the whole idea of heterosexual relationships as being supportive and equally rewarding into question and suggested that she might be better off without men.

The ascription of responsibility for conflict within the family was a key issue in the second study in which we interviewed women who had experienced acute conflict in their childhood family relationships and who had also often experienced abuse in adulthood within heterosexual relationships. The experience of abuse and disruption within close family relationships presented these women with a marked dissonance between their own experience of family life and their expectations of it. They were thus faced with a major problem in accounting for the breakdown in the family and assigning responsibility for it. In making sense of family conflict the women made frequent comparisons between their own family life and that of "normal" families. "Normal" families, in contrast to their own, were described as unproblematic and mutually rewarding.

The women again appeared to be interpreting the experience of family conflict (in this case of childhood abuse and/or disruption) against a framework of assumptions of what family life ought to be, which placed central responsibility on the woman as mediator of conflict and as caretaker of the quality of family life, and which characterized the heterosexual relationship as inherently supportive. This construction of "normal" families as relatively unconflicted, together with an adherence to a traditional view of women's responsibility for the maintenance of unproblematic family relationships, meant that the women's attributions of responsibility were strongly influenced by the gender of family members. For example, they had more elaborate expectations of mothers and mother figures than of fathers and father figures, and were far more likely to censure mothers and hold them responsible for the family's failure to live up to the norm.

Women who had suffered a family breakdown gave accounts which presented their mothers as responsible for the breakdown of family relationships. In the face of conflict, mothers were expected to stay and maintain the family. Mothers (but not fathers) who abandoned families were heavily censured, as in the following extract in which one woman describes her abandonment by both natural parents.

DI My Mum and Dad got divorced when I was new born. My Mum, I don't have anything to do with my Mum any more because she is a very immature woman. I went through three years of saying you know, "be my Mum, you are supposed to be my bloody mother," and she wasn't. So I thought, "if I don't have you as a mother I don't want you at all," because that's what I needed.

Fathers were never blamed either for abandoning mothers before birth or for the decision to relinquish custody of children following marital separation. Fathers were not expected to take up the mantle of responsibility if mothers left, or to resume responsibility on remarriage. No blame was imputed to fathers who had been unwilling or unable to care for their families after they had separated from their wives. In these accounts, the heterosexual partnership was again cast as the norm, and the expectation was that women should derive support from it, and that those who were unable to do so were personally culpable. For lone mothers to abandon their children was seen as excusable since it gave them the chance of being parented in a "proper" family. None of the women who had been given up by lone mothers in early childhood presented her mother as culpable.

SHARON She could have had an abortion and I wouldn't even be here so I am just glad she made that decision. She has done it for both of us, for herself and for me so I don't hold that against her at all.

ENID I do have a lot of respect for her that she put me into care for the best I could get out of life. I don't feel bitter towards her or angry because at the end of the day she did what was right.

In contrast, mothers who walked out on heterosexual relationships (even when these were abusive) were seen as culpable. Although the women found some explanation and mitigation for mothers who abandoned them while they were lone parents, stressing the situational pressures associated with lone parenting, social stress was not seen as an adequate explanation for abuse or abandonment in families in which mothers were enjoying all the "benefits" of a heterosexual relationship.

PAULA She says like she was young and all that lot and she had so many kids, but that's not a real answer. I just blame her for the way that my life has turned out, for the way I feel.

Women who had been abused also held their mothers, rather than fathers, responsible for their abuse. Where women had been abused by male carers, nonabusive female parent figures were often seen as at least partly responsible for the abuse. Sixteen of the twenty-two women who had been abused by male family members and who had not been abused by female family members represented mothers or stepmothers as either partly or wholly responsible for their abuse. Similarly, although all perpetrators of sexual abuse were male, all but three of the women who had been sexually abused saw their mothers or stepmothers as at least partly responsible for the abuse. However, male parent figures were never seen as responsible when the perpetrator of the (nonsexual) abuse was female and in two out of the three cases in which both natural parents had been physically abusive, the mother was seen as more to blame.

Thus while fathers and father figures were more likely to abuse and to severely abuse they were also more likely to be excused and exonerated than mothers and mother figures. These attributions appeared to cut across the women's tendency to give accounts that exonerated natural parents (Croghan and Miell 1995). In these accounts, abuse was recast as a relational problem in which mothers' failures to fulfill their family obligations were seen as factors that explained the male perpetrator's propensity to abuse. For example, mothers were presented as to blame for failing to prevent abuse even if they themselves were being physically abused.

IRENE There is no bond there or anything. She would never stop him and that's what I didn't like.

BETH I know my Mum should have stopped it or even talked to him about it or even stuck up for me when it actually came out in the open but she didn't.

UNA I couldn't stand there and let someone beat my little boy up. It just goes to show what kind of Mum she is.

Sexual abuse was also frequently ascribed to the mother's failure to satisfy her spouse's sexual needs, either by being unfaithful or by being otherwise unavailable.

ENID My mum has changed slightly, but I think it (the abuse) was basically because of problems within their marriage.

NICKY My Mum wasn't being exactly true to him. She should have been the wife. She shouldn't have been doing the things that she was doing. She could have been a bit more caring toward us and maybe things like this wouldn't have happened.

THEA She had moved away see, and run after my step-dad and left me and my sister and my brother with my real Dad. That's when it started you see, and she couldn't accept that if she had stayed there it might not have happened, he might not have had the urge sort of thing.

In contrast, the women presented accounts that limited the father figure's responsibility for family conflict, employing a range of justifications and excuses for the behavior of the men. Abused women tended to emphasize their own contribution to the abuse, particularly if they had a strong emotional investment in the relationship, for example with a natural father.

DI He's got to be really pushed to do it. He didn't like hitting me he just did it for my own good I suppose.

SALLY I know it sounds bloody stupid, and I still don't like him, but we did deserve it. We were right little bitches me and my sister, we used to do really bad things.

CLAIRE I thought I was to blame. Should I have been walking around the house in my dressing gown you know.

Or they might emphasize their mothers' or stepmothers' responsibility for instigating the abuse.

ANJI He wasn't violent violent, but plus his wife would wind him up a lot as well.

DI I feel sorry for my Dad. My Dad has even told me she (my stepmother) drives him to drink, literally. My Dad is an alcoholic. There's no excuse for hitting, but I can forgive my Dad where I cannot forgive my stepmum.

Male abusers were again represented in ways that mitigated their responsibility, either because of damaging early experience, current social stress, or because of a "natural" propensity to find their violence or sexuality difficult to control. Such excuses were not employed in relation either to the women themselves or to other women in the family.

CLAIRE He was actually undergoing a lot of stress as well. He was I suppose knocking on 40, I mean he got made redundant twice in a year or something and started up his own business. He's not a bad man, this is one thing I would really emphasize, he is a kind, giving, loving man.

The women appeared to find no mitigating circumstances that explained abuse when it was carried out by mothers in a stable heterosexual relationship, which was presented as the "ideal" setting for raising children. They stressed their mother's innate predisposition to violence and abuse rather than looking for interpersonal or situational factors that might explain the abuse. Domestic violence, in which mothers and stepmothers were abused, was presented as a problem for which mothers held at least joint responsibility. Of the thirteen women whose mothers or stepmothers had been abused by fathers or stepfathers, only one of these women saw this as a mitigating factor that explained either her mother's inability to care for her children or to protect them from abuse. The others gave accounts in which their mothers were represented as equally responsible for the violence in the family, or were seen as contributing to their own abuse.

LIZ They told me that my Mum had accused my Granddad of interfering with her sexually when she was younger and they were scared it would happen if I moved in with him. I couldn't see him laying a finger on her. Well, I could if she encouraged it.

OLIVE I do blame my Mum. My Mum seems to take up with really bad people. There are a lot of women it seems to me that choose to be victims. OK they choose to take that role onto themselves but then it's not fair to their children.

## DISCUSSION

The women in these studies related their understanding of family conflict to their understanding of "normal" family relationships, and of women's roles within them. Although there were variations in individual accounts, there were certain key themes that underlay the construction of the "normal" family, in particular the assumption of mutuality and support with the heterosexual nuclear family, the abnormality of severe conflict and of family breakdown, and women's responsibility for the maintenance of the emotional tenor of family life. The family was presented as a private and personal arena in which problems arose through difficulties in interpersonal adjustment rather than through any fault in the way family life was constructed. Mothers accepted a high degree of personal responsibility for family conflict and failure and judged other mothers according to these criteria. In spite of their experiences of acute family conflict, the women drew on discourses that implied distinct yet equal gender roles and unproblematic fulfillment for women within heterosexual relationships. These were presented as the optimal setting in which to raise children. These high expectations of women in heterosexual relationships appeared to hold good even when women were under severe emotional pressure, or where the women or their mothers were being beaten or abused by their sexual partners. Women were seen as primarily responsible for the quality of the relationships within the nuclear family, a setting that was seen as usually unproblematic. They were therefore seen as responsible for preventing family conflict, and were given a key role in diffusing conflict when it did arise. Both studies echo the findings of critiques of family policy that suggest that similar assumptions inform much public intervention into family life (Williams 1989). However, the studies discussed here highlight the way in which these discourses are dealt with at a personal level. Drawing on the discourse of the "normal" family as supportive and unproblematic as a key resource in making sense of family conflict tended to reinforce women's responsibility and to put the onus for change onto her as an individual.

Thus, this discourse had a very real effect, both on new mothers who blamed themselves for their experience of stress and were unable to question their lack of support effectively, and for women who experienced abuse in the family and who saw either themselves or other women in the family as responsible. For example, women whose mothering was considered to be problematic by welfare professionals tended to present accounts in which they attempted to distance themselves from other "problem" mothers (Croghan and Miell 1995). However, in doing this and in failing to recognize the common conditions that underpinned problems in mothering, they were implicitly accepting individual responsibility for the stress they experienced within the "normal" family. This not only added to their sense of guilt and helplessness but also isolated them and cut them off from support either from nonabusive female family members, or from other women in similar circumstances. The notion of individual maternal responsibility was particularly punishing for women who were currently suffering from acute material disadvantage and abuse, who found themselves hampered not only by their high expectations of themselves but also by the expectations of welfare professionals who assumed that they could overcome both abuse and disadvantage and mother effectively if they simply attained the "right" attitudes or skills.

The act of resistance was itself deeply enmeshed in existing cultural representations, and engagement with these representations was an integral part of creating an alternative view. Refuting a negative version of events involved the account maker in an implicit appeal for sanction to an audience which, together with the authors of these accounts, was immersed in common cultural values, locating themselves within those values while at the same time struggling to establish an alternative version of events. Though prevailing discourses of the normal family and maternal responsibility were at times challenged, these challenges were hedged about by expectations of what was due to women within the normal family. These expectations appeared to override both mothers' experience of the negative aspects of family life and their commitment to overtly feminist models of the organization of gender roles. Thus, while these women were aware of and struggled with the high expectations surrounding women's roles within the family, they often found their challenges overthrown by their core commitment to "normal" family life.

Both the studies reported here raise questions about the relationship between subjectivity and social representations, the relative autonomy of the individual, and the way in which ideas of the "normal" family are formed and challenged. As Billig (1987) has pointed out, argument and dialogue are crucial to the formation of subjectivity. Although some representations of family life may be more powerful than others, we cannot assume that family life will be experienced by everyone in the same way or that the meaning attached to family life will remain constant over time or even within one account. It is necessary, therefore, to focus not simply on shared social representations but on the formation of subjectivity within different circumstances and contexts. We need to understand how the personal history, the immediate context, and the existing cultural representations come together in the production of accounts and the ways in which resistant discourses engage with and refute such representations. It is also necessary to understand more about (a) the extent to which discourse can be subverted from within, (b) which parts of discourse appear to be essential and (c) which parts may be more easily expendable.

These are issues that are being explored in research that we are currently undertaking into the way in which women construe maternal stress. This research examines some of the influences on mothers' understanding of maternal stress and child abuse by interviewing women who share a common experience as mothers but who differ in their experience of childhood abuse and disruption, of professional social work training and in their current levels of social and relational stress. Of particular interest is the ascription of responsibility within the family and the connections between personal experience, professional training and issues of maternal blame. In our current research we are also looking at differences between lay and professional theories of the causes of child abuse, and at the influence of an alternative feminist discourse of family life and gender roles on maternal subjectivity.

In the late twentieth century, the meanings ascribed to family life and to gender roles are at a crucial point of transition. Many discourses around family life are emerging through which previously unarticulated experiences are being heard. These discourses, which arise from the individual's struggle with contradictions between experience and representation, are likely to draw on, yet subvert, previous discourses around the "normal" family. As such they offer an opportunity to examine the formation of subjectivity and to understand the way in which social change occurs.

## NOTE

1 Research funded by the Economic and Social Research Council, UK.

## BIBLIOGRAPHY

Barrett, M. (1980) *Women's oppression today*, London: Verso.

Barrett, M. and McIntosh, M. (1982) *The anti social family*, London: Verso.

Billig, M. (1987) *Arguing and thinking: A rhetorical approach to social psychology*, Cambridge: Cambridge University Press.

Brannen, J. and Wilson, G. (eds) (1983) *Give and take in families*, London: Allen & Unwin.

Burman, E. (1990) "Differing with deconstruction: A feminist critique," in I. Parker and J. Shotter (eds) *Deconstructing social psychology*, London: Routledge.

—— (1992) "Feminism and discourse in developmental psychology: Power, subjectivity and interpretation," *Feminism and Psychology* 2: 45–60.

Caplan, P. (1981) *Barriers between women*, Lancaster: Falcon Press.

—— (1985) *The myth of women's masochism*, London: Methuen.

Chodorow, N. (1978) *The reproduction of mothering: Psychoanalysis and the sociology of gender*, Berkeley: University of California Press.

Croghan, R. (1993) "A task for life: Coming to terms with childhood disruption in family relationships," paper presented at the INPR Conference, Milwaukee.

Croghan, R. and Miell, D. (1995) "Blaming our mothers, blaming ourselves: Women's accounts of childhood abuse and disruption," *Feminism and Psychology* 5: 31–47.

Fraser, E. (1992) "Teenage girls reading Jackie," in P. Scannell, P. Schlesinger and C. Sparks (eds) *Culture and power: A media, culture and society reader*, Newbury Park, CA: Sage.

Gergen, K. (1991) *The saturated self*, New York: Holt, Reinhart & Winston.

Giddens, A. (1994) "Elements of the theory of structuration," in *The Polity reader in social theory*, Cambridge: Polity Press.

Gill, R. (1995) "Relativism, reflexivity and politics: Interrogating discourse analysis from a feminist perspective," in S. Wilkinson and C. Kitzinger (eds) *Feminism and discourse: Psychological perspectives*, London: Sage.

Graham, H. (1983). "Caring: A labor of love," in J. Finch and D. Groves (eds) *A labor of love: Women work and caring*, London: Routledge & Kegan Paul.

Griffin, C. (1990) "The researcher talks back: Dealing with power relations in studies of young people's entry into the job market," in W. Shaffir and R. Stebbins (eds) *Experiencing fieldwork*, Newbury Park, CA: Sage.

Hollway, W. (1984) "Gender differences and the production of subjectivity," in J. Henriques, W. Hollway, C. Urwin, C. Venn and V. Walkerdine (eds) *Changing the subject: Psychology, social regulation and subjectivity*, London: Methuen.

La Rossa, R. and La Rossa, M. (1981) *Transition to parenthood: How children change families*, Beverley Hills, CA: Sage.

Nice, V. (1992) *Mothers and daughters: The distortion of a relationship*, Macmillan: London.

Oakley, A. (1981) "Interviewing women: A contradiction in terms," in H. Roberts (ed.) *Doing feminist research*, London: Routledge & Kegan Paul.

Parker, I. (1992) *Discourse dynamics: Critical analysis for social and individual psychology*, London: Routledge.

Pleck, J. H. (1982) *Paid work and family work adjustment*, Wellesley, MA: Center for Research on Women.

—— (1985) *Working wives, working husbands*, Beverley Hills, CA: Sage.
Potter, J. and Wetherell, M. (1987) *Discourse and social psychology*, London: Sage.
Pleck, J.H. and Lange, L. (1978) *Men's family role: Its nature and consequences*, Wellesley, MA: Wellesley College Centre for Research on Women.
Shotter, J. (1993) *The cultural politics of every day life*, Milton Keynes: Open University Press.
Weedon, C. (1987) *Feminist practice and poststructuralist theory*, Oxford: Basil Blackwell.
Wetherell, M. (1995) "Romantic discourse: Analyzing investment, power and desire," in S. Wilkinson and C. Kitzinger (eds) *Feminism and discourse: Psychological perspectives*, London: Sage.
Wetherell, M. and Potter, J. (1992) "Mapping the language of racism," in J. Potter and M. Wetherell (eds) *Discourse and the legitimization of exploitation*, Hemel Hempstead: Harvester Wheatsheaf.
Wilkinson, S. (1981) "Personal constructs and private explanations," in C. Antaki (ed.) *The psychology of ordinary explanations of social behavior*, New York and London: Academic Press.
—— (1988) "The role of reflexivity in feminist psychology," *Women's Studies International Forum* 11: 493–502.
—— (1991) "Feminism and psychology: From critique to reconstruction," *Feminism and Psychology* 1: 5–18.
Williams, F. (1989) "Social policy: A critical introduction," in F. Williams (ed.) *Issues of race, gender, and class*, Cambridge: Polity Press.

Chapter 4

# Budding happiness

## The relational dynamics of the abuse of girls and young women by their boyfriends

*Renée Römkens and Sylvia Mastenbroek*

Renée Römkens got her academic training in criminology and psychology at the Catholic University of Nijmegen. She combined her early activism in developing women's studies within the university during the 1970s with her interest in wife abuse and the shelter movement in the Netherlands. From the 1980s onward she has been doing research on violence in the family. She has conducted an in-depth national survey on wife abuse among a representative sample of 1,016 women in the Netherlands. The combination of quantitative and qualitative methods in the field of violence in the family is her special interest. Her current research focuses on sociolegal aspects of battered women who kill their spouses. Currently she is an associate professor of women's studies at Utrecht University.

Sylvia Mastenbroek is a clinical psychologist who received her training at the Free University of Amsterdam. Her involvement with violence against women began during her university training when she was working in a self-help organization for raped women. Motivated also by feminist interests she conducted research on wife abuse for several years, in particular on dating violence and the development of therapeutic methods for abused women. Furthermore she is looking for ways on how to apply her insights about abusive relationships when raising her own children. She currently teaches in a postdoctoral program for family therapists on wife abuse and works in a private conjoint psychotherapy practice in Amsterdam.

*The authors hope to raise awareness of the need for early education in schools on how romance, domination and control in Western culture easily intersect in abusive heterosexual courtship relations.*

Violence against young and old is on the increase (Kester and Junger-Tas 1994) and is predominantly the work of boys and men (Junger-Tas 1995; Römkens 1995). Concern about this increase in violence concentrates on *public* violence: vandalism, theft, and the recent phenomenon of group rape. A topic which is hardly discussed in the Netherlands, however, in contrast to the United States and Canada, is abuse and rape of a girl *by her boyfriend*. Yet if we consider the violence that occurs in relationships between young people, as well as the physical and psychological damage it causes, there are grounds for concern. Previous exploratory research already indicated the binds in which girls find themselves when they are abused by their boyfriends at an early stage in the relationship (see Levy 1991). These relationships are marked by rapid alternations between romantic expectations and hope, on the one hand, and shame and fascination, on the other. Add the growing social isolation because they do not dare to talk about it for a long time, and a number of crucial ingredients are present which further complicate the decision on whether to continue the relationship or not. So far systematic empirical research on the process of "symbiosis," in which the boyfriend and girlfriend become entangled, is lacking.

Two aspects of the issue are tackled in the present article. First, we review research on prevalence of abuse of girls in dating relationships. "Dating violence" is defined as violation of a girl's *physical* integrity by her boyfriend. This means that the girl is subjected to pain or harm against her will by physical violence or force, and/or that she is forced to engage in sexual intercourse. In relation to this first aspect, we present an international survey of the main results of research on the prevalence and nature of dating violence.

In the light of this quantitative outline, we proceed to deal with the question of how girls experience relationships in which their boyfriends are violent, especially the difficulties they encounter in deciding whether or not to continue with the relationship. In discussing this question, we will present results of a recent qualitative study conducted in the Netherlands among a group of twenty young women who were interviewed in depth about the dynamics of their abusive relationships (Mastenbroek 1995).

## DATING VIOLENCE IN INTERNATIONAL PERSPECTIVE: PREVALENCE AND NATURE

### Physical abuse of girls by their boyfriends

During the first half of the 1980s it became clear that a lot of dating violence takes place among young people during the period of getting to know one another, which is usually associated with romantic feelings and love (Makepeace 1981; Henton *et al.* 1982; Legg *et al.* 1984). Estimates of the scale on which it occurs differ widely. It was also unclear whether and in which context both partners resorted to violence, and how serious that violence was. There were no reliable statistics on prevalence because of the lack of representative research and because data was collected in different ways.

Representative Dutch research conducted among 1,016 women between the ages of 20 and 60 years (oral interviews) in 1989 revealed that almost one out of every four (23 percent) young unmarried women (up to 24 years) had experienced *unilateral* violence from a boyfriend at some time. Previous indications in American research—that violence is relatively more common among unmarried and cohabiting couples than among married couples—were confirmed in the Dutch research. Young unmarried women reported not only more cases of abuse (23 percent compared to 17 percent among married women), but also *significantly more serious* cases of abuse, by (former) boyfriends (Römkens 1989, 1992, 1997; see also Yllö and Straus 1981).[1]

A recent Canadian survey (written questionnaire) among a representative sample of 1,835 female students between the ages of 17 and 24 years confirmed the impression that violence against young women is certainly not exceptional in terms of prevalence. One out of three female students (34 per cent) claimed to have been subjected to violence by a boyfriend at some time. In more than one in five cases (22 percent), this had taken place within the previous year (Kelly and DeKeseredy 1994). Unfortunately, this research fails to specify the seriousness of the violence; nor does it make clear the extent to which the violence was unilateral and originated from the boyfriend.

Research also shows that girls regularly hit their boyfriends (see White and Koss 1992); however, this should not be taken to imply that violence among young people is an equally serious problem for boys and girls. Various studies have demonstrated a gender bias in self-reports of violent behavior. Girls and women tend to "overreport" violence, whereas boys and men tend to underreport. Girls and women also tend to feel more responsible for their own violence, whereas boys and men who use violence put the blame on girls and are more inclined to view their violence as "reciprocating." This gender bias can result in a distorted picture in which prevalence and severity of male violence is downplayed, while female violence is overemphasized (Szinovacz 1983; Edleson and Brygger 1986; Riggs *et al.* 1989; Stets and Straus 1990; LeJeune and Follette 1994). For the time being it may be assumed that girls can certainly be violent toward their boyfriends, but that this is usually in the sense of the proverbial slap which can fall anywhere. Compared to that, the average violence of boyfriends toward their dates tends to be more severe.

**Undesired sex and rape**

The American survey by Koss *et al.* (1987) among 3,187 female college students provides the most reliable data on girl rape for the time being. A total of more than one out of every four female students interviewed for that survey (27 percent) in the United States claims to have been raped (15 percent) or to have experienced an attempted rape (12 percent) after the age of 14 years. A large majority (80 percent) of the rapists were friends or acquaintances of the girls. *Rape* in this case is defined as undesired sexual penetration accompanied by violence or threatening behavior, or when the victim was under the influence and could not give her free assent.[2] Only 5 percent of the raped female students reported it to the police, and half of them did not mention it to anyone. Incidentally, in the case of rape by an acquaintance, not talking about it is a general tendency among rape victims (Russell 1982).

In a recent Dutch survey held among 457 female students in Amsterdam on sexual violence *"in dating situations,"* almost one out of five (19 percent) claimed to have had undesired sexual contact at some time with the person they were going out with. More than half of them (10.5 percent of the entire sample) had experienced a rape or attempted rape at some time while dating a male friend (Dhalganjansing and Raams 1995).

The figures in these studies cannot immediately be compared with one another because of the differences in methodological approach and in the definitions followed. However, they convincingly demonstrate that date rape is by no means exceptional. The high figures have led to heated debates in the United States for a variety of "methodological" reasons,[3] and out of sheer disbelief. Since sex between adolescents and youngsters is inevitably a matter of uncertainty and ambivalence, exploring one another's boundaries and sexual desires is an activity in which things can indeed easily go wrong. Among young women there have been voices accusing their peers of labeling every disappointing sexual encounter *post hoc* as rape, turning their sexual ambivalence into a simple victim claim (Roiphe 1993). In particular, the category of "rape under influence" in Koss's research has come in for criticism. The American researchers have meanwhile revealed that, if this category is disqualified as "rape," the figure drops by one-third. This leaves 8 percent of girls who have experienced an attempted rape, and 11 percent who have experienced an actual rape, after the age of 14 years, usually by a friend or acquaintance (Koss and Cook 1993). The latter statistics are close to the figures from the research among female students in Amsterdam.

## THE DYNAMICS OF DATING VIOLENCE: THE DILEMMA OF STAYING OR LEAVING

The large-scale inquiries referred to above also show that it is not always easy to break off a violent relationship. In the research by Koss *et al.* (1987), a large number of the female students indicate that they still had sex with the boyfriend in question after the rape, with 87 percent of those raped eventually breaking off the relationship for good. Secondary analyses of research material from the large-scale Dutch research on the abuse of (young) women (Römkens 1989) reveal a similar tendency. One out of four young women who are abused by a boyfriend experience ongoing violence for a period of two to five years. The following sections deal with the qualitative Dutch study into the bonding dynamics in abusive relationships and the dilemmas which girls have to face (Mastenbroek 1995).

### Theoretical background

The Dutch study includes aspects of the psychological and relational dynamics which throw light on why girls experience the problem of whether to continue a relationship with a violent boyfriend or not as a *dilemma* in which outsiders seem to have just one natural reaction: leave him (cf. Römkens 1991). Various theories offered guidelines for conducting the research into the relational and psychological dynamics of abusive relationships.

The psychoanalytic and system-oriented theory of Willi (1987) claims that serious relational conflicts are caused by polarized processes of transference which already come into play at the start of the relationship. In a so-called "autonomy–dependency collusion," both partners (often unconsciously) have to deal with the desire for and the fear of dependence or independence. In order to resolve this conflict, they transfer their dependence or independence to one another. In the intimacy of the relationship, they can both experience the desired and feared property at close quarters without having to recognize it as such. Goldner *et al.* (1990) remarked that such patterns of transference display a gender arrangement and play an important role in relationships in which women are abused. The partners try to find in one another those capacities that they have more or less lost during the process toward culturally acceptable forms of masculinity or femininity. The man tries to find his capacity to be vulnerable. This provokes considerable anxiety about his reduced "masculinity," resulting in violent actions to counter it. The latter researchers noted a tendency to take over the "masculine" ideal of strength and autonomy on the part of abused women. They, too, are seized by serious anxieties when it comes to opposing culturally transmitted definitions of "femininity." The ambivalent transferences can seriously complicate a woman's decision on whether to continue or end a violent relationship.

Paradoxically enough, two crucial factors in a violent relationship *reinforce* the process of *traumatic bonding* between the partners (Dutton and Painter 1981; also Dutton and Painter 1993). The first is *intermittent reinforcement*: the violent partner alternates positive–remunerative with negative–punitive strategies. Second, the asymmetry of power and dependence prevents a relationship from being broken off quickly, no matter how painful it may be. A bonding to a person who is perceived as more powerful than yourself leads in the short term to a more positive image of yourself, but in the long run it makes you extremely vulnerable to abuse of that asymmetry of power. This only increases the difference in power between boy and girl, and the boy assumes omnipotent qualities in the eyes of his girlfriend.

Against the theoretical background of these insights, in-depth interviews were conducted in 1994 among a self-selected sample of twenty women who agreed to participate in a study on experiences with physical violence as teenagers or young adults at the hands of a former boyfriend.[4] They were asked about the course of the relationship from the moment of making acquaintance. Developments in the early stage, especially the positive aspects of the partner, subsequent ambivalences, and transference processes which get under way in the relationship are scrutinized in the light of the violence that came later.

The physical violence experienced by the twenty young women in this study was (very) serious in all cases. The frequency varied from a single incident with serious injury to systematic abuse over a number of years. One-third of the girls were already subjected to physical violence by their boyfriend during the early stage of the relationship, others as it developed. Almost two-thirds of the girls were abused when they were still attending school or further education. The names of the interviewees are fictional to protect the privacy of the women involved.

## RESULTS

### Romantic attachment, control and violence

In many cases, the girls in this study feel flattered by the encompassing attention boyfriends initially pay: they want to be with the girl all the time and will not take "no" for an answer; they want to know who they have met, what they have been doing, etc. A young woman may feel flattered if her boyfriend often phones unexpectedly, drops in, or suddenly appears while she is supposed to be going somewhere on her own. If the boyfriends tell their dates to behave differently because they do not want other boys to start pawing, most of the girls experience this as a sign of caring. During the early stage of the dating most interviewees report the transition from this universal and enclosing attention to a demanding, controlling, and isolating behavior. This throws girls into confusion. Mary is often unexpectedly picked up by her boyfriend to go for a ride in his car. She feels that she is very important to him and thinks that the feeling of being entirely surrounded by him is love. Later in the relationship her boyfriend demands all her attention, criticizes and controls her eating and dressing habits, and isolates her from other social contacts.

MARY At first we were so attached to one another. But later it becomes clear to you, the control and having to do everything together.

In many cases, a boy is eager to get a relationship going quickly. For example, he wants to give a ring at one of the first dates or to tell others that he has a relationship with the girlfriend without discussing it with her. At parties he emphatically puts his arm around her, pulls her away from other people with a joke to annex her, or stands between her and other people. Boys often rush personal intimacy or force it by repeatedly asking very personal questions. Many girls indicate how far they are prepared to go, but they are often still unable to hold on to the boundaries they initially set for themselves if the boys are persistent, and give in. Even physical violence can become extremely romanticized in the beginning.

MAISY Because you don't use force and violence to stop a person from going somewhere unless you love that person. You want that person to stay with you: You are mine, I love you, you're staying here.

Social isolation can set in at an early stage in the relationship, leading to a reduction in the possibilities of comparing the relational standards of the boy with those of others. The romantic interpretations and the feeling of being flattered by the boy because of his "all-embracing" attention make it difficult to get the restrictive aspects into focus, even though many girls can already feel them at an early stage. They become imprisoned in a symbiotic "everything together."

### Confusion in the sexual relationship

All girls are in love at first and enjoy the sexual excitement. A girl may see her boyfriend's sexual attention as a sign of passion and love, even though she may feel uncomfortable about it. Most boys tell their girlfriend that "good sex" is the most important thing in a relationship. For half the girls, sex becomes sharply split off from the rest of the relationship. A girl may feel appreciated by her boyfriend in their sexual relation (even though priority is usually given to the boyfriend's sexual wishes), while the rest of his behavior is often coarse. She may then try to cope with the confusion arising from this by generalizing the positive experience of sex to the whole of the relationship or to the "nature" of the boyfriend, and shut herself off from the feelings and thoughts about the humiliating, menacing or sometimes simply violent behavior of her boyfriend. Sex becomes a straw to clutch at.

If, on the other hand, a girl makes it clear that she is not (yet) ready for sexual intercourse, she does not usually make any further agreements on this point with her boyfriend. They both seem to expect the boy to take the initiative. According to the interviewees, their boyfriends think up all sorts of reasons to get them to have sexual intercourse with them. Often they refer to the fact that they are males, and "thus" have more knowledge or sexual experience. Some of the girls have been grilled for hours about why they do not (yet) want to have intercourse or other forms of sex with them. A few girls report to have experienced physical violence at an early stage when their boyfriends forced them to have sex. Signals of pain by the girl during (anal) sex are completely ignored by some boys. Sometimes sexual intercourse is imposed as a punishment for "disobedience," for example, if the girl was talking to another boy. These circumstances make sexual contact an extremely ambivalent experience for many of the interviewees. Here, too, many of them are confused about what romantic sexual behavior is supposed to be like.

**Ambivalent transference of power by the girl**

The girls in this study often make their acquaintance in the first instance with the extremely self-confident side of their boyfriends' personality. Out of a need for security and protection they seem to focus exclusively on this aspect of their character. This need can play a role in the development of the relationship and in surviving the subsequent abuse.

When the girls pass through the stage of detaching themselves from their parents or guardians, this is almost always accompanied by feelings of insecurity and uncertainty about whether they will manage to build a life of their own. They try to find help and support in a boyfriend who does not seem to be bothered by these feelings and exaggerate his perceived imperturbability.

If girls have an injured sense of self, often as a result of extremely painful experiences in their childhood (such as psychological, sexual and/or physical violence by parents/caregivers, which is the case for almost half of the interviewees), they can solve their anxieties and feelings of helplessness by associating (and projectively identifying) with a powerful, protective boyfriend. This enhances their self-image.

LINDE The most attractive thing in my eyes was his macho behavior. It made him stronger than my parents. And I had such an influence over him that he would stand up for me. If anyone touched his family, he was beaten up. He was very proud to talk about it. I just saw a strong man who wouldn't get taken in by anybody. And who gave as good as he got. He did things I'd never done. I should have, but I was afraid. It's as if he was a mirror to me, showing me what I would have liked to be.

Linde was physically abused by her mother and sexually abused by her grandfather. The abuse came to an end once she had a romantic relationship. The sense of being "freed" by her boyfriend continued long after his psychological and physical violence had begun.

A third aspect that appeared to be of great importance for almost all interviewed girls in their need for protection is their fear of sexual harassment and rape by other boys. Strikingly enough, most of the interviewees mentioned some kind of perceived risk of being sexually victimized as a fact of life for girls and (young) women.

RONDA I felt safe and protected with him. Because once when someone pinched my bottom he beat him up completely. It was terrible, that boy was bleeding from his eyes and so on. I thought: "He takes care of me, he makes sure no one touches me."

On the other hand, Ronda does not think it right that her boyfriend's "protection" should be combined with such heavy violence. In the course of the relationship, several interviewees find themselves in the paradoxical situation of protecting themselves against (potential) violence from third parties by attaching themselves to an aggressive young man. In many cases the parents also contribute to the process by which a girl regards her boyfriend as a protector or bodyguard. Many of the girls immediately acquire more freedom when they are dating a boyfriend, freedom which also enables them to develop further. In some cases the role of supervisor or protector is literally assigned to the boyfriend by the parents.

Two-thirds of the girls are extremely fascinated by the strength of their boyfriend. On the one hand, they leave that side up to him; on the other, they want to use that strength as an *example* for themselves.

ARLETTE I just watched him: how he does it, that heroic behavior and not caring about anything at all. It fascinated me. I wanted to pick some of it up as well. I didn't just want to carry on admiring it in him.

Many girls are caught up in this field of tension between the wish to be more autonomous and its transference to a strong, apparently autonomous man. They find themselves in the impossible situation of wanting to be more powerful in a relationship with a man who feels extremely threatened by this desire.

**Between strength and vulnerability: Transference by boys**

Based on what the interviewees report, there seems to be a strong splitting evident among the violent boyfriends between their strength and their vulnerability. Strength is expressed in extremely forceful behavior based on (what the girls perceive as) a perfect self-image, which is regularly taken to be inherent in being a male.

LYDIA He thought he never did anything wrong because he was older and a man.

Half of the girls experienced a constant alternation between very self-assured and very powerless and hurt behavior from their boyfriends.

IRENE He sometimes said that he felt like a crying giant.

One side of him is the self-assured "giant": omniscient, omnipotent, up to anything. The other side is a crying, fearful and hurt person. Since the two sides are not integrated, it is very difficult for the girl to form a coherent image and set of feelings about her boyfriend.

If a girl comes into contact with the vulnerable side of her boyfriend, he makes it clear to her that she is the only person to whom he dares to show that side of his personality, that she is the only one who understands him, and that he needs her.

HANNAH He longed for someone with whom he could be himself intimately. That's what I've become for him. I have to care for him, back him up, be there when he needs me, make love a lot with him . . .

A girl feels flattered if this apparently strong young man lets her into the secret of his vulnerable, powerless side. She will increasingly aim at the satisfaction of his needs. She does her utmost to spare him. She feels that she is growing into the role of "saviour," often at precisely the moment at which she feels weaker and weaker *vis-à-vis* her "omnipotent" boyfriend. Most of these girls take care of their boyfriend not only to maintain their image of his strength, but also out of pity, loyalty or a sense of guilt, and increasingly out of fear of his violence.

Sooner or later, the boys shift the responsibility for their (emotional) wellbeing to a large extent onto their girlfriends, and many girls increasingly assume that responsibility. They start to feel guilty about not being able to satisfy the demands of their boyfriends, despite the great efforts they make.

IRIS It was all my fault. It wasn't his fault that he felt so depressed and unable to cope with life. I simply didn't do my best. I was in fact responsible for his happiness. That's what he said as well. He said it, honest!

If it does not work out, the overwhelmingly positive projections which the boy at first makes onto her are gradually transformed into overwhelmingly negative projections. While the girlfriend was his hope of salvation at the start, sooner or later she becomes his big disappointment. As a result, the boy starts to feel strong again and the girl feels weak again. She alternates between feeling that she is a saviour and a major disaster. Many girls are blamed for the violence of their boyfriends.

ARLETTE I was blamed for his aggression right from the start of the relationship. If I just behaved properly, he wouldn't have such a miserable life in which he had to abuse somebody. I felt like a bastard.

A turn toward (extreme) confusion of boundaries in the relationship is due to the boy's demand for "total" care and lack of responsibility on the one hand, and the girl's assumption of the responsibility to help him on the other.[5] Later on, she often does this too in her attempts to prevent his violence. Through sharing the boy's secret about his feelings of fallibility and dependence, the girl often covers up his violence for a long time. The boy's behavior often escalates from more and more serious forms of psychological violence (such as insults and verbal abuse, isolation, blackmail and threats of violence or rape) to increasingly serious physical and sexual violence.

## Ambivalence and the development of strength among girls

Strong ambivalences and discrepancies arise among all interviewees between their emotions and their intellect. On the one hand, they are in love with the attractive aspects of their boyfriends, but more or less from the start; on the other, they all have feelings of astonishment, anxiety or fear about their unpredictable, threatening or violent behavior. Girls may do "everything" to try to prevent violence, to help their boyfriends to change, and to adjust their own behavior; but they may become very confused and for short or long periods *deny* the seriousness of the situation. They selectively focus on the positive aspects of their relationship.

SANDRA I started to doubt my feelings. Feelings, they were something strange, I couldn't do anything about them. He had so many contradictions.

IRENE I should have listened to my feelings at the times when I was so frightened.

What is striking is the *strength* with which most girls put up a verbal and sometimes violently physical resistance to a boyfriend's pressure and violence. This strength also often acts as a camouflage; it may make the girl feel for a long time that she is as strong as he is, because "I'm not the kind of girl who puts up with being beaten." This disguises the humiliating idea that the relationship is no longer one between equals and that, despite her (feeling of) putting up a resistance, she gives in more and more often and makes concessions in order to avoid conflicts and violence.

CHERYL I said fairly soon: "You can't stay the night here." "Of course I can stay, why not!," he replied. So I said: "Well, OK, go and lie on a mattress somewhere." And in the end he stayed the night and we had sex.

Among girls who have been brought up in a feminist setting, the struggle against violence is a bitter one, and the denials of the humiliations are correspondingly vigorous.

Many girls feel that they have landed in some kind of "funnel" right from the start of the relationship: they experience less and less control over their own lives. In almost all cases the girls' self-confidence in relationships decreases. Some of them can maintain their self-confidence in other aspects of their life—for instance, because they do well at school—but many often have problems with concentrating and studying. Contacts with fellow pupils decline. Some girls report being kept awake until late at night, for example, explaining why they do not want to have sex. As a consequence, they are unable to get up in time to go to school the next morning. Some of them drop out of school under the pressure of circumstances and due to the violence of their boyfriends.

## Getting out

The girls (most of them are by that time young women in their twenties) gradually arrive at the conclusion—often exhausted—that whatever they do will not change the behavior of their boyfriends, that despite all their efforts they will *be able neither to help nor to change their boyfriends,* and that they still get (literally and metaphorically) beaten. It is only when they have reached this conclusion that they manage to break through their denial of the humiliations and of their insecurity. Step by step, they re-establish contact with feelings of emotional and physical self-preservation. More and more they break through the transference of their protection and face up to their fear

ELLEN Just at the moment when I felt I'd hit rock bottom, I felt a strength somewhere inside: "Now I'm going to go it on my own." And that pulled me out of it. That driving force is very important.

The young women are then increasingly able to discriminate and weigh up the positive and negative sides of their boyfriends, even though their inner turmoil is sometimes prolonged long after the end of the relationship. When Cheryl breaks off the relationship and reports it to the police, her anger at her boyfriend's excessive violence ebbs away, and suddenly she feels overwhelmed by feelings of love for him.

CHERYL I had no idea how to cope with that. Because I didn't consider going back to him again for a moment.

The process of distancing is also complicated by the fact that it is precisely during this stage that a boyfriend's violence and threats can increase. If, nevertheless, the girls leave, many boys re-assume the behavior of romantic conquest and remorse. Hope of improvement and the old feelings of being in love may return to the girls, which goes some way to explaining the well-known phenomenon that many abused women break off the relationship and then come back again, time after time.

But there is another process too which affects the phenomenon of leaving and then going back to the partner which outsiders often find so hard to understand. After breaking off a relationship, an emotional process of coming to terms starts once the girls are really in a safer situation. An integral component of the psychological coming to terms with traumatic experiences is the alternation between periods of re-experiencing (for example, in nightmares), and periods of denying the violence (by which women start to doubt the seriousness of what happened). During the periods of denial, a woman is more likely to go back to her boyfriend, especially if he tries to contact her at that time, lays a claim on her and promises to improve. However, as the return takes place within the process of coming to terms, she often assumes a more detached attitude toward the relationship. In the end, all but one of the interviewees broke off the relationship.

## CONCLUSIONS

International research data indicate that physical and sexual abuse is a problem in many dating relationships. If we follow conservative estimates, we must assume that *at least one out of ten girls* is confronted by (unilateral) abuse and/or is forced to have sex with a boyfriend or partner. The idea that violence is a "marital problem" which arises "later" is a romantic illusion. Many girls and boys learn this the hard way. The fact that a large group of schoolgirls are the victims of physical and sexual violence at the hands of their boyfriends should especially alert teachers to noticing it and opening it up for discussion (parents too, of course, but some of them are themselves entangled in violent abuse). Information and prevention programmes as developed in the United States and Canada may be helpful in this respect (see: NiCarthy 1986; Levy 1993).

The Dutch in-depth study, as presented here, shows that breaking off a relationship with a violent boyfriend proves to be a far-reaching and difficult task for a girl. The mixture of sociocultural notions about sharing each other's company romantically, infatuation, passion, and violence makes teenagers vulnerable as a social group. They run the risk of slipping when they take their first steps on the road to forming relationships. Sexuality often turns out to be a world to which boys and girls attach different expectations and meanings. Boys are offered numerous legitimations for dominant and aggressive "captivating behavior" (Larkin and Popaleni 1994). The shift in their behavior from overwhelming, captivating attention to controlling, annexing, jealous, and violent behavior usually takes place gradually, so that girls hang on to their initial romantic interpretations for a long time (see also Browne 1987). Public education and information services must continue to critically analyze this interweaving of romanticism and violence. But given the fact that the mixture of violence against women and romance is culturally acceptable and legitimated in many movies and video clips, efforts to counteract this require a paradoxical effort as well.

The dilemma of whether to stay or to go is intensified by processes of transference between the partners which bring about a confusion of the boundaries between them. The results presented here are in accordance with theoretical notions about the *polarized transference of strength and vulnerability* (Willi 1987) along gender-determined lines (Goldner *et al.* 1991) both during the stage of partner choice and in the development of conflicts. Girls are caught in a field of tension between developing their own strength and identity on the one hand, and being fearful and uncertain about it on the other. They often continue to look for strength and security in what they regard as "strong" boyfriends. It gives a lot of the girls who were interviewed an illusion of security to have relationships with boys who are prepared to defend them—with violence if necessary. This implies a self-image of being "weak." They feel stronger because their demand for security is met. It is possible that girls who are mistreated by their boyfriends have a greater need for security and safety—and are thus more vulnerable—than girls who do not experience violence at the hands of their boyfriends (see Verhoeven 1991). Second, girls try to find their strength and identity by taking the self-assured, emotionally resilient behavior of their boyfriends as an example for themselves. As a result of the polarized transference of strength and vulnerability, however, a relational dynamics is created in which they are unable (and not allowed) to develop the role of strong woman, but become more and more vulnerable and dependent. In discussing the developments in their relationship, we could see a lot of girls carrying on—though ambivalently—to try to get power again in their own hands. In the end most break through the transference of strength and come into contact with their own desire for independence (van Rappard 1988).

Although the boys were not interviewed, the stories of the interviewed women reflect many tensions in the boyfriends' behavior between their strength and vulnerability. On the one hand, many of them seem to explore their vulnerable and dependent sides to some extent within the intimacy of the relationship. They make it clear to their girlfriends that they do not dare to do this with anyone else. On the other hand, the public expression of the one-sided strong role indicates that this exploration in the intimate relationship is highly conflict-ridden. This can also be seen from the transference of the responsibility for their problematic behavior and from the extreme claims they make on their girlfriends. The way the boys control and socially isolate their girlfriends, and the violent way they behave, can be seen as a resistance to the fear of being dominated and made subordinate. The boys try to sublimate their own wish for dependence by making others dependent on them. A boy's fear for his own dependence will increase in the relationship, with the risk that it will be resisted with even more tyrannical behavior. One of the symptoms of this is the shift from psychological to physical violence. The "autonomy–dependence collusion" (Willi 1987) and the alternating behavior of the boy (caring, captivating, repentant, alternating with humiliating and violent) lead to a "traumatic bonding" (Dutton and Painter 1981, 1993).

The confusing combination of concern about his problems, the sense of being important for him in that way, of being physically abused and held responsible, is often fatal for breaking out of the relationship (see also Römkens 1991). One of the reasons for this may be the fact that many girls are parentified in their family of origin, i.e. have learned to sense the (emotional) needs of their parents and often try to "take care" in that respect of their parents, disregarding their own needs as a child (Draijer 1990). Further research is required to throw more light on this in connection with relationships of abuse.

There is no need to argue that upbringing and education should pay more attention to the development of "strength" as a vital part of femininity, and *mutatis mutandis* "vulnerability" in masculinity. Only too often girls simply muddle on too long, vainly hoping for that budding romantic happiness which was once there but which fails to return.

## NOTES

1 Incidentally, there has been an increase in the number of fatal victims (partner killings) among unmarried couples in the United States since 1976, while there has been a corresponding decrease among married couples. The increase concerns mainly female victims (Browne and Williams 1993).

2 The recent Canadian survey by Kelly and DeKeseredy (1994) reported that more than 44 percent had experienced a rape, an attempted rape, or an "undesired" or "forced" sexual contact. In view of this broad definition, it is difficult to compare these statistics with data from the quantitative study by Koss *et al.* (1987).

3 Gilbert (1993) presented as "methodological" criticism of this definition of rape that, if the boy did not *intend* to rape the girl, and had not understood that no "really" meant no, then it was not a case of rape. Under cover of a "methodological discussion," sexist views about women, men, and sex are repeatedly aired in this research field (see Römkens 1990, 1994).

4 This is an exploratory research project based on oral in-depth interviews of young women who were interviewed in retrospect about their experience of violence (Mastenbroek 1995). The women responded to advertisements in national dailies, magazines, university magazines, a radio programme, and practices for psychotherapy. The selection criteria were: Dutch-speaking women, preferably below the age of 35, who had experienced one-sided violence in a heterosexual relationship. In view of the retrospective character of the research, measures were taken to prompt recall and to counter selectivity in the recollections. Interviews were held using a semi-structured questionnaire covering: the family of origin, the period prior to the relationship, the course of development of the relationship in which they had experienced violence, and their present situation. Attention was also paid to aftercare.

Three-quarters of the women were below the age of 35 at the time of the interview. The average level of education of the research group was fairly high: two-thirds of them had been through higher (general, vocational or academic) education. In every case, except one, the relationship was a thing of the past. The duration of the relationships varied from 4 months to 15 years. Three-quarters of the group were teenagers (14 years or older) when they started the relationship. Almost all of them were in secondary school or had just started further training. The boys were four years older on average.

5 It may be the case that a specific individual background factor among girls is connected with this tendency to assume the responsibility for the emotional happiness and violent behavior of their boyfriends. Secondary analysis of the research material revealed that many girls were allocated tasks in the parental home which adults should have performed. At a young age they developed a constant awareness of the sensitive points and/or (often implicit) needs of their guardians (parentification).

## BIBLIOGRAPHY

Browne, A. (1987) *When battered women kill*, New York/London: The Free Press.

Browne, A. and Williams, K. (1993) "Gender, intimacy and lethal violence: Trends from 1976 through 1987," *Gender and Society* 7: 78–98.

Dhalganjansing, S. and Raams, S. (1995) "Date rape: sexueel geweld in uitgaanssituaties," unpublished Ph.D. thesis, Universiteit van Amsterdam.

Draijer, N. (1990) *Seksuele traumatisering in de jeugd. Gevolgen op lange termijn van seksueel misbruik van meisjes door verwanten*, Amsterdam: SUA.

Dutton, D. and Painter S. (1981) "Traumatic bonding: The development of emotional attachments in battered women and other relationships of intermittent abuse," *Victimology: An International Journal* 1: 139–155.

—— (1993) "Emotional attachments in abusive relationships: a test of traumatic bonding theory," *Violence and Victims* 8: 105–120.

Edleson, J. and Brygger, M.P. (1986) "Gender differences in reporting of battering incidents," *Family Relations* 35: 377–382.

Gilbert, N. (1993) "Examining the facts: Advocacy research overstates the incidence of date rape," in R.J. Gelles and D.R. Loseke (eds) *Current controversies on family violence*, New York and London: Sage.

Goldner, V., Penn, P., Scheinberg, M. and Walker, G. (1990) "Love and violence: Gender paradoxes in volatile attachments," *Family Process* 29: 343–364.

Graham, D.L. *et al.* (1995) "A scale for identifying 'Stockholm syndrome' reactions in young dating women: Factor structure, reliability, and validity," *Violence and Victims* 10: 3–22.

Henton, J., Cate, R., Koval, J., Lloyd, S. and Christopher, S. (1982) "Romance and violence in dating relationships," *Journal of Family Issues* 4: 467–482.

Junger-Tas, J. (1995) "Het raadsel van de vrouwencriminaliteit," in A. Fuldauer *et al.* (eds) *Gevangen vrouwen: Essays over criminaliteit en detentie*, Amsterdam: Nemesis.

Kelly, K.D. and DeKeseredy, W. (1994) "Women's fear of crime and abuse in college and university dating relationships," *Violence and Victims* 9: 17–30.

Kester, J. and Junger-Tas, J. (1994) *Criminaliteit en strafrechtelijke reactie*, Arnhem: Gouda Quint.

Koss, M. (1993) "Detecting the scope of rape: A review of prevalence research methods," *Journal of Interpersonal Violence* 8: 198–222.

Koss, M. and Cook, S.L. (1993) "Date and acquaintance rape are significant problems," in R.J. Gelles and D.R. Loseke (eds) *Current controversies on family violence*, New York and London: Sage.

Koss, M.P., Gidycz, C.A. and Wisniewsky, N. (1987) "The scope of rape: Incidence and prevalence of sexual aggression and victimization in a national sample of higher education students," *Journal of Consulting and Clinical Psychology* 55: 162–170.

Larkin, J. and Popaleni, K. (1994) "Heterosexual courtship violence and sexual harassment: the private and public control of young women," *Feminism and Psychology* 2: 213–227.

Legg, J., Olday, D.E. and Wesley, B. (1984) "Why do females remain in violent dating relationships?," paper presented at the Second National Conference for Family Violence Researchers, Durham, NH.

LeJeune, C. and Follette, V. (1994) "Taking responsibility: Sex differences in reporting dating violence," *Journal of Interpersonal Violence* 1: 133–140.

Levy, B. (ed.) (1991) *Dating violence: young women in danger*, Seattle: Seal Press.

—— (1993) *In love and in danger: A teen's guide to breaking free of abusive relationships*, Seattle: Seal Press.

Makepeace, J.M. (1981) "Courtship violence among college students," *Family Relations* 30: 97–102.

Mastenbroek, S. (1995) *De illusie van veiligheid: Voortekenen en ontwikkeling van geweld tegen vrouwen in relaties*, Utrecht: Van Arkel.

NiCarthy, G. (1986) *Getting free: You can end abuse and take back your life*, Seattle: Seal Press.

Pape, K.T. and Arias, I. (1995) "Control, coping and victimization in dating relationships," *Violence and Victims* 10: 43–55.

Pirog-Good, M.A. and Stets, J.E. (eds) (1989) *Violence in dating relationships*, New York: Praeger.

Rappard, M. van (1988) *Tot hier en niet verder: Verzet van mishandelde vrouwen*, Baarn: Ambo.

Riggs, D.S., Murphy, C.M. and O'Leary, K. (1989) "Intentional falsification in reports of interpartner aggression," *Journal of Interpersonal Violence* 2: 220–232.

Roiphe, K. (1993) *The morning after: Sex, fear and feminism*. London/New York: Little, Brown & Co.

Römkens, R. (1989) *Geweld tegen vrouwen in heteroseksuele relaties: Een landelijk onderzoek naar de omvang, de aard, de gevolgen en de achtergronden*, Amsterdam: WOSG.

—— (1990) "Methodologie of ideologie? Een reactie op het besprekingsartikel over onderzoek naar meisjes en vrouwen als slachtoffer," *Tijdschrift voor Criminologie* 4: 378–381.

—— (1991) "Het onbehagen over geweld tegen vrouwen: Projectie en internalisering van verantwoordelijkheid en schuld," in P.B. Defares and J.D. van der Ploeg (eds) *Agressie: Determinanten, signalering en interventie*, Van Gorcum: Assen/Maastricht.

—— (1992) *Gewoon geweld? Omvang, aard, gevolgen en achtergronden van geweld tegen vrouwen in heteroseksuele relaties*, Amsterdam/Lisse: Swets en Zeitlinger.

—— (1994) "Wie is bang voor geweld? Over dwang en drang tot zwijgen en dilemma's in het feministisch denken over geweld," in J. Da Lima (ed.) *Het klappen van de zweep*, Utrecht: Van Arkel.

—— (1995) "De partnerdoodster als statistische rariteit," in A. Fuldauer *et al.* (eds) *Gevangen vrouwen: Essays over criminaliteit en detentie*, Amsterdam: Nemesis.

—— (1997) "Prevalence of wife abuse in the Netherlands. Combining quantitative and qualitative methods in survey research," *Journal of Interpersonal Violence* 12: 99–125.

Russell, D. (1982) *Rape in marriage*, New York: Macmillan.

Stets, J. and Straus, M.A. (1990) "The marriage license as a hitting license: A comparison of assaults in dating, cohabiting and married couples," in M.A. Straus and R.J. Gelles (eds) *Physical violence in American families. Risk factors and adaptations to violence in 8,145 families*, New Brunswick/London: Transaction Publishers.

Szinovacz, M.E. (1983) "Using couple data as a methodological tool: the case of marital violence," *Journal of Marriage and the Family* 45: 633–644.

Verhoeven, D. (1991) "Ontaarding van romantiek. Een onderzoek naar het gedrag, de kenmerken en de aantrekkingskracht van later mishandelende mannen in de beginfase van de relatie", unpublished Ph.D. thesis. Katholieke Universiteit Brabant.

White, J.G. and Koss, M.P. (1992) "Courtship violence: Incidence in a national sample of higher education students," *Violence and Victims* 6: 247–256.

Willi, J. (1987) *De partnerrelatie: Ontstaan, ontwarren en verhelderen van conflicten*, Rotterdam: Ad. Donker.

Yllö, K. and Straus, M.A. (1981) "Interpersonal violence among married and cohabiting couples," *Family Relations* 3: 339–347.

# Part II

# Extended family

Chapter 5

# Family conflict in France through the eyes of teenagers

*Didier Le Gall*

Didier Le Gall is Professor of Sociology and Director of The Laboratoire d'Analyse Socio-Anthropologique du Risque (Research Center for The Social-Anthropological Analysis of Risk) at the University of Caen, Basse-Normandy.

*I received my academic training in sociology at the University of Caen where I got my* doctorat *(Ph.D.) in 1984. I completed my second thesis (what we call* habilitation à diriger des recherches*) at the University of Paris V – Sorbonne in 1993. I also have a* licence *(M.A.) in philosophy and in educational sciences from the University of Caen.*

*I am interested in the topic of my chapter because I have been working on families for a long time (traditional families, single-parent families, and stepfamilies). I encountered family conflict very often—between husband and wife, during divorce, and so on. Now, I work more specifically on affective ties and, of course, I encountered conflicts again. The main representation of family is always the same: "In the family, everybody loves each other," although that is not true. So what is the family today? What does it take to make us feel a sense of belonging to a family? Around which values and norms did the family revolve during two decades of change? In order to answer these questions, this chapter focuses on the conflicts that disturb the foundations of the family, a focus that is based on the idea that these conflicts are the potential indicators that may reveal ties between family members. And because I think it's not possible to approach these conflicts from all sides at once, I chose (that's one option among others) to look at family conflict as viewed by the youth. I choose this focus also in order to show that family conflicts are quite different from other conflicts. The slightest differences can have resounding effects which can easily transform into radical conflict. Thus, family conflicts differ from other conflicts because the idea of "Family" is associated with the idea of unity.*

*I would obviously like the reader to see and understand all this, but not only this. I would also like him or her to understand that social regulation within the family differs between social classes because in each social class we have different representations of what "Family" is or must be—something like a family norm. Therefore it is difficult to have only one discourse about all family conflicts. We find here what we know about divorce: the upper class is better armed to find the way to negotiation. There is conflict, but it less often results in (physically) violent explosion.*

## FROM THE "CRISIS" OF THE FAMILY TO THE "RELATIONAL" FAMILY

In the 1960s and the 1970s, there was the issue of the "crisis," be it the deterioration or the break-up of the family unit (Autrement 1975); some scholars even went as far as prognosticating its death (Cooper 1972). The hegemonical influence of Parsonian thinking, the social and cultural movements of the era, as well as the rapid changes that weakened the institution of the family explain this phenomenon. The family is alive and well and plays a major role today as research from those very years underlines, in the USA as well as in Europe; namely those studies that showed the persistence of relationships and exchanges in the center of the kinship network (Bossard and Boll 1956; Young and Willmott 1957; Rémy 1967; Mogey 1976; Roussel and Bourguignon 1976; Pitrou 1978). The family showed the persistence of relationships and the exchanges within the parental network. A retrospective analysis (Chalvon-Demersay 1989) of about fifty surveys conducted between 1968 and 1988 demonstrates that the French never ceased to consider family an essential value. And the recent infatuation with genealogy shows how much family still is and always will be at the heart of the social imagination (Michelat and Segalen 1991). Beyond the crisis discourse, the family lived on and the French were attached to it. Today, the family appears to be an inevitable reality.

However, it is no longer the family of the 1950s. The high divorce rate, the drop in birthrate, the decreased number of legal marriages, increase in cohabitation and the number of births out of wedlock, the growth of single-parent and stepfamilies as well as longer life expectancy, have obviously transformed the family. Slowly, new balances are established (Segalen 1993). Furthermore, economic growth is over. From a period of near full employment, we moved to an era of recession with endemic unemployment. In spite of such a precarious environment, hopes for greater individual autonomy born from a time of economic growth were not abandoned. Moreover, the rise of individualism, though somewhat dependent on social class, weakened the "communist family" as the traditional family had been called (Roussel 1989). In this sense, the state of the family seemed "uncertain." However, it is not so much the family that is undergoing a crisis as the marital couple. As conjugal disagreements easily bring about separation (Kaufmann 1993), matrimony becomes fragile. But blood ties and intergenerational ties live on, though in different forms as they are restructured along with changes in the family (Le Gall and Martin 1996).

Of course, this "uncertain" family can cause difficult social encounters. For example, following a divorce we almost always see a drop, either temporary or ongoing, in the standard of living of the custodial parent, and in particular for women, who form the majority of custodial parents (Lefaucheur 1988). For the most disadvantaged families, economic instability often goes along with interpersonal vulnerability. But otherwise, the recognition of individual autonomy, the increasing emphasis on emotions in the regulation of family relationships, as well as the greater importance given to the quality of interpersonal relationships contributed to a more egalitarian family that pays more attention to individual well-being and the education of children. Therefore, with reference to E. Durkheim (1975), de Singly (1993) sees the modern family less as a "conjugal" family and more as an "educational" family, and joins those who characterize the contemporary family as "relational"—a development that renders the family no less sensitive to the need for mutual support and solidarity.

Mutual family aid can come in various forms (contribution or loans, emotional support, assistance services, etc.). Types of support differ depending on the changes the family has undergone. Although cohabitation of different generations is less common, living apart does not mean that there is no solidarity. Although children nowadays enjoy more freedom *vis-à-vis* their parents, they tend to postpone leaving home. In well-to-do families, this event involves a form of investment (e.g. college education) that facilitates the children's social success. In less affluent families, it is a waiting period, even withdrawal. In the latter case, the family plays "a considerable role as a shock absorber against the increasing difficulty of social integration" (Galland 1985: 43). Though the increase of three-generation families living together tends to modify the terms of social support (e.g. presence of grandparents, parents, and grandchildren), the importance of social exchanges is in no way diminished. Nowadays, grandchildren, often less numerous than grandparents, are not the only ones to benefit from this restructuring. Considering these changes, it may not be easy to determine whether today's family is more or less united than it used to be. It is obvious that the family still plays a major economic role, and recent research on intergenerational solidarity emphasizes the extreme vitality of family life (Attias-Donfut 1995).

Uncertain but more relationship oriented, smaller but more long-lived (i.e. fewer children; coexistence of several generations), apparently always concerned to fulfill the requirements of solidarity, even though conjugal instability sometimes provokes irreversible ruptures—today's family appears as a multifaceted universe that is not easy to understand and it will be a delicate matter to define its essential qualities. What is the family today? What does it take to make us feel we belong to a family? Around which values and norms does the family revolve after two decades of change ? In order to try to offer some answers to these questions we chose to focus on the conflicts that "trouble" the family—a choice that may surprise but is based on the idea that conflicts may reveal the ties that keep the family together.

## FROM CONFLICT TO FAMILY CONFLICT

According to German sociologist Georg Simmel, conflict is first and foremost a fundamental force of social life because it is an integral part of socialization and the search for social equilibrium.

> If all human interaction is socialisation, then conflict, which is one of the most active forms of interaction has to be considered a form of socialisation . . . Once conflict escalates . . . , it becomes in fact a protective process against the divisions that separate and a way towards a form of unity.
>
> (Simmel 1908/1995: 19)

Hence, at the center of Simmel's theory is the notion that, instead of being a factor of division, conflict is actually a form of socialization that promotes unity. "Conflict in itself is already a solution of the tension between adversaries" (*ibid.*: 20). In other words, all interaction creates some form of connection, even conflict. From this perceptive, struggle appears to be a factor of unity as illustrated by Simmel with a number of cases where unity between two nations emerges after being at war. This tension between antagonism and unity seems to account for all forms of conflict.

In the context of the family, conflict arises amidst "loved ones," people belonging to the same group. We tend to think that this closeness reduces the risk of clashes and misunderstandings. Simmel argues that, on the contrary, this is not the case.

> It is the close family ties, the social and economic solidarity, the presumed unity, that can give rise to violence against the individual. They favor the creation of frictions, tensions and oppositions. We can even say that family conflict is a form of conflict sui generis.
>
> (Simmel 1908/1995: 85–86)

In fact, the slightest differences can have a resounding effect, which can easily develop into full-fledged conflict. Commentating on Simmel's work, Alois Hahn argues that

> Sameness is mundane reality in the midst of a group. What is the same becomes less important for conscious awareness. What is noticed is difference, however small it may be. Whatever is common among individuals only plays a secondary role in our preoccupations and finds itself in the background of our attention not adding to our gratification. One could then speak of a decline or crumbling of gratification from which normal or ordinary forms of satisfaction suffer. Simmel observed that family conflicts quite often are trivial misunderstandings that trigger intense hatred.
>
> (Hahn 1990: 379–380)

Family conflicts differ from other conflicts because the context of the "family" is associated with the idea of unity and solidarity and appears to be the perfect haven of close relationships. In 1908, G. Simmel pointed out that

> The cause, the intensity, the way of influencing all unimplicated persons and the form of quarrels as well as reconciliation are completely peculiar. The reason is that there is a foundation of organic unity born out of a thousand connections, both internal and external, impossible to compare with other conflicts.
>
> (Simmel 1908/1995: 86)

Despite this uniqueness, we have to admit that family conflicts have rarely caught the attention of sociologists. Even less so if by "family" we mean a larger group of people related by blood or marital ties and not simply the nuclear family (man, woman, and their children) or those living under the same roof (some of whom may not have any blood relations with the others). Research on family conflicts is limited mostly to the analysis of conflict at home, primarily marital conflict or conflict between parents and children. There is more, and more interdisciplinary, research on conflict that leads to violence (battered wives and children, even battered parents, Chartier and Chartier 1990), and particularly research on sexual violence (*Dialogue* 1992; Welzer-Lang 1992; Perrone and Nannini 1995). This violence attracts public intervention (Gruyer *et al.* 1991; Chemin *et al.* 1995) when the abuse "spills out" of the privacy of the home and breaks the "law of silence."

In other words, "family conflict" almost always refers to conflicts at home and hardly ever to conflicts in the extended family, a trend not restricted to the social sciences. For instance, Alison Lurie's 1974 novel *The War between the Tates,* depicting Mr and Mrs Tate and their household, was translated in French as *Conflits de famille* (Lurie 1990). In fact, although the family did not develop along the lines delineated by the discourse about its "crisis," this very discourse, as well as actual changes in the institution of marriage, has contributed to a focus on what seems to be the family's least stable component, the marital union, while neglecting the larger and more stable family system in which the marital union is embedded. Therefore, it is not surprising that sociology, in contrast to anthropology and history (Daumas 1988), is more interested in conjugal and parental conflict than in family conflict. However, this is changing; now, a pluralism of approaches prevails that according to Déchaux (1995) is concerned with diverse understandings of modernity.

## FAMILY CONFLICT IN THE EYES OF THE YOUTH

This chapter focuses on conflicts in the family. These conflicts might come in the form of a simple misunderstanding or a radical and violent disagreement, and may oppose individuals or groups of individuals. We will consider the family as a specific "social context," like other contexts such as education, vocational training, work, and leisure, knowing that due to its particularities (closeness of members, solidarity) such conflicts will oppose groups of individuals at least as much as individual family members. We will treat these groups as "social circles," drawing on the approach of Célestin Bouglé (1910), a colleague of Emile Durkheim. Bouglé described "circles" as the result of processes that blend the thinking of individuals, who initially were only loosely connected, "towards a common end." We will try to shed light on such normative systems, or the "common spirit " (Degenne 1987), of opposing "camps" in the family in order to pinpoint conflict dynamics in the context of the family.

For the purpose of this study, we decided to tackle the analysis of family conflicts from the point of view of the youth—that is, teenage boys and girls between 17 and 22 years of age, coming from different social classes. The higher ranges of the social ladder are represented by those whose parents belong to the upper middle class (e.g. father a medical specialist, and mother a lawyer). The lower ranges are represented by those whose parents can be considered disadvantaged (e.g. father unemployed and mother a housewife). The data on which we will draw is part of a larger study and consists of ninety in-depth interviews ranging from 3 hours to 11 hours 15 minutes in length.[1]

It would no doubt be tiring to try to do justice to the diversity of factors causing family conflicts. We can compile only an incomplete inventory. In any case, the same cause doesn't always produce the same effects. Similarly, when we try to classify the conflicts by degree, ranging from simple disagreements to those that manifest themselves in violence, we risk overlooking important distinctions such as that between home and family, men and women, and among social classes. As O. Schwartz has shown, acts such as marital violence, which are viewed as violent in the middle class, are not always viewed in the same manner by the working class. "To a certain extent, slaps on the face would not be perceived by men as an act of violence but rather as a normal end to an increased aggression coming from women" (1990: 425). Men resort more quickly to violence when they can no longer contain a verbal attack which is a more feminine technique of contesting. The root of this behavior can be found in the notion of the supposed reputation of masculine authority and the already fragile social status of men. Verbal attacks easily turn into violence when men are not supposed to be overpowered by their wives, even if it is the wife in the first place who assumes most of the domestic affairs. "There is a contradiction in family life. Governing of household affairs is feminine and the fiction of authority should rest masculine" (*ibid.*).

Our research focuses on conflicts in the wider family. Our primary informants are teenagers. We did not intend to categorize or classify their views, as such an approach would put an end to our goal of capturing the reality of family conflicts. In fact, our data resemble the near-truths of "family novels" (Freud 1909) in that our teenage narrators both revise and elaborate their stories. Sociologically speaking, Vincent de Gauléjac's work on the junction of sociological and clinical case interviews (1987, 1990, 1994) emphasizes the facts about "family novels."

> History means two things. First, what really happened and second, how it is interrelated. History is always a reconstruction, an account of what had happened. This account is sometimes objective and sometimes subjective. It recounts what had occurred and at the same time the manner in which the family narrates it.
>
> (Gauléjac 1996: 202)

Our study tries to show, without claiming to be exhaustive, what seems to be the youth's specific perception of family conflicts. It is likely that these accounts do not correspond completely to the way the wider *family* sees the events nor to the version of the family *faction* to which the narrator feels close.

## WHEN THE IDYLLIC FAMILY CRUMBLES ...

In accordance with the common ideal of a united rather than conflictual family, young people are generally predisposed to accentuate the "stitches" rather than the "ruptures." Whatever concerns the family is considered private and shall not be shared with strangers. However, with more probing, small tensions become topics of conversation. "*The thing that pisses me off is the disagreeable manner in which my mom criticized the family of my dad.*" It is dangerous to associate this type of tension with conflict. Quite often, the young people warn us against this implication. "*Yes, there is someone whom I swear at every time I see him . . . But that doesn't mean that I don't get along well with him."* When these tensions involve not only individuals but groups, the same caution should be applied. Tension then becomes distance—a distance we can understand when family members are geographically separated. In fact, regular visits with those who live close by are likely to produce feelings of being less close to others, but when weak ties cannot be explained in terms of objective factors like geography, they become more difficult to define. Our participants, both boys and girls, admit to the problem of affinity. Still, in their discussions they emphasize closeness with certain family members in order to justify distance from others. "*Our ideas are somewhat similar . . . We do things together*." Differences in relationships almost always result from being "too" close to some rather than excluding others. However, this reluctance to focus on what separates family members when there is no real conflict is not always present. "*They are not close to my dad, that's why they are not close to us either*." But even here, the narrators prevent any risk of interpreting the situation in terms of conflict. "*It can be said that there is goodwill when there is no conflict*." In other words, distance does not signify hostility.

Yet, we need to be aware that the absence of conflict in a family is sometimes the result of a past conflict, which, as Simmel suggested, led to a new balance within the family. After a full-blown conflict, reconciliation may be possible only after permanently breaking off relationships with some family member(s). In these cases, out of sight, out of mind. Ultimately, they may no longer be considered part of the family such as in the case of Sabine, "*Yes, for me, I like my family*."[2] It is clear that she does not include the ones with whom contact was broken off a long time ago. In answer to our questions, she only hinted that,

> *There's a lot of them that I don't see because my dad is not with them anymore . . . Between my dad and his family, well, there were many conflicts following the death of my grandma, I mean his mom . . . . And a lot of quarrels followed after . . . . Now, I have almost forgotten about them.*

This might be paradoxical. Even where there were past conflicts, the young people tend to present a conflict-free picture of their family. For them, the notion of the family evokes primarily the ones with whom they are still in contact.

Because we focus not so much on family conflict *per se* but on the youth's perception of family conflict, it is necessary to illuminate an often masked, yet important element in their stories: we discover conflict as we are growing up. In fact, except in families shattered by very pronounced, even violent, conflicts, which seems to be more common at the bottom of the social ladder, everything is done to spare children the experience of conflict. However, in trying to maintain the ideal of communitarian happiness the family can create illusions and, for some, even becomes an illusion. "*When I was a child, my family was extraordinary because everyone loved each other. The more you grow older, the more you see that this isn't so.*" At the moment of their discovery, even harmless conflicts turn into a personal drama. When the feeling of having been duped resides, what remains are the deception and bitterness that mark the start of a slow process of mourning. A very different vision of the family emerges, less idyllic, and at times leads some to no longer want to hear anymore from those who lied to them in order to protect them.

> *This is done slyly, my mom talks to us and that's what's disturbing me. I always tell her, "Listen, if you want to talk about it . . . I know you do it to the best of your ability. But just leave me alone. I don't want to listen to what you think of it !"*

It is not easy to maintain one's stand of total neutrality.

Once the true color of the idyllic family is revealed, a page is turned. It remains to admit that family unity is not without fault. A painful observation that cannot but incite the imagination as to what the future might bring. At times, the young people anticipate future scenes.

> *There might be a problem when my grandma dies. Then there'll be a huge problem because there is a house to be shared, there's a lot of furniture, land, and there's a lot of people. Some people more sly than others would want a bigger share. Others will be disgusted . . . I dread that time. Sometimes, my sister Marie and I talk about it and we say, "the day when it happens will be catastrophic."*

It is not surprising that once we discover the fragility of the family we are predisposed to anticipate and imagine potential conflicts. In contrast, it is surprising to see that boys or girls are sometimes completely aware how some pieces in the family puzzle are more decisive than others in maintaining minimal coherence. "*When grandma is no longer here to hold the family together, conflicts can flare up again, or else be created. There will be gaps between family members. There will be no longer a place to rally around, because that's what my Grandma's house* is." A place (the family house) or a person (grandmother) symbolically constitutes a force that is strong enough to regulate centripetal forces—in short, to avoid implosion. It may be surprising that a person who barely left the illusion of a happy community behind, is aware of this state of affairs. However, it underlines that a conflict cannot always be reduced to opposing individuals or groups, particularly within the family context. Due to their standing in the family, some members can, if not play the role of a mediator, at least contain the risks of confrontation for some time.

There is no doubt that family elders often occupy key positions in limiting the amplitude of conflicts because they represent the "go-betweens." This is not always due to their charisma, their authority, or their talents at mediating, but the affection we have for them requires moderation. If that is not the case, then it is based on empathy: just as we protect the youngest from family troubles, we try hard not to show the oldest who will follow them.

## TYPE OF FAMILY COHESION, SOCIAL CLASS AND ROLE EXPECTATION

Yet, sometimes the stories about grandparents are critical, to say the least. As Virginie commented,

> *I have a grandma that I don't like much because I don't really consider her as one. She doesn't play the role of a grandma. She doesn't act like one. Like for example, for our birthdays, she never calls us. For me, that's not a grandma. She's my grandma because it's written on paper. But in my heart, she's not my grandma.*

For Virginie who is quite a family-oriented person and whose parents belong to the middle class, this attitude of the grandmother doesn't correspond to the image she has about the relationships between grandchildren and grandparents.

Sometimes, the position assigned to each family member according to the rules of kinship engenders specific role expectations. This is the case with low-income families whose family organization Kellerhals and Montandon described as "bastion" type families:

> The bastion type family is characterized by its close-mindedness and fusion. Here, withdrawal into the family group is perceived to be the norm. Contact with the external world is considered frustrating and dangerous. Instead, family members share as many beliefs and activities as possible. They share one life, deriving satisfaction from each other.
>
> (Kellerhals and Montandon 1991: 40)

When in these families, where tradition legitimizes the rights and obligations of each member, the attitude of a close relative does not conform to what one could expect, feelings of deception mixed with hostility arise, which quickly give room to disapproval.

In contrast, "association" type families more often come from an upper-middle-class background and are characterized by openness and autonomy. The fate of the individual only partially depends on the family. Status-related role expectations are a lot less marked. Young people in these families are more open to the idea of having "young" grandparents who are dynamic and less focused on the family. Séverine is a senior student in economics and social studies; her father works as a medical researcher, her mother is a physician. Comparing her maternal and paternal grandparents, Séverine comments, "*My maternal grandma is someone who is very dynamic for her age. And the other (paternal grandma), she's an old grannie, a real grannie! One of them goes skiing while the other never does anything.*" Whereas Séverine, the well-to-do, criticizes the lack of dynamism in her paternal grandmother, Virginie, from a less well-to-do background and a "companionate" type family that combines features of both "bastion" and "association" type families, would have preferred a more "grannie-ish" grandmother, one that is, no doubt, like Fanny's: "*My grandma is a myth . . . She's the grandma we read about in books.*" Considering these different role expectations we need to re-examine the notion that contemporary families are more "relational." Though individuals from very well-to-do backgrounds nowadays are in fact less influenced by family pressures, this is not always the case for those from less well-to-do backgrounds where status-related rights and obligations continue to dictate the terms of conduct. With this in mind we can say that the same image of "model grandmother" elicits enthusiasm in some and disapproval in others. We should note in particular that Virginie's criticism of her grandmother is related to the restructuring of intergenerational contracts that we see nowadays.

Though at times perceived as "old" by the younger ones, due to higher life expectancy grandparents often are relatively young, "young elders" in a way. It is not rare to see them realize their long-awaited dreams, most of all travel, as soon as they retire. In these cases, freedom from work obligations does not necessarily translate into that greater availability so much wished for by grandchildren like Virginie, and by those parents who wish to take advantage of their own parents to take care of their grandchildren. Most of the time, the dynamism of some grandparents is considered a positive factor to bridge the generation gap. Sometimes, however, it becomes a factor of tension between the generations—first, because it reveals a certain autonomy from the family and, second, because it very concretely translates into less availability for the family.

## THE IMPOSSIBLE NEUTRALITY

One peculiar feature of the teenagers' stories is that they are, so to speak, always on the "good side." "*They fight for the heritage. Since this does not interest us, we became distant.*" As soon as they are more or less involved in a conflict, the young men and women tell us quite clearly that no bad intentions should be attributed to the "camp" they belong to. Although this camp is almost always involved at the heart of the conflict, it is presented as disinterested and resolved to not take part in the hostilities, as is the case in the examples below.

The wording of a narrative gives us a bird's eye view of who are the "good ones" and the "bad ones," specifically when the speaker is directly or indirectly involved. And just as the speaker's sagacity always leads to an exemplary decision, events unfold as though our informants were exempt from all criticism. In other words, only individuals "beyond reproach" can discuss family conflicts, for the simple reason that they cannot evoke a conflict of which they are part without properly justifying their position or that of their camp. The conflict discourse, above all, is a discourse of justification, particularly within the context of the family.

Emotional closeness as well as enmity do not permit a neutral stand for long. They constitute a strong reminder to join those we feel close to. In that case, serious arguments need to be presented in order to justify the change of heart. Stéphanie's story is illustrative:

> *I adored my Grandma until the age of 15. Soon after, I saw . . . Well, let's put it this way, that she did not have a good relation with her children* (including Stéphanie's parents) *and her children had warned me saying, "Be careful with your grandma. She's a bitch! She'll do you some bad turns!" and well, until 15, I stuck up for her against all odds.*

But could Stéphanie have stood alone for a long time? Could she have maintained her neutrality when her parents, whom she adores, are depicted as the "victims" of this cruel mother? Without a doubt, no. And that's what happened.

Sure, her grandmother is perhaps not exempt from all criticism. But to explain this change of heart, Stéphanie has to advance numerous arguments:

> *And then, she did some nasty things to me. And well, for sure, it all ended! She did some dirty tricks on me. She's a woman who masters excellently the art of messing up other people's lives . . . . She had done a lot of harm and as for me . . . . She has a forked tongue. Nobody can change her . . . . She sows discord among others. I almost got mad with Manou* (a young paternal aunt) *because of her. One day, I stopped by Manou's place. I hadn't seen my aunt for 15 days. And she slammed the door in my face. She didn't want to see me anymore. I didn't even know why. My grandmother had been there not long ago . . . . Once she said that I had stolen the keys of my other grandma's house and that I had stolen some money . . . all lies.*

We interrupt this inventory at this point, although it is not yet complete; it clearly indicates that Stéphanie felt obliged to justify her change of mind.

Sooner or later the dynamics of the family forces individual members to choose whether to be "for" or "against" other members. This is obviously the case when one is alone against the others. But it is also the case when one adopts a position of "benevolent neutrality," that is, when one does not want to be part of a conflict. And even if the cause of "the loved ones" does not incite us to join their camp, it so happens that the adversary camp "pushes" us towards it. Friendly relationships between the "neutrals" and the enemy camp rarely last for long. Hence, we wonder whether the family context is, *par excellence*, one of "impossible neutrality."

So far, our examples often featured grandparents; also, the tensions and conflicts occurred almost always within the paternal branch of the family. Most of our data confirm this asymmetry, though less markedly: distancing, tensions, and conflicts are, in effect, a little more frequent with the paternal branch of the family. In our data we find again what others have underlined: that relationships with the maternal branch of the family are often calmer and closer. In their work "Les réseaux de solidarité dans la famille (The networks of solidarity in the family)," Coenen-Huther *et al.* observed that "The husband has a tendency to put his parents-in-law on the same pedestal as his own parents while the wife makes a clear distinction between them" (1994: 68). This observation led them to the following statement: "Women confine their affection within the structure of the biological frontier . . . which men, being less selective on this issue, do not" (*ibid.*: 69).

Bawin-Legros and Gauthier write from a perspective closer to ours as they also try to understand adolescents' representations of their grandparents. According to them, "In a number of families, the more vivacious attachment of women to their mothers directly reflects on the preferences of the adolescents" (1992: 256). In other words, being more implicated than men in the maintenance of intergenerational relationships, women tend to, voluntarily or involuntarily, favor their own branch of the family; in doing so, they implicitly influence their children's preferences. According to the authors, this distinction will be particularly marked when the two branches of the family come from different social backgrounds. "It seems easier to forgive maternal grandparents their modest origins" (*ibid.*: 258). We have mentioned the "impossible neutrality" with regard to conflict but perhaps we also should re-examine, with regard to favoritism, the notion of "impartiality".

## FRATERNAL CONFLICTS: CONFLICTS BETWEEN ADULTS?

In their survey "Proches et parents" (Next of kin and parents) Bonvalet *et al.* asked one question aiming at family dysfunctions: "Is there any person in your family or family-in-law that you would rather avoid?" Twenty-six percent of the respondents answered affirmatively, a substantial portion of the entire sample. Even more interesting is that such avoidance strategies concerned some members of the family more than others.

> The expression "hostile brothers" is illustrative here because avowed enmities concern, first of all, members of the same generation. Parents and members of the previous generation come into play second. Contrary to what we might think it is not conflicts *between* generations that appear to be more common but rather conflicts *within* the same generation.
>
> (Bonvalet *et al.*1993: 105)

We wonder whether we have put too much emphasis on the role of grandparents and not enough on that of the siblings.

We should not forget that these family conflicts were evaluated from the viewpoint of teenage boys and girls, the majority of whom are still living at home. Due to their young age they are not quite adults yet but rather on the threshold of adulthood, which they are about to enter, each in their own way. Halfway between adolescence and adulthood, they have not yet developed the autonomous and well-established relationships of adult siblings with regard to their brothers and sisters; relationships like those between their parents and their parents' brothers and sisters. This particular stage in life may explain why it seems that they have fewer conflicts with their siblings than the survey cited above implies.

Naturally, there are frictions, oppositions, rivalries and jealousies. But, in general, all our participants talk a lot more about the affection they have for their siblings than about any hostility they may feel. "*I adore my little sister.*" Except for a few cases, when they mention a disagreement with a younger brother or sister it is most often trivial and never the result of a direct confrontation that would involve more than one person.

> *My younger sister, Marion, can be irritating at times, specially the way she takes my parents for a ride. At meal times, she is very difficult to handle. I remember when we had soup and, well, even if we didn't like it . . . . I remember one time, staying at the table until 9 o'clock at night just to finish my soup. And Marion, if she doesn't eat it, uh, my mom cooks up something else for her. . . . Among the three of us, she is the most difficult one! They haven't been tough enough with her!.*

In this example, the conflict is related, as is almost always the case, to differential treatment of the siblings by their parents. Sometimes this creates a collective sibling opposition, but one that affects her, who for all of them remains the "little Benjamin," only indirectly: "*Often, Mathieu* (the brother) *and I ally against Dad and Mom, for the way they're raising Marion.*"

In contrast, disagreements with older brothers or sisters seem more distinct. Due to our participants' young age such disagreements involve an adult and a youth who is about to enter adult life. Hence, different issues are at stake. They often involve defending, even asserting, one's life choices—a common problem among immigrant families in the process of integration. The case of Yamina, 20, is a good example.

> *My brother Lared wants to run my life, he plays too much the role of the elder one who. . . . It pisses me off! He was born back in Algeria. And he acts as if he's still in Algeria. And yet, I have other brothers who were born there. But Lared, specifically, is the type to not put up with my brothers being with French girls, things like that. Ever since my dad is not here anymore, my brother wants to impose his laws on everyone. He even wants to dominate my mom. It's completely stupid! Any moment there could be conflict with him.*

Here, two distinct camps oppose each other for what, as we can see, family means to them: some family members value and practice the customs and traditions of their country of origin, while others clearly have opted for those of their adopted country.

Be that as it may, conflicts between boys and girls and their younger or older brothers and sisters seem quite rare. Another indicator that supports this statement are the responses to the first question in our interview: "Who are the persons that are actually important to you, who actually counts in your life?" The purpose of this question had been to assess, unobtrusively, any close interpersonal ties, regardless of the different social contexts that we would touch on subsequently. We have to admit that brothers and sisters are very often among those considered important.

Given the contradictions between data from the adult population and our sample of young people between 17 and 22 years of age, a major conclusion seems possible, though it needs further verification: taking all things together, conflicts between brothers and sisters take real shape during adulthood. In other words, whether or not there had been any disagreements during childhood or adolescence, significant differences emerge or reach full proportions when siblings, as adults, are equipped with fully developed reasoning powers. And even though the work of Klagsbrun (1994) on brothers and sisters shows that in childhood hatred can go along with sibling alliances, we would like to emphasize that this finding is based only on the testimony of adults.

There is no point denying that, from childhood onward, siblings are capable of hating each other for reasons like parental favoritism or because one of them always served as the scapegoat of the family (Le Gall 1995). Looking at our data from almost a hundred young people of diverse social backgrounds, the relatively small number of sibling conflicts mentioned was indeed surprising—all the more so, given that conflicts among members of the previous generation are fairly common. Now, as there is little reason to assume that the parent generation is more predisposed to conflicts, we believe that sibling quarrels are more likely to develop and become manifest during adult age. This implies that the entry into adult life will be a time of recomposition of sibling ties, and/or that the stakes of adult life are likely to let old disagreements re-emerge or to let us reconsider our old alliances in the light of new interests that did not bother us during childhood and adolescence.

However, all this needs to be verified by more detailed sociological research. Although psychologists, psychoanalysts, psychiatrists, ethnologists, family therapists and social workers have been interested in sibling relationships, that is hardly the case for sociologists. A case in point is an issue of *Dialogue* (1991) entitled "Moi, mon frère; moi, ma soeur" (Me, my brother; Me, my sister). Besides the two authors who did not indicate their field of specialism, among five psychoanalysts, four therapists, two psychologists, two ethnologists, a psychiatrist and one social worker, we counted only two sociologists. Moreover, even though the article by A. Langevin was appropriate for the theme of the issue, as she compared the lives of brothers and sisters in two different generations, that was not the case with the other sociologist.

Owing to the fact that sibling ties weave through childhood, and almost always indicate great closeness, they acquire a powerful symbolic meaning in our imagination. From the Bible and mythology to fairy tales and novels, everything emphasizes the uniqueness of sibling ties. Caïn killed Abel and Romulus did the same with Remus. Dostoievski, Cocteau, Rilke, De Maupassant, Simenon and others have written about brotherhood and sisterhood in different ways but never leaving us indifferent. And when we leave the realm of fiction, we think of those who have collaborated as siblings such as André and Marie-Joseph Chénier, Auguste and Louis Lumière, Edmond and Jules Goncourt, the Troisgros brothers, de Broglie, etc. We are less inclined to focus on those who excelled in different fields such as Paul and Camille Claudel.

It often seems as though sibling ties could only represent either perfect alliance or insurmountable hatred. Even if these extremes reflect reality to some degree, they can obscure the fact that, in ways similar to other family ties, sibling ties recompose over time and are therefore open to change.

## EVERYDAY CONFLICT WITHIN THE SAME GENERATION

Recounting conflicts within their parents' generation, many of our participants seem to support the idea that intragenerational conflicts emerge with the transition to adult life. *"Sophie, my maternal aunt, was not well accepted by Martine and Gilles* (maternal aunt and uncle) *because she's a newcomer in the family. . . . Anyway, it has been two years. She's quite fun-loving by temperament and this does not please the other two."* In this case, the tensions were born the moment when one of the brothers got married.

We sometimes forget that the love relationship of a sibling means that a new person will join the family (sister-in-law or brother-in-law). And if this new person is not well received, in particular by the other brothers and sisters but also by their spouses, old ties can deteriorate. The explanations offered for these conflicts are often couched in terms of "differences," arguments that are not explicit but show that the "circle" of the others is structured along a set of specific norms.

Those whose marital choice did not incite the enthusiasm of their brothers and sisters have not much choice but to take the side of their spouse. Thus, matrimonial ties compete with sibling ties. This scenario is quite typical, with sometimes long-lasting effects.

> *On the wedding day of my parents, he (my mom's brother) insulted my dad by calling him a shilly-shaller . . . . No fight ensued. None. But it was obvious that they didn't like my dad. Well, anyway, that's the way it happened. . . . The family, hmm, it's us, the kids, with dad and mom . . . . Well, my mom still talks to her sisters. But she does not see her brothers any more. She says hello to them and that's all. This is how the groups were formed.*

Aside from the conflicts mentioned in this chapter, there are the more classic cases related to questions of inheritance. In France, equality among siblings is mandatory, except in cases where the father or the mother, by their testament or donation and within the limits of the available amount, favor or disfavor one or more of the children. In other words, in accordance with the norm of equality well implanted in the family ideal, all children are supposed to receive equal parts. This equality is not without absurd side effects (Gotman 1988) in an era where the decreased importance of economics is counterbalanced by an increased importance of affective relationships.

> Shares established according to strictly economic criteria make this affective asset incomplete and unsatisfying. The equality of values can become absurd and arbitrary, in the sense that this option precisely consists of not taking into account the differences. This can bring about a sense of frustration, of not being distinguished, chosen or recognized in his own difference if specific choices were not embellished.
>
> (Gotman 1990: 98)

This led Anne Gotman to conclude: "Inheritance is to a certain point impossible sharing" (*ibid.*).

Even though the intricacies of inheritance are not always quite clear, our respondents, boys and girls, have their own version of these conflicts. *"These people are very much interested, financially speaking," "there are those who want a bigger share,"* etc., comments which, on the one hand, illustrate that even without having complete knowledge of the details we take sides, and, on the other, that there is always at the very least the problem of financial equality.

But often the story is more complicated. For example, the claim of mere equality is at times the cause of conflict. Because it is equivalent to the denial of differences, as noted by Gotman.

> *I know that my uncle Yves has some big problems with his brothers and sisters because he had inherited the farm. But the house was divided among brothers and sisters. The fact is that he has a brother with whom he gets along very well but he has two sisters who are more interested in the money than in the wellbeing of their brother. For a long time they wanted to sell the house even if it meant that he becomes homeless. At that point, he went through a period of hopelessness; as a farmer he doesn't make much.*

In this case, no one is suspected of wanting more than his or her share. The problem is more delicate. The two sisters demand their respective share of the inheritance at this very moment, but the two brothers are opposed to the idea of selling the family house, which serves as a vital source of income for the brother who is not only a farmer but also the less affluent of the family.

Two norms of justice conflict here. In the eyes of the law, the claims of the sisters are legitimate. But from a perspective of "family ethics" that takes the emotional side into account, it is necessary to show support for siblings in need. Even though the family ethics does not really oblige same status members to compensate for any inequalities existing between them, it nevertheless forbids behaviors that provoke conflict. The legitimate demand to be treated equally is only acceptable if it does not create inequality elsewhere. The dilemma here is the wish of some family members to assert an "egalitarian logic" within the very context that makes this assertion impossible.

At times, this dilemma is revealed when a dependent elderly family member needs daily intensive care. "*There are some who want to put her* (the grandmother) *in a home for the elderly, and others who do not want this treatment. Then, there is conflict.*" The more family-oriented generally oppose such placement. They easily express their refusal to those who are ready to pay to "get rid of" the problem. The less family-oriented ones, somewhat more pragmatic, signal the moralizers below their breath that insisting on the idea of the family-in-charge will implicitly mean volunteering for the job. Confrontations rise fast between those who, in the name of "filial love," defend family responsibility and those who argue that constant medical attention is necessary and thus prefer professional care. This type of conflict re-emphasizes close as well as distant relationships between brothers and sisters and their elderly parent—in particular, when the family finally is in charge of taking care of the elderly parent. For the "comfort" of the dependent parent, it is preferable that the "closest" child devotes himself or herself to the parent's care—an argument that those who feel they were the "victims" of their parents' favoritism will rarely pass up.

In some cases, when the family is very family-oriented, members of the extended family are authorized to intervene in the affairs of others, even if it concerns their very private life. This is the case with Thierry's family who are a "companionship" type of family. His father, the one most empowered to intervene due to his social position, is solicited by a "quasi family council." Duly mandated, he tries to uphold the norms of family justice.

> *There had been some problems with Sylvie* (an aunt whose husband was killed in a car accident). *My dad intervened. She had gotten a huge amount of money and my dad wanted this amount to be placed under the account of Cédric, Mathieu and Angélina* (nephews and nieces) *until they reached legal age. But Sylvie never consented.*

The young widow completely rejected the intervention by the head of the family, which she sees as an intolerable interference. We must not forget that the death of a family member always brings about a recomposition of the family structure. With regard to the death of her husband, this process of recomposition presented an opportunity to get rid of her in-laws' influence, which she judged to be a little too inquisitorial.

Career differences do not favor sibling ties either. Even if the siblings' status in the family remains equal, there is still a gap. From this point of view, professional success can, at times, weaken long-standing alliances. If that success is due to "betrayal," such as the refusal to "be married" to the family profession or enterprise, communication between siblings becomes particularly difficult:

> *My father was the cleverst of the family. It was a family of fishermen. And my dad was into computers. In doing so, he made it . . . . As soon as this became the subject of conversation, misunderstandings occurred, so . . . he was not like the others . . . .*

The truly intolerable fact is more than the social and economic differences. It is flaunting the success. Such behavior is not well-received by siblings or cousins.

Brigitte had undergone some training before working in a dry-cleaning store. Her dad had died and she lives with her mother, a housewife. They live precariously, unlike the rest of the family. Her maternal uncle, a retired employee of a provincial airport is married to a tennis teacher who comes from a relatively "good family." They have two children, Brigitte's cousins. One of them is a manager in a company while the other is a doctor specializing in geriatrics. Both are "well-married." The following statement indicates the gap that separates Brigitte from her cousins and their respective spouses.

> *They* (female cousins and the wife of a male cousin) *are snobs. With their remarks, they try to make us jealous by saying things like, "I went to Disneyland in Martinique" and others. But we don't care. It doesn't matter. Ever since that time, we're immune to it.*

When such differences become too large while family ties require that we follow certain rituals, we can understand that the circumstances can breed hatred.

> *Jacques* (one of the cousins) *is always on vacation. He says, "think of me when I go to the Landes to stay with friends. We'll do this and that." This is not a subject of conversation. Normally, we don't talk about it. It seems like he is doing it intentionally . . . . He seems to be mocking our situation. They don't give a damn to what happens to us as soon as they become well-off and own beautiful houses. So, the cousins and the aunt, eh . . . !*

In this case, it is obvious that in order to escape from the "sadistic treatment" of those who are better off, the only option is conflict. It is also surprising that up to this point, there is no rupture yet. Perhaps this is another peculiarity of having kinship ties across geographic distances. It is unlikely that, had they lived closer to their kin, Brigitte and her mother would have accepted this type of "maltreatment" for long.

## SOCIAL CLASS, FAMILY REPRESENTATION AND CONFLICT

Although these examples of everyday conflicts among peers of the same generation give a good idea of the diversity of conflicts that can weaken the family structure, we cannot detect one single dominant characteristic, even if we look quite closely at our acquired data. We would put it this way: While family conflicts exist in all social classes, their probability of emerging, and the form in which they are manifested, reflect differences between classes.

Families that exert only little influence over individual autonomy seem less predisposed to conflicts, or at least better equipped to regulate and contain them. As soon as they enter a "zone of disturbance" such "association" type families (typically affluent) prefer to have dialogues and negotiations. According to the "principle of contract" that guides them "[conflict management] is only an allocation of rights and responsibilities corresponding to what the concerned individuals have decided on their own accord" (Coenen-Huther *et al.* 1994: 33). Being more "open-minded," more adaptable and more inclined to recognize individual autonomy, these families possess a margin of maneuverability to resolve conflicts or find acceptable compromises. Hence, it is not surprising that boys and girls from this social background have less to say on the subject of conflicts. Their families have certainly undergone more tension than accounted for. But many of these disagreements have not really taken the form of conflict since they have never been mentioned. The traces of present or past quarrels are nevertheless visible in that some sections of the family are avoided, or are absent from the account. Moreover, when we insisted on this point our participants admitted to tensions. However, they do not systematically liken them to conflicts. Instead, they would comment: "*There's a coldness that reigns within the family. So we are more distant.*"

At the opposite end of the social ladder, in "bastion" type families, what counts is the "principle of status"; "It is the principle of equality applied to different kinship categories" (*ibid.*). Here, the risk of confrontation is a lot higher. Being more enmeshed, more close-minded and rigid, these families are also, as Simmel clearly recognized, more sensitive to making the smallest mistake and, hence, more predisposed to conflict. Even the most trivial factor can become magnanimous, especially when the family memory links them with conflicts from the past. Family events like the death of a loved one, rituals like baptism or communion of a young one, and holidays like Christmas often are periods when hostilities arise.

Notwithstanding these opposing family types, we should not forget the "companionate," middle-class families where the contrast is less striking as they combine elements from the other two family types. For example, as "companionate" type families are very family oriented, much like "bastion" type families, an apparently trivial event can, for its symbolic meaning, trigger a conflict of long-lasting impact—as in the case of Ophélie whose father is a supervisor and the mother an employee:

> *Before, we got along well. We spent good times together. But now, it is not as good. My cousin, 21, made a fuss about the grave of my grandma. She broke everything. Just because my dad had put up a cross on her grave, which he had brought back from Lourdes. And it said on it, "for my grandmother, from the children and grandchildren" and my aunt, she phoned: "Yeah, what right do you have to place the cross there and all those writings on the grave . . . . But, excuse me, I'm also a grandchild." She's not the only one , huh . . . and then she asked someone to remove the cross and since that day, there was a cold war in the family.*

As a matter of fact, collectively, everyone is an "owner" of the grave of a parent. Everything that concerns it will be the subject of discussion. In this case, one side of the family, without any prior consultation, took the initiative to place a crucifix, bought in a highly symbolic place, on the grave of the grandmother. The engraved dedication certainly included all grandchildren, but some of them had not been associated with this project. During a visit to the cemetery, they discover it and become upset. The cross *per se* is not the problem. Yet, it symbolizes the appreciation of only some and not other family members. At this point, the declaration of affection became intolerable.

Despite all this, the terms of conflict are kept within reasonable limits, which is not always the case in less affluent families. At the lower end of the social ladder, what is said is not always related to the conflict only, and the arguments used are often exaggerating the facts. Nathalie shared her story. Her father is deceased while her mother is a housewife.

> *We* (mother and daughter) *are mad at everyone, all the family of my dad . . . . Because just after the death of my dad, his mom reproached my mom, saying that it was her who pushed him to drink and that she had lovers and patati and patata . . . . At the funeral, well, uh, she stole the calling cards . . . Yes, like that, in her bag and of course, this didn't please my mom. Afterwards, one day, she phoned my mom at work. She started insulting her with names! Well, when we heard this . . . they are all against my Mom. All is her fault . . . . She's the reason why he drank, the reason why he was miserable.*

When we consider that the paternal grandmother had not been in favor of this marriage, it is easier to understand how the father's death could elicit such behavior. If, according to Maurice Halbwachs (1925), family memory is an element of family cohesion, a sign of belonging, shared values, and norms, it also contributes to reactivating and magnifying those differences of which we thought they had been forgotten. But once the differences cross a line, ancient hatred reignites like glowing embers hidden under the ashes.

The "strength of lineage" can also be found in families "recomposed" after divorce who may suffer from lack of "institutionalization" (Cherlin 1987; Théry 1991). Geared toward first marriages, society offers little institutionalized support for families with children from a previous marriage. Moreover, without being able to rely on their old habits or on institutionalized rules, these families are obliged to find rules adapted to their particular needs (Le Gall and Martin 1993, 1995). Within affluent milieux, the recomposition unfolds somewhat continuously in new and complex rules: the parental union survives even when the conjugal one fails. The new spouse progressively establishes a place within the family without encroaching upon the prerogatives of the noncustodial parent. The role of the stepparent becomes what I have called a "friendly patronage" (Le Gall 1992, 1993). Among less affluent families, this recomposition occurs with more ruptures: ties with the noncustodial parent become blurred, then disappear. The "new family" presents itself as the "original family." The stepfather embodies the role of a "substitute";

effectively he takes the place of the biological father with whom the children have no or almost no relationship any more. Here we also see conflicts between children who are becoming adolescents and their stepfathers.

This is the most common case: due to the fact that in the majority of cases the mother is granted custody (Muñoz-Perez 1987), children more often live with a stepfather than with a stepmother. Nevertheless, when the stepfamily consists of the custodial father and his new spouse the situation is hardly any easier. As the division of labor in low-income families is relatively traditional, domestic chores and the education of the children fall to the stepmother (Le Gall 1996). For her, there are few "emotional" rewards if the children remain factually or in their minds (in cases of abandoned children) attached to their biological mothers. In addition, if the stepmother has children of her own from a previous marriage, she often favors them, a situation that inevitably leads to conflict. This confrontation usually pits the stepmother (and sometimes her children) against the stepchildren. Considering that domestic affairs are his partner's problems, the father often stays in the background. In these cases, the comments of our young participants tend to underline the mean and obnoxious character of their stepmothers. We were sometimes reminded of the old fairy-tale image of the cruel stepmother (e.g. Cinderella, Snow White), as is illustrated in Borris's account, whose father is a mariner living with a cleaning woman, who works part time, and their two daughters.

> *My real sister, she can't take it anymore* (the stepmother). *She left at 18 with her boyfriend because she had suffered a lot. My stepmom gave her a hard time. She was really tough with her. Even I myself, had to leave home twice. Now, I'm more respected. Well, she has three daughters and there is always some sort of jealousy. All for her daughters and nothing for us . . . . Anyway, my stepmother, she doesn't say anything openly, but she criticizes everything. They are all the same. Right now, I'm sure, as I have brought my laundry. I'm sure I'll hear about it this morning: "He could have washed his own clothes. He comes home only to bring his laundry!" But I don't listen anymore because it pisses me off. It's a stupid mentality.*

## CONFLICT WITHOUT WORDS AND THE ABSENCE OF WORDS TO EXPRESS CONFLICT

Family ties are also blood ties. Although an adopted child is almost always wholly accepted and integrated into the family, this is not always the case with those who are "living proof" of a "past mistake." In traditional middle-class families, this type of situation seems to pose more problems than usual.

Within the affluent class, the choices made by individuals are recognized as legitimate. Hence, stigmatization against an individual whose path does not conform to the traditional norm is very rare. All the more so as stigmatization would affect a child who is not to blame for the problem. In less affluent families, birth origin is not a problem either, but for different reasons. At least, that is the case as long as there is no other conflict. Whenever there is a dispute, it is likely that whatever is considered abnormal resurfaces because of the tendency to exaggerate everything. But in the middle class the desire to conform, which prompts people to "denounce" those who do not, sometimes clashes with the necessity to admit the choices of loved ones; for example, a son's decision to adopt the illegitimate child of his spouse. The pressure of having to accept a choice that is otherwise not acceptable often engenders tensions, perhaps not verbalized but inevitably transparent in behavior. A tension that is experienced as real violence by the primary target in the case of Yoann, 22 years of age, whose adoptive father works in a factory and the mother in a hospital:

> *Yes, I don't get along at all with the family on my father's side. Well, they've never considered me their grandchild since we have no blood relationship. That's to say my dad is not my dad. My mom had me before they were married. Then, he adopted me when I was five years old, after the wedding, when my younger sister was born; so we will have the same last name. There are always some differences, especially when my brother and my sister were born . . . and I don't like it when they say they're my stepbrother or stepsister because for my little sister, whenever someone says that, it means that I don't love her or something like that . . . . That's to say, for this reason, I was isolated. Well, now that I'm grown up, I'm more interesting, I don't know; well they try . . . . The last time, I called them up because I was invited to the 40th birthday celebration of my uncle. They came to talk to me but well, I can't renew the ties.*

We sense here that conflict, even violent conflict, may sometimes be preferable to a conflict without words, which seems to be more of a "mute tension" rather than a veritable conflict. In contrast, there are family conflicts that cannot even be mentioned in front of a stranger. These are conflicts that involved physical violence and where there is a victim: In other words, conflicts without the words to describe them; this is a limitation of our study. When a family conflict has crossed the limits of what can be admitted, a sense of decency and sometimes shame seem to prohibit any mentioning of the facts. Only confidants and professionals handling such cases such as social workers, psychotherapists, doctors, lawyers, and judges are allowed to listen to these accounts. Still, within the limits of our research these rare conflicts, even personal tragedies, are sometimes mentioned; but always with such discretion that it is almost impossible to develop a clear understanding of them.

Lydie, 22, dropped out of school at a young age and lives with Marie, a 38-year-old psychiatric nurse. Lydie's father, an employee with a telecommunications company, and her mother, a cleaning woman, separated when she was still young. Lydie lived for a while with her mother and stepfather, a retired military man with children from a previous marriage. Her biological father died two years ago. She discovered her homosexuality at an early age. She says: *"I will tell you right now since I think we will talk about it later; I am a homosexual . . . . Marie, I live with her . . . . Yes, we have a sexual relationship, we are a couple."* Then, without presenting herself as a militant homosexual, she lets us know clearly that she is perfectly well integrated in the homosexual milieu. *"This is the homosexual world. There are the exits on the right and on the left . . . . We come to know each other like this and we have bars and that's it. Yes, there are organizations, but here, they are simply bars."* Then, on the subject of her mother, Lydie declares, *"My mom, she buys me with money . . . . But I'm still close to mother. I need my mom even if we have a troubled relationship. We still need each other."*

During the interview, we learned that Lydie was placed in a home at the age of 15. Later, she was hospitalized for six months when she was more or less *sans domicile fixe* (homeless).

> *With mom, we haven't seen each other for four years and that didn't bother me . . . I was hospitalized for six months . . . . Yes, it allowed me to be closer to my mom, but for her, she felt a little obliged. I had a nervous depression. That was why I was hospitalized for so long. The only way out for me was to be housed in someone's home . . . . It was the doctor who called my mom . . . and there, my mom got me out of the hospital because at that time I was considered an SDF* (homeless person). *I worked illegally, sold newspapers like* Macadam, S'en sortir *and all that !*[3]

At this point of the interview, it is evident that there are some dark zones in Lydie's life. What type of relationship does she have with her mom and stepfather? Why did she leave her mom's place so early (voluntarily or involuntarily) to go to a home? Why hasn't she seen her mom for the last four years? Why was it that her mom doesn't have much choice ("she felt a little obliged . . . ") in welcoming her home after a long period of hospitalization?

Other bits of information, without being more explicit, nevertheless outline what seems to be Lydie's major problem, and, we should note, not an ordinary case.

LYDIE I filed a complaint against my mom and my stepfather. It passed through the courts . . . . It was for beatings and deliberate injury . . . .

There was an outcry within the family. But for me, when I sued my stepfather and my mom, his four children did the same.

INTERVIEWER For the same reasons?

LYDIE Yes . . . but for them, it allowed them, more than me, to free themselves from a lot of things . . .

Further along the interview, the interviewer returned to the topic from a different angle:

INTERVIEWER You and your mother, can't you get reconciled after the decision of the court?

LYDIE No, I was already living in the home then.

INTERVIEWER And was it against your mom or mainly against your stepfather?

LYDIE I sued both of them.

Obviously, Lydie wants to evoke the violence she had lived through but she couldn't say any more. Based on the information we could gather we can advance merely the outline of an interpretation. At 15, Lydie leaves her mom and stepfather to live in a home. She sues them for beatings and deliberate injury. Her stepfather's children from a previous marriage lodge their complaints for the same reasons even if they haven't been living with him for some time. To have made public such a private matter seems "to have liberated them from a lot of things." Possibly, Lydie had been sexually abused by her stepfather and her mother was a silent accomplice to it, for fear of losing her husband. This scenario is plausible, especially when the steps taken by Lydie allowed the children of her stepfather to accomplish, though delayed, the same objective and for the same reasons.

It is also likely that Lydie's stepfather, knowing she intended to reveal his behavior, resorted to physical violence to force her to shut up. At the end of the interview, Lydie said, *"I am leaving for another professional project. COTOREP proposed it to me because I'm recognized as a disabled worker."*[4] Off the record, the interviewer asked her about her disability because she had never mentioned it. Lydie replied *"I have a glass eye."* This handicap has prevented her, on many occasions, from getting a job. She finally decided to accept the offer by COTOREP.

To be sure, this is conjecture based on the bits of information that Lydie had skillfully distilled. Nevertheless, even if reality does not correspond to this scenario, the violence of the conflict had reached a point of crisis where the victim was barely able to find the right words to account for it within the artificial setting created for our research purposes.

While there are conflicts without words, there are also conflict for which no words can be found to express them. Conflicts without words illustrate one of the particular forms of family conflict. The absence of words to describe conflicts sketches the outlines of what is socially acceptable in family conflict.

## CONCLUSION

From this approach to family conflicts through the eyes of teenagers, it seems possible to draw some general conclusions. The family continues to be symbolized as a coherent and homogeneous whole; this is apparent in the readiness of the youth to emphasize ties even when they are asked about conflicts. In general, we need to admit that some families do not seem to be "touched" by serious conflicts, even though sometimes it is longstanding conflicts that contribute to this impression. Still, even in the absence of conflicts, it is clear that the family comprises different "circles." There are a few very close relationships that illustrate, if that was needed, that the family is elective, and which by the way confirm recent quantitative surveys. For instance, according to Bonvalet *et al.* (1993), the French designate five members of the family as "close." This finding agrees, *ceteris paribus*, with the results of the Swiss survey by Coenen-Huther *et al.* (1994: 65) who noted that

> The density of affinities is quite weak .... It is not indifference nor hostility that characterise the majority of potential relationships ...; simply, for the most part, family ties ... are luke-warm. We do not feel detached from the others but we do not wish their company either.

From our perspective, for those who have been involved in conflict against their will (e.g. due to a divorce), the conflict is an adolescent experience that is often painful and almost always a form of initiation. The beginning of adolescence, the age when adults believe that the younger ones are "ready to understand," tolls the bell of revelation. "Family unity" appears with all its dissensions. In this universe of tension a neutral outsider's position is impossible: the family context becomes, in fact, that of "impossible neutrality."

Across the diversity of conflicts, some consistencies are apparent. For instance, splits often occur along different branches of the family with more conflicts in the paternal branch. Similarly, disagreements tend to pit same generation peers against each other. Differences seem to become veritable conflicts only once sibling ties have been "reworked" at the entry into adult life. At this point in life, sibling ties are sometimes rudely challenged by competing conjugal ties that did not exist before.

Finally, the same event can have rather different implications depending on social class and family cohesion, two interrelated factors. Those who are in the normative grip of their family are most susceptible to awkward family events; whereas those who are less subject to normative influences enjoy an autonomy that makes them less susceptible to conflicts related to role expectations. The latter ones are better equipped to regulate conflict to the extent that they employ, as is the case in more affluent circles of society, communication and negotiation based on contractual relationships. Moreover, more affluent families seem to be less conflictual. Less affluent families, although concerned about family cohesion and more dependent on family solidarity—"without family, you don't get very far"—are in fact more prone to turbulent family conflict.

In the light of these factors, we need to consent that the expression "relational family" is a little abusive. It certainly indicates changing norms of family life. But the assertion of a democratization of parent–child relationships (Fize 1990), so comforting to many, needs to be put in perspective. As Blöss remarked aptly: "The ideological success of the thesis of the renewal of family values masks the fundamental inegalitarian character of family relationships in general" (1996: 178). Also, this general approach concerns "family conflict," whereas we move to the analysis of "conflict in families" (family types) in order to better understand the significance and function of family conflicts and their modes of expression. Moreover, the notion of the "socially acceptable" in family conflict, which we deduced from the impossibility, or simply the refusal to talk about a violent conflict with a third party who is neither a professional nor confidante, should not obscure that our mode "of entry" into the world of conflicts (e.g. perceptions of teenagers) also partly determines the outcomes of our research. Obviously, even though it is difficult to achieve, an approach to family types that included different members of the same family (overlapping accounts) would constitute an ideal framework to refine our analysis.

## NOTES

1 The general objective of this research project that involves two research centers (the LASMAS-IDL/CNRS and the LASAR/Department of Sociology) is to find out how adult life begins for youth in an certain age group (longitudinal survey, data collection every three years; Bidart *et al.* 1993). This research underlines a specific point: it takes into account the diverse contexts of social life from school to work including family, leisure, activities, etc. It emphasizes the reorganization of relationship networks with the passage of time. Principles and origins of the project have been described in Bidart (1994) and its first results in Bidart and Le Gall (1996).
2 The procedure of making a systematic inventory of family connections in the interviews permitted the researchers to take a census and at the same time "go back" to existing old conflicts.
3 This refers to newspapers sold by individuals living on the street. Selling newspapers allows the vendors, often SDF, to earn some money and benefit from social protection, started in France in 1993. Cf. Collectif (1994).
4 Commissions Techniques d'Orientation et de Reclassement Professionnel. These commissions decide on the recognition of disabled employees to direct

them towards appropriate jobs such as Ateliers Protégés (AP, Protected workshops), Centres de Distribution du Travail à Domicile (CDTD, Center for Home-work or industry) and the Centres d'aide par le Travail (CAT, Centers for special jobs).

## BIBLIOGRAPHY


Attias-Donfut, C. (1995) (ed.), *Les solidarité entre générations: Vieillesse, familles, Etat*, Paris: Nathan.

Autrement (1975), "Finie la famille," special edition, Paris.

Bawin-Legros, B. and Gauthier, A. (1992) "Les relations inter-générationnelles: Grands-parents dans la rupture et la continuité," *Famille et contextes sociaux: Les espaces et les temps de la diversité*, Conference papers, Lisbon 10–12 April 1991, GREF/ Association Internationale des Sociologues de Langue Française, Portugal.

Bidart, C. (1994) "Insertion sociale, sociabilité et cycle de vie," *Cahiers de la Maison de la Recherche en Sciences Humaines, Université de Caën* 3: 91–107.

Bidart, C. and Le Gall, D. (1996) "Les jeunes et leurs petits mondes: Relations, cercles sociaux, nébuleuses," *Cahiers de la Maison de la Recherche en Sciences Humaines, Université de Caën* No. 5: 57–76.

Bidart, C., Degenne, A., Lavenu, D., Le Gall, D. and Mounier, L. (1993) *Sociabilité et insertion professionnelle: Analyse comparative du réseau de relations de jeunes scolarisés et de jeunes en voie d'insertion*, research project, LASAR/LASMAS-IDL, MRSH, Université de Caën.

Blöss, Th. (1996) "La 'démocratisation' des relations parents–jeunes," in Arléa-Corlet (ed.) *La famille malgré tout*, Panoramiques, No. 25: 177–182, Paris: Le Seuil.

Bonvalet, C., Maison, D., Le Bras, H. and Charles, L. (1993) "Proches et parents," *Population, INED, Paris* 1: 83–110.

Bossard, J.H.S. and Boll, E.S. (1956) *The large family system*, Phildelphia: University of Pensylvania Press.

Bouglé, C. (1910) "Qu'est-ce la sociologie?," in *Qu'est-ce que la sociologie*? (1897, Revue de Paris), Paris: Félix Alcan.

Chalvon-Demersay, S. (1989) "Cette famille toujours indispensable," Informations Sociales, Paris, CNAF, 4: 68–76.

Chartier, J.-P. and Chartier, L. (1990) *Les parents martyrs: Passions, haines et vengeances d'adolescents*, Toulouse: Privat.

Chemin, A., Drouet, L., Geoffroy, J.-J., Jezequel, M.-Th. and Joly, A. (1995) *Violences sexuelles en famille*, Paris: Eres.

Cherlin, A. (1987) "Le remariage comme institution incomplète" [*The American Journal of Sociology*, 1978, 84: 634–650], Paris, Dialogue, AFCCC, No. 97: 50–64.

Coenen-Huther, J., Kellerhals, J. and Von Allmen, M. (1994) *Les réseaux de solidarité dans la famille*, Lausanne: Réalités Sociales.

Collectif (1994) *Macadam Blues*, university thesis, in D. Beynier and D. Le Gall (eds) *Action sociale et études locales*, Université de Caën.

Cooper, D. (1972) *Mort de la famille*, Paris: Seuil.

Daumat, M. (1988) *L'affaire d'Esclans: Les conflits familiaux au XVIIIe siècle*, Paris: Seuil.

Déchaux, J.-H. (1995) "Orientations théoriques en sociologie de la famille: Autour de cinq ouvrages récents," *Revue Française de Sociologie* 36: 525–550.

Degenne, A. (1987) *L'acteur social et son réseau. Un niveau intermédiaire: Les réseaux sociaux*, Paris: CESOL.

*Dialogue* (1991) "Moi, mon frère; moi, ma soeur," Paris, AFCCC, No. 114.

—— (1992) "Impensables violences," Paris, AFCCC, No. 117.
Durkheim, E. (1975) "La famille conjugale" (1892 lecture, published in *Revue de Philosophie* 1921), in E. Durkheim, *Textes III*, Paris: Minuit.
Fize, M. (1990) *La démocratie familiale: Évolution des relations parents–adolescents*, Paris: Les Presses de la Renaissance.
Freud, S. (1973) "Le roman familial des névrosés: Névroses, psychoses et perversions," in *Le mythe de la naissance du héros d'O. Rank 1909*, Paris: PUF.
Galland, O. (1985) "Formes et transformations de l'entrée dans la vie adulte," *Sociologie du Travail* 27: 32–52.
Gauléjac (de), V. (1987) *La névrose de classe*, Paris: Hommes et groupes.
—— (1996) "Le roman familial," in Arléa-Corlet (ed.) *La famille malgré tout*, Panoramiques, No. 25: 201–204, Paris: Le Seuil.
Gauléjac (de), V. and Aubert, N. (1990) *Femmes au singulier ou la parentalité solitaire*, Klincksieck.
Gauléjac (de), V. and Taboada Léonetti, I. (1994) *La lutte des places*, Paris: Epi.
Gotman, A. (1988) *Hériter*, Paris: PUF.
—— (1990) "L'impossible partage," in *Des soeurs, des frères. Les méconnus du roman familial*, Paris, Autrement, No. 112: 95–99.
Gruyer, F., Fadier-Nisse, M. and Sabourin, P. (1991) *La violence impensable: Inceste et maltraitance*, Paris: Nathan.
Hahn, A. (1990) "La sociologie du conflit," *Sociologie du Travail* 32: 375–385.
Halbwachs, M. (1925) *Les cadres sociaux de la mémoire*, Paris: PUF.
Kaufmann, J.-C. (1993) *Sociologie du couple*, Paris: Presses Universitaires de France.
Kellerhals, J. and Montandon, C. (1991) *Les stratégies éducatives des familles: Milieu social, dynamique familiale et éducation des pré-adolescents*, Neuchâtel/Paris: Delachaux et Niestlé.
Klagsbrun, F. (1994) *Frères et soeur: Pour le meilleur et pour le pire* [*Mixed Feelings* 1992, New York: Bantam Books], Paris: Bayard éditions.
Langevin, A. (1991) "Des couples de frères et soeurs, ou la sexuation des itinéraires," *Dialogue* 114: 54–63.
Le Gall, D. (1992) "Secondes amours: Aimer la raison?," *Revue Internationale d'Action Communautaire* 27/67: 69–79.
—— (1993) "Formes de régulation conjugale et familiale à la suite d'unions fécondes,"*habilitation* thesis, Université de Paris V – Sorbonne.
—— (1995) "Samia, Delphine, Franck et les autres: Discours de l'exclusion ordinaire," Technical report for the Délégation interministérielle auprès des jeunes, la CAF et l'EPE du Calvados, LASAR, Université de Caën.
—— (1996), "Beaux-parents au quotidien et par intermittence," in D. Le Gall and C. Martin (eds) *Familles et politiques sociales*, Paris: L'Harmattan.
Le Gall, D. and Martin, C. (1993) "Transitions familiales, logiques de recomposition et mode de régulation conjugale," in M.-Th. Meulders-Klein and I. Théry (eds) *Les recompositions familiales aujourd'hui*, Paris: Nathan.
—— (1995) "Construire un nouveau lien familial: Beaux-parents et beaux-grands-parents," in M. Gullestad and M. Segalen (eds) *La famille en Europe: Parenté et perpétuation familiale*, Paris: La Découverte.
—— (eds) (1996) *Familles et politiques sociales: Dix questions sur le lien familial contemporain*, Paris: L'Harmattan.
Lefaucheur, N. (1988) "Les conditions et niveaux de vie des enfants de parents séparés," L'enfant et ses parents séparés, IDEF, Paris.
Lurie, A. (1990) *Conflits de famille* [*The War Between the Tates*, 1974], Paris: Éditions Rivages.

Michelat, C. and Segalen, M. (1991) "L'amour de la généalogie," in M. Segalen (ed.) *Jeux de familles*, Paris: Presses du CNRS.

Mogey, J. (1976) "Residence, family and kinship: Some recent research," *Journal of Family History* 1: 95–105.

Muñoz-Perez, B. (1987) "Le divorce," in *Données Sociales*, Paris: INSEE.

Parsons, T. (1955) "The kinship system of the contemporary United States," in F. Bourricaud, *Eléments pour une sociologie de l'action*, Paris: Plon.

Perrone, R. and Nannini, M. (1995) *Violence et abus sexuel dans la famille*, Paris: ESF Éditeur.

Pitrou, A. (1978) *Vivre sans famille? Les solidarités familiales dans le monde d'aujourd'hui*, Privat: Toulouse.

Rémy, J. (1967) "Persistance de la famille étendue dans un milieu industriel urbain," *Revue Française de Sociologie* 4: 493–505.

Roussel, L. (1989) *La famille incertaine*, Paris: Odile Jacob.

Roussel, L. and Bourguignon, O. (1976) *La famille après le mariage des enfants*, Cahiers No. 78, Paris: PUF, INED.

Schwartz, O. (1990) *Le monde privé des ouvriers: Hommes et femmes du Nord*, Paris: PUF.

Segalen, M. (1993) *Sociologie de la famille*, Paris: Armand Colin.

Simmel, G. (1908/1995) *Le Conflit*, Paris: Circé.

Singly, F. de (1993) *Sociologie de la famille contemporaine*, Paris: Nathan.

Théry, I. (1991) "Trouver le mot juste: Langage et parenté dans les recompositions familiales après divorce," in M. Segalen (ed.) *Jeux de familles*, Paris: Presses du CNRS.

Welzer-Lang, D. (1992) *Arrête ! Tu me fais mal ! La violence domestique, 60 questions, 59 reponses . . .*, Montreal: VLB Éditeur.

Young, M. and Willmott, M. (1957) *Family and kinship in East London*, Boston: Routledge & Kegan Paul.

## Chapter 6

# The discourse of philotimo and conflict resolution in an urban Greek family

## A psychosocial approach

*Vana Theodossopoulou-Papalois and Mara Theodossopoulou*

Vana Theodossopoulou-Papalois was trained in Greek classical studies, has an M.A. in school psychology, and a Ph.D. in social psychology. Mara Theodossopoulou's academic training was in psychology, counseling, and career guidance in the M.A. program at the School of Philosophy, University of Athens.

*Philotimo is a distinct Greek value. The question is how this value operates as a conflict resolution and mediation strategy in family conflicts. This chapter analyzes the dynamics of a family conflict episode at the intersection of psychosocial and cultural factors. We describe how members of an urban, nuclear family in Greece formulate an intrafamily mediation strategy that is based on the value of philotimo. We use a qualitative methodology to investigate family members' attitudes during a family discussion in which a philotimo-oriented mediation strategy is developed. A conceptual framework that describes the distinct psychosocial characteristics of the modern Greek family sets the ground for the discussion of findings of this study.*

*As regards our research approach we believe that the study of naturally occurring language behavior is the most authentic and objective way to analyze the attitudes of various parties involved in family conflict.*

*What we would like the reader to take home from this chapter is the idea that informal family conflict resolution strategies, outside the legal system, are shaped by the distinct cultural values that operate in a society.*

*A Greek saying relevant to this chapter is: "You cannot turn blood into water." In other words, because of the difficulty to exit family relationships, due to strong biological and psychological bonds, people involved in family conflict situations, especially the Greeks, search for informal rather than formal (i.e. legal) conflict resolution strategies that promise not to hurt feelings, and not to damage the social identity of the family members. It is better for a family to exercise all its power and "contain" a conflict within its network rather than officially ask for society's intervention. In a word, the exercise of good will is the best guarantee for the peaceful resolution of family conflict.*

## INTRODUCTION

The purpose of this paper is to describe how members of an urban, nuclear Greek family formulate a philotimo-based mediation strategy to deal with a family conflict situation. Philotimo ("love of honor") is a polysemantic, traditional social value that characterizes Greeks more than other nationalities and accounts for a set of human qualities such as: honesty, morality, respect, love, duty, obedience, success, progress and humaneness. The family conflict analyzed in this chapter is about an economic transaction made between family members in a spirit of trust and good faith rather than using formal legal procedures. In what follows, we discuss the issue of family conflicts in general, sketch a psychosocial portrait of the modern Greek family, and provide a brief overview of the family conflict situation analyzed in this case.

### Family conflicts: Definition and characteristics

Conflict has been defined as "the interaction of interdependent people who perceive incompatible goals and interference from each other in achieving those goals" (Hocker and Wilmot 1985). We understand family conflict as perceived incompatibility of goals between people who are related to each other by strong biological and psychological bonds. According to Emery (1992), the main characteristics that distinguish family conflicts from other social conflicts are:

- Opportunity for conflict and difficulty to exit the family: members of the family live in close physical proximity and share many life experiences and conditions that make conflict of interest more likely to occur among them. Also, there is no easy way for family members to escape their biological bonds, besides death.
- Dynamic change in family life: human relationships are dynamic phenomena and individual members of the family are involved in a cycle of constant evolutionary and developmental change. Within this cycle, development brings change and change in turn generates conflict.
- High stakes: family conflicts usually have significant consequences for the individual because they are associated with the control and distribution of emotional, social, and economic resources.
- Few alternatives: family conflicts prescribe a restricted set of conflict resolution alternatives to individual members of the family. The unique personality type and life history of individual family members along with everyday family rituals, socialization practices, and identity claims are all factors that potentially limit the choice of conflict resolution strategies among family members.

## The Greek family and the value of philotimo: A conceptual framework

Industrialization in Greece started during the 1950s and was accompanied by migration of the rural population to the large urban centers, particularly Athens. These social changes have left a profound effect on the Greek family system and its values. A shift from the extended family system characteristic of the small and isolated Greek communities to the nuclear family system characteristic of urban areas resulted in the gradual rejection of collectivistic and the adoption of individualistic values among members of the Greek family (Georgas 1991).

In the traditional, collectivistic Greek family, a hierarchical system of family roles and the values of a broad in-group are dominant. In the traditional Greek family, the father controls the economic power and is authoritarian in his relationship with the spouse and the children; the mother is submissive to the father and has the duty to care for the home and the children. Also, in the traditional Greek family, the values as well as the authority figures of the in-group are dominant. The Greek in-group includes all relatives, in-laws, and friends who have the distinct characteristic that they show concern and "will come to aid" when members of the family are "in time of need" (Campbell 1964; Triandis and Vassiliou 1967; Vassiliou and Vassiliou 1973; du Boulay 1974; Polemi-Todoulou 1981; Doumanis 1983; Dragonas 1983; Katakis 1984).

Philotimo is the key social value that dominates the relationship between family members and the in-group in the traditional Greek family. Also, philotimo is a central part of the Greek self-concept and a social value that characterizes Greeks more than other nationalities. The word philotimo literally means "love of honor" but is a polysemantic concept associated with honesty, morality, respect, love, duty, obedience, success, progress and humaneness (for a detailed discussion see Lee 1953; Friedl 1962; Sanders 1962; Campbell 1964; Vassiliou and Vassiliou 1966, 1973; Triandis and Vassiliou 1967; Adamopoulos 1977).

The modern nuclear Greek family constitutes the particular social unit in which the transition from a collectivistic to an individualistic culture takes place. Systematic cross-cultural research findings indicate that Greece is in the middle position between collectivistic and individualistic cultures and that the traditional, hierarchical family values are gradually rejected, especially by young people who live in Athens and are members of nuclear families (Hofstede 1980; Triandis *et al.* 1985; Georgas 1989, 1991). With respect to the value of philotimo, research findings indicate that it is still functional among parents in the small communities; it is not rejected by Athenian parents but it is "no longer an integral part of the value system of the young people," and it is torn from its context of the traditional in-group "due to the diminished influence of the extended family and the in-group" (Georgas 1989, 1991).

### A brief overview of the case

A young couple decided to buy a new car and asked for a loan (of approximately $7,000) from the wife's parents. Relying on good faith rather than formal legal procedures, the wife's parents agreed to give the loan. The only condition was to receive their money back within two years because this sum was their only economic security for their elderly years. Three years passed and the parents had not received their money. The only answer the parents received from the young couple was "you should be able to get the money within a month." However, a period of eight months went by and the parents still had not received their money back. In this case, one thought bothered both parents most: "When they were in need we gave them the money. Now, we are in need and they don't give us back our own money." The parents attributed the young couple's behavior to a lack of philotimo and asked their older daughter Irene, the wife's sister, to mediate the conflict.

In this chapter we describe what happened in the older daughter's family during the discussion of the appropriate conflict mediation strategy. The case closed when Irene's intervention in the dispute was successful. A month later the parents got their money back and rebuilt their relationship with their younger daughter.

This case is interesting for three reasons. First, it illustrates an intrafamily mediation in which the primary cause of the conflict is attributed to a psychological entity with great sociocultural implications in the Greek milieu (i.e. philotimo). Second, it shows how the relationship between the nuclear and the extended family in Greece influences intrafamily mediation. Third, it describes the dynamics of conflict resolution and decision making within the context of the modern Greek family.

## THE CASE STUDY

### Materials of the study

Analysis of the case is based on the transcript of a discussion between members of Irene's nuclear family including Irene, her husband and her daughter. The discussion took place at the family's home in Athens on a Sunday afternoon in the presence of a family friend (the principal investigator of this study). The discussion was tape recorded with the consent of all family members. The transcript of the family discussion was translated into English by two bilingual psychology students who had been instructed to translate the materials as close to the Greek original as possible.

### Members of the family: A brief introduction

The initial parties to the conflict were Maria, her husband Takis and Maria's parents. Maria, 37, was born and raised in Athens. She co-owns an antique shop with her husband. Takis, 41, was born and raised in Athens as well. Maria and Takis had asked Maria's parents for the loan. Maria's father, 78, is a retired taxi driver. He was born and raised in a small town in the northern part of Greece. The mother, 72, is a housewife; she was born and raised in a village in northern Greece.

Maria's parents asked their older daughter Irene to mediate the conflict with their younger daughter Maria. Also involved in the mediation effort is Stasa, 44, a cousin of Irene and Maria; Stasa is married and has three children. Stasa has studied law but has never worked as a professional lawyer. She is Irene's paternal cousin and was also born and raised in Athens. Stasa has a very good relationship with all three nuclear families: Irene's, Maria's and Irene's parents.

The nuclear family who are discussing the appropriate mediation strategy are Irene, her husband John, and Helen, their adult daughter. Irene, 43, works as a teacher at the kindergarten of a private school in Athens. She was born and raised in Athens. John, 44, works as an architect in his own construction company. He was born and raised on a small Greek island. Helen, 21, the only child, is a biology student at the University of Athens.

### The family discussion

VISITOR So, how are things now between Maria, Takis and your parents?

IRENE The same, I suppose. My parents haven't got the money yet and I am their only hope. I haven't spoken to Maria yet. I am supposed to be the one who will make Maria and Takis give the money back to mom and dad. My question is, how can I possibly do that? And if my parents are right, and Maria and Takis don't have philotimo at all in their heart, then I don't think there is much for me to say or do in this case. Based on my experience, in cases like this the only thing one could do is either go to court or end the relationship forever. The question is: How can you do that to your own daughter? Besides, to the best of my knowledge at least, there isn't yet a textbook written in Greek that could teach me how to deal with people who don't have philotimo and are your sister and brother-in-law. I really don't know what I should do.

JOHN That's right, dear. In my opinion, philotimo is something people are born with. It's a gift from God. I mean, look at your family: Your parents are people who do have philotimo, you do have philotimo as well, and here it is: Maria doesn't have philotimo. Can you explain that? Two sisters from the same family, the same home, the same parents, the same school, the same friends, the same everything. . . . How can you possibly explain that? And I agree with you that there isn't much you can do if Maria and Takis are people who don't have philotimo in their hearts—especially for their own parents. And in this case, it's not only that you don't have philotimo; it's that your behavior hurts other people's philotimo.

IRENE Listen, John, deep down in my heart I want to believe that Maria must have some kind of philotimo. I don't know about Takis. It's just that her philotimo is only directed toward her new home and her husband. She mostly cares about her own home and her relationship and I couldn't ever blame her for that. The problem is that she uses the people who love her so much, she uses her own parents. She takes their love for granted and she, mistakenly of course, thinks that she isn't supposed to give anything back in return. That's her big mistake. That's what happens I think in this situation.

HELEN I think that no one should take anything for granted in life, mother. Philotimo is something you should only share with people whom you know you can trust. I mean, you need to know for sure. People whose behavior can prove you that they do have philotimo in their heart. And philotimo isn't something that has to do only with your relatives, mother. You can find people who are philotimo at your school, at your work, everywhere, in Greece, in America, in China, everywhere. If you don't know that, then you simply take your chances.

IRENE Well, maybe you are right. But our question here is: how can you possibly talk and deal with people who don't have philotimo? What could I say or do to Maria and Takis to make them give the money back to grandma and grandpa?

JOHN Maybe your parents should have brought them to court in the first place. That might be a good reason to awaken philotimo in their hearts, and drastically, I suppose. The problem though, is that I doubt if your parents have made any written agreement with Maria and Takis before they lent them the money. It's a transaction made out of good will. That's the problem.

IRENE Oh come on now, John. You've known mom and dad for so many years. Even if they had the papers, do you think they could do that to their own child?

HELEN Why not?

IRENE Oh come on now, Helen. You know grandpa and grandma. They have so much philotimo. And besides, for them money is not the real issue in this case; it's rather Maria's apathy toward their request that hurts them the most.

HELEN Sure. But, listen mom. We already have enough problems in this family. Do we need this one as well? I don't need to remind you, I suppose, that this is an exams period for me and I don't need this home to become a battleground. What I want is a peaceful and quiet environment to study. And definitely, I don't need all this noise and the arguments and the race of phone calls between you, dad, the grandpas, Maria, Takis . . . . Gosh! I can even picture what will happen right now. That's what I hate. How am I supposed to succeed in my exams this way? And you know, what? I should expect grandma and grandpa to have some philotimo and don't have us involved in problems like that in the first place. Do we call other people to solve our problems? Then, why should other people call us to solve theirs? I cannot understand this.

IRENE Helen, these other people just happen to be your own grandparents.

HELEN All right, all right! Let's stop it before it starts. I just wanted to say that you've got your own family now and your own problems. And that you should care for us more than you should for anyone else. Besides, I am very concerned about your blood pressure. You shouldn't get involved in a frustrating situation like this. Your parents should have thought about that, as well—since they do have philotimo themselves. Don't you think so?

IRENE OK, OK. Let's not argue about this now. Be sure that I am very well aware of my situation. I take good care of my health and please don't worry. I promise you, nothing will affect your study for the exams. That's a promise.

HELEN In other words, what I am saying is just try to stay cool with everyone and don't get upset. I am confident that Maria will give the money back in the end and that she will also explain the delay and that your parents will live happy ever after.

JOHN I do think that Helen is right about that, Irene.

IRENE I know. I am sure Maria must have some kind of philotimo in her heart. There must be an explanation behind all this. I don't want to believe that she could have done that on purpose. Maybe it would be a good idea for us to invite them for dinner sometime this week. And then I could talk to Maria while you, John, could talk to Takis. And we will take things from there. I also think that Stasa might be the perfect person to talk to Maria as well. They are still very close to each other and they do listen to each other.

JOHN I think that's the right thing for us to do. You could also tell your parents not to worry about a thing. Let them know that we do love them and let them also know that we will be right behind them all the way. If they need some money, they can always give us a call. Anytime. And in the end, they can count on us for taking care of them if the need calls. We are rich enough to afford two more dishes on the table; that isn't such a big deal. On the contrary, it is our pleasure. But just make sure that they get the message. Tell them how much I love them and how much I care for them. Because they are nice and sensitive people and I know how much they must suffer for all this. After all, they are old people. That's what they are thinking all the time: old age and their children. All the time. I know. As far as Maria and Takis are concerned: they have done nothing wrong to us personally and I don't think we should break our relationship with them. Just let Maria know—and I could also talk to Takis about that—that we could lend them some money if they are in need. This way they could give the money back to your parents and everybody will be happy. Of course, we will sign a contract for the loan; just to make sure. Tell Maria also that she should sit down sometime and talk to your mother, your parents. I am sure they do have a lot of understanding. Besides, they love her so much. She always will be the little Benjamin in their family. I think, that's the only way we could bring them to philotimo. What would you say Irene?

IRENE I absolutely agree. This way, we can always give them a chance to prove whether they do have philotimo or not and at the same time we are doing the right thing for my parents, and we can have our conscience clear that we did the right thing.

HELEN I think it will work.

### Research questions and procedure

We were interested in how members of this nuclear family reached their decision about a common mediation strategy and how personal, relational, and group concerns played a role in that decision. At the personal level, we investigate how individual members of the family view their role in the conflict resolution process. At the relational level, we investigate how members of the family view the role of each other in the conflict resolution process. Finally, at the group level we investigate how members of the family perceive their role as a unit in the conflict resolution process.

To pursue our research questions we used a newly developed methodology for the qualitative analysis of attitudes (Papalois-Theodossopoulou 1996). This methodology is called Psycho-Social Lexical Orientation (PSLO) and uses naturally occurring language data (oral statements, written documents, conversations) to capture the psychosocial concerns, life experiences and rationales associated with people's (individuals, social groups) evaluative statements.

In principle, PSLO methodology can provide researchers and practitioners with a natural rather than an artificially made scientific tool for investigating attitudes. PSLO methodology follows the natural mechanisms of the language people use to communicate their attitudes, and it analyzes evaluative statements as they are made in the respondents' own words. The result is a better understanding of the language people use when communicating their attitudes and, based on that, a better quality of communication and strategic decision making.

With regard to conflict and mediation, PSLO methodology can provide researchers and practitioners with a simple and cost effective tool that can capture people's views of the conflict situation, the opponent(s) and themselves, which may help generate consensus or facilitate negotiations and third party intervention efforts.

The PSLO follows a free association procedure in which the speaker either expresses her attitudes in a natural way or is asked by the investigator to respond to the question: "What is your opinion about X?" The investigator makes sure that the speaker takes sufficient time to fully express her opinion.

We analyzed the present case in four stages: Coding, analysis, outcome, and verification. First, we coded all statements for the use of first (I, we) and second (you) person pronouns. Second, we analyzed each speaker's message in terms of: agenda items (i.e. which aspects of an issue does the speaker raise as relevant to her concerns); input (i.e. which life experiences and arguments does the speaker associate with each agenda item); and connection (i.e. what is the rationale that connects agenda items to each other). Third, we identified the tone of language (information, emotion or action-oriented) as well as the principle (rationale, in terms of an if . . . then . . . statement) on which evaluative responses are made. Finally, we searched for linguistic evidence of how personal, relational, and group concerns are reflected in the development of the family mediation strategy.

## Findings of the study

### *Irene*

At the personal level, Irene deals with feelings of uncertainty ("I really don't know what I should do," line 16) and responsibility ("I am their only hope," line 4) as she tries to come to a decision and develop an effective mediation strategy and action plan. The focus of Irene's concern during the decision making revolves around three agenda items: her relationship with members of the extended family; her relationship with members of the nuclear family; and the success of her mediation effort. The concept of philotimo is associated with all three of the above items.

With respect to her relationship with members of the extended family, Irene cares deeply for her parents and wants to help them resolve their dispute with her sister ("they have so much philotimo . . . hurts them the most," lines 64–66). She also recognizes that the essence of this family conflict has to do with emotions rather than money ("money is not the real issue in this case; it's rather Maria's apathy toward their request that hurts them the most," lines 64–66). According to this view, Irene's mediation efforts should not only focus on settling the economic transaction but rather on rebuilding the interpersonal relationships between the family members. She recognizes that the difficulty of her mediation task is related to her parents' view that "Maria and Takis don't have philotimo at all in their heart" (lines 7–8). To overcome this difficulty Irene develops her own evaluation toward the conflict situation. This revised view is based on intuition and the idea that "Maria must have some kind of philotimo" (line 30); thus, Irene's mediation effort should be designed to target Maria's hidden feelings of philotimo ("deep down in my heart . . . this situation" (lines 29–38), "I am sure Maria . . . on purpose," lines 101–104). Irene supports her idea by stating that, although hidden, Maria's philotimo is still there but has taken a new direction ("her philotimo is only directed toward her new home and her husband. She mostly cares about her own home and her relationship and I couldn't ever blame her for that," lines 31–34). However, according to Irene, in cases like this one problems start to arise when people decide to accept only the benefits rather than the responsibilities related to their relationships with members of the extended family (lines 34–38). With regard to Takis, Irene, although she admits that she does not know whether or not he has philotimo in his heart ("I don't know about Takis," lines 30–31), is willing to develop a mediation strategy that treats him and his wife on an equal basis, as if they both had philotimo in their hearts ("and then I could talk to Maria . . . to Takis," lines 105–106).

With respect to her relationship with members of the nuclear family, Irene assumes responsibility and promises John and Helen two things:

her mediation effort will not harm the climate of their home; her mediation effort will harm neither her health nor the wellbeing of members of her family (lines 91–94, 135–138). With respect to the success of her mediation effort, Irene works toward two directions: she develops a mediation strategy and action plan based on good will and full support of members of the immediate family (John, Helen, Stasa); she develops a mediation strategy and action plan that combines the elements of emotion and rationality, intuition and realism (lines 101–109).

At the relational level, Irene tries to balance and accommodate in her mediation strategy and action plan the needs and interests of both the extended and the nuclear family. To achieve this, Irene works toward two directions: she involves the members of her own nuclear family in her decision-making process by inviting them to air their views as well as misconceptions regarding the family conflict and the people involved in it; she is open to new ideas and is willing to incorporate them into the development of her mediation strategy and action plan (lines 16, 48, 106, 135–138).

At the group level, Irene presents her mediation strategy and action plan as a joint family effort rather than an individual task (lines 104–109). She also assures members of the nuclear family that her mediation strategy and action plan are specially designed to protect all parties' interests on a long term and on a short term basis (lines 135–138). Specifically, Irene submits her mediation strategy and action plan for approval. It is worth noting that Irene formulates her strategy and plan as a tentative proposal rather than a final decision ("maybe it would be a good idea," line 104).

*John*

At the personal level, John focuses his concerns on the concept of philotimo and its relevance to the family conflict at hand. According to John, philotimo is an innate quality of human beings and is not subjected to social learning ("people are born with. It's a gift from God," line 18). Applying a deductive syllogism to support his view, John uses Irene's family as an example ("I mean, look at your family: Your parents are people who do have philotimo, you do have philotimo as well; and here it is, Maria doesn't have philotimo. Can you explain this? Two sisters from the same family, the same home, the same parents, the same school, the same friends, the same everything . . . ," lines 18–23).

The above view of philotimo is closely related to what Irene's parents think about this conflict. According to this view, there is no easy way to resolve a conflict, if the people who are involved in it don't have philotimo in their heart ("and if my parents are right . . . this case," lines 7–9, "and I agree . . . their hearts," lines 24–26).

With respect to the mediation strategy, John's opinion is relevant because he understands the difficulty of Irene's task and he feels responsible to help her, and to care for and support her in her decision-making effort and action plan (lines 17, 110, 134 "and I could also talk to Takis about that," lines 125–126). Furthermore, John stresses the problematic situation of the family conflict by expressing his doubt that legal documents exist to confirm the economic transaction between Maria and Takis, and Irene's parents ("I doubt . . . that's the problem," lines 55–58).

In addition, John expresses feelings of empathy as well as sympathy for Irene's parents ("and I agree with you . . . their own parents," lines 24–26; "tell them how much I love them and how much I care for them . . . I know," lines 118–120; "I am sure they have a lot of understanding," line 131).

At the relational level, John focuses his attention on the details of the mediation strategy and the implementation of the action plan. As regards the mediation strategy, John expresses the view that Irene's proposal to use a tit-for-tat philotimo mediation strategy is the only viable alternative because breaking off the relationship or going to court are unacceptable and *de facto* not possible (line 57). Also, John expresses his agreement with Helen's suggestion regarding the frame of mind in which Irene should approach the mediation task. His wife should not jeopardize her health and emotional wellbeing during her mediation efforts (line 100). Moreover, John believes that Irene should assume the most active role in the mediation effort because the two opposing parties belong to her side of the extended family network (lines 110, 125, 134).

Regarding the implementation of the action plan, John suggests to Irene a series of specific directions by making a synopsis of his own understanding of the conflict situation and his family's involvement in it (lines 110–134). According to John, he and his wife are the two members of the nuclear family who are responsible to develop and implement the mediation strategy. The only difference between them is the role each assumes during the decision-making process: the woman submits and evaluates alternative proposals while the man selects, confirms and asks for the final approval of the proposed course of action.

At the group level, John assumes the responsibility of a democratic leader who expresses the needs, interests, and views of all members of the nuclear family as they interact with members of the extended family and their conflict. Specifically, John focuses his attention on three issues: the relationship between his nuclear family and Irene's parents (lines 110–122)—here the message is "we do love them and we will be right behind them all the way" (lines 112–113); the relationship between his nuclear family and the family of Maria and Takis (lines 122–133)—here the message is "they have done nothing wrong to us personally and I don't think we should break our relationship with them" (lines 123–125);

a legally binding procedure for a possible proposed economic transaction between his nuclear family and Maria and Takis—here the message is "we could lend them some money if they are in need . . . of course, we will sign a contract for the loan; just to make sure" (lines 126–129).

*Helen*

At the personal level, Helen expresses her own view about philotimo as well as her concerns regarding the role of the nuclear family in the mediation effort. According to Helen, philotimo is a value that may be found in every culture and social relationship and is not exclusively related to the family network. Also, Helen considers philotimo a value related to personal commitment rather than social privilege ("philotimo is something . . . your chances," lines 40–47). Helen associates the family mediation effort with negative feelings and harsh criticism. On the one hand, she is almost sure that Irene's mediation effort will bring noise, frustration, arguments, and tension to the climate of her nuclear family and will finally destroy the privacy and peace of mind she needs to pass her exams ("and definitely, I don't need . . . this way?," lines 71–76). On the other hand, Helen's criticism has to do with the fact that her mother, and thus herself and her father, are involved in the middle of a family crisis by social obligation rather than by personal choice. Helen has difficulty understanding why people in her nuclear family resolve their differences without asking for help from the extended family and why members of the extended family do not do the same thing ("I should expect . . . can not understand this," lines 76–80, "why not?," line 62).

At the relational level, Helen directs her attention toward two aspects: Irene and Irene's parents. Helen reminds Irene of her role and responsibilities in Irene's nuclear family ("you've got your own family . . . anyone else," lines 84–86) and criticizes, with a dose of irony, her grandparents for not respecting their own daughter's privacy and health problems ("your parents . . . don't you think so?," lines 88–90). Because of Helen's view that Irene has been involved in the family conflict not by free choice but by responsibility to her aging parents she insists on giving Irene a lot of advice as well as moral support for her mediation effort. Helen recognizes that her own advice and reminders of obligation to her mother stem from her deep concern and love for her mother (lines 86–88, 95–99).

At the group level, Helen uses the pronouns "I" and "we" interchangeably. In this way, she links her own life and concerns to her nuclear family as a whole ("we already have enough problems in this family. Do we need this one as well? I don't need to remind you, I suppose, that this is an exams period for me and I don't need this home to become a battleground," lines 67–70). The only responsibility Helen assumes during the mediation is her tolerance of the situation; the family mediation strategy and action plan described by John does not account anywhere for Helen's active role in the conflict resolution process.

With respect to decision making in the nuclear family, Helen believes that her own views of the conflict situation and the mediation effort are in congruence with her nuclear family's interests and for this reason they should be respected and taken into account in family decisions; consistent with this stand, she accepts family decisions that incorporate her views (line 139).

## DISCUSSION AND CONCLUSIONS

We will summarize how the attitudes of individual members of the nuclear family contribute to the development of a philotimo-oriented mediation strategy.

With regard to the nuclear family's decision-making process one view is shared by all family members despite their differences in opinion: When one of us is in trouble, all of us are in trouble. Thus although it is only Irene who undertakes the mediation task at the social level, the entire nuclear family is involved in the decision-making process at the family level. The nuclear family as a whole is the one who sets the criteria and guarantees the success of Irene's mediation effort.

Each family member's contribution to the mediation strategy is directly related to his or her views about the value of philotimo. Below follows a profile of all philotimo-related views expressed during the family's decision-making process:

Irene uses an emotional tone of language to support the view that the success of the mediation strategy will be guaranteed if it secures the rebuilding of the relationship between Maria, Takis and the old couple. According to Irene, philotimo is a quality that people do not lose but redefine during their life time. In our case, Maria has redefined philotimo, from her old to her new family. Therefore, success of the mediation strategy is guaranteed when Maria realizes how much hurt she has caused to her old parents.

John uses an action-oriented tone of language to support the view that if the mediation strategy incorporates the short- and long-term interests of both the extended and the nuclear family, then its success is guaranteed. According to John, philotimo is an innate tendency in human nature. In our case, a philotimo-oriented mediation strategy is the only viable option for the nuclear family.

Helen uses a belief-oriented tone of language to support the view that if the mediation strategy defines the limits between the interests of the nuclear and the extended family, then its success is guaranteed. According to Helen, philotimo is a value that people achieve through their actual behavior in everyday life; philotimo is not something imbued on people by virtue of their social relationships. In our case, a philotimo-oriented mediation strategy should be designed especially to secure the interests of the nuclear family.

With regard to the philotimo-oriented mediation strategy, we summarize what it is, how it works, and what it does.

- A philotimo-oriented mediation strategy puts special emphasis on the long term benefits of both the mediator and the opposing parties. In our case it targets the continuation of the relationship among relatives and meets the mediator's criteria of justice and fairness.
- A philotimo-oriented mediation strategy seems to be suitable in this case because it helps to resolve the deep causes rather than contain the family conflict. Besides returning the money the ultimate goal of the mediation strategy is rebuilding the emotional and social relationships between the two opposing families.
- In a case where the family conflict has been defined at its core as "lack of philotimo," a tit for tat mediation strategy should be adopted. The rationale of a philotimo-oriented mediation strategy implies: When philotimo does not show by itself, it must be hidden somewhere; people who deeply care about someone have to find a way to awaken it.
- Personal contact, open communication, and sharing of family bonds are the main elements for the creation of a philotimo climate during the implementation of the mediation strategy.
- A philotimo-oriented mediation strategy works in two phases. First, building trust and commitment between the mediator and the opposing parties. Second, removing the barriers to people's kind and moral feelings. The nuclear family's action plan secures all of the above by incorporating the following elements: private discussion between Irene and her parents, warm welcome of Maria and Takis at Irene's family's home, proposal of Irene's family to offer Maria and Takis a loan, suggestion for a private discussion between Maria and the old couple.
- In our case, a philotimo-oriented mediation strategy is actively implemented by two people: John and Irene. John assumes the role of the democratic leader who carefully listens and considers the views of all members of his nuclear family, articulates the details of a family mediation strategy and action plan, and finally asks for his wife's feedback on his proposal. Irene, the mother of the family, does all the thinking and arguing to support her proposal for the development of a mediation strategy and action plan but passes the responsibility for the final decision to her husband.

Our observations in this case are in agreement with other findings in the literature regarding the gradual rejection of collectivistic, and the adoption of individualistic values among members of the Greek family (Georgas 1991). Our case also illustrates that the value of philotimo is torn from its context of the traditional in-group (Georgas 1989, 1991).

With respect to the function of the philotimo value in family conflict, the evidence of the present case supports the following conclusion. Although the meaning of philotimo follows the transformations of the Greek family, its impact remains strong and emotionally loaded for family members of all ages.

Our objective for the future is to further establish the significance of the value of philotimo and explore its dynamics in relation to conflict situations at the interpersonal, intragroup, and intergroup level in the Greek milieu. Our challenge for the future is to investigate the application and relevance of the Greek value of philotimo in negotiation and conflict resolution episodes that occur between individualistic and collectivistic cultures.

## BIBLIOGRAPHY


Adamopoulos, J. (1977) "The dimensions of the Greek concept of philotimo," *Journal of Social Psychology* 102: 313–314.

Campbell, J. (1964) *Honor, family and patronage*, Oxford: Clarendon.

Doumanis, M. (1983) *Mothering in Greece: From collectivism to individualism*, New York: Academic Press.

Dragonas, T. (1983) "The self-concept of adolescents in the Hellenic context," unpublished Ph.D. thesis, University of Aston.

du Boulay, J. (1974) *Portrait of a Greek mountain village*, Oxford: Clarendon.

Emery, R.E. (1992) "Family conflicts and their developmental implications: a conceptual analysis of meanings for the structure of relationships," in C.U. Shantz and W.W. Hartup (eds) *Conflict in child and adolescent development*, New York: Cambridge University Press.

Friedl, E. (1962) *Vassilika*, New York: Holt, Rinehart & Winston.

Georgas, J. (1989) "Changing family values in Greece. From collectivist to individualist," *Journal of Cross Cultural Psychology* 20: 80–91.

—— (1991) "Intrafamily acculturation of values in Greece," *Journal of Cross Cultural Psychology* 22: 445–457.

Hocker, J.L. and Wilmot, W.W. (1985) *Interpersonal conflict*, Dubuque, IA: Wm C. Brown.

Hofstede, G. (1980) *Culture's consequences*, Beverly Hills, CA: Sage.

Katakis, H. (1984) *Oi tris tautotites tis hellenikis oikogenias* [The three faces of the Greek family], Athens: Kedros.

Lee, D. (1953) "View of the self in the Greek culture," in UNESCO (ed.), *Cultural patterns and technical change*, New York: UNESCO World Federation of Mental Health.

Polemi-Todoulou, M. (1981) "Cooperation in family and peer group: A study of interdependence in a Greek island community," unpublished Ph.D. thesis, Bryn Mawr College.

Sanders, I. (1962) *Rainbow in the rock*, Cambridge, MA: Harvard University Press.

Theodossopoulou-Papalois, V. (1996) "Using language documents to investigate human attitudes: A database," unpublished manuscript, The London School of Economics and Political Science.

Triandis, H.C. and Vassiliou, V. (1967) "A comparative analysis of subjective culture," unpublished manuscript, University of Illinois.

Triandis, H.C., Leung, K., Villareal, M. and Clack, F. (1985) "Allocentric vs. idiocentric tendencies: Convergent vs discriminant validation," *Journal of Research in Personality* 19: 395–415.

Triandis, H.C., Vassiliou, V., Vassiliou, G., Tanaka, Y. and Shanmugam, V. (1972) *The analysis of subjective culture*, New York: John Wiley.

Vassiliou, G. and Vassiliou, V. (1966) "Social values as psychodynamic variable: preliminary explorations of the semantics of philotimo," *Acta Neurologika Psychiatrika Hellenika* 5: 121–135.

Vassiliou, V. and Vassiliou, G. (1973) "The implicative meaning of the Greek concept of philotimo," *Journal of Cross Cultural Psychology* 4: 326–341.

# Part III

# Cultures and communities

Chapter 7

# Gender stereotypes and beliefs about family violence in Poland

*Anna Kwiatkowska*

Anna Kwiatkowska received her Ph.D. in clinical and social psychology from Warsaw University.

*I am interested in the topic of this chapter because the basic thing about domestic violence in Poland are permissive attitudes toward violence in the family. The main questions are why people tolerate acts of violence in Poland and to what extent this is connected to Polish culture. I chose my research approach because gender stereotypes might be something like vehicles carrying cultural/national values, so that they create a permissive climate for domestic violence. To begin to do anything about domestic violence, you must know what is in people's minds about it and why, and how various beliefs are blended or mixed.*

*What I think is important for readers to understand is that there is a Polish specialty regarding domestic violence, as well as a broader social context within the patriarchal order of the world. My favorite quotation in this regard is from Anne Tyler's book* Breathing Lessons: *"But Maggie remembered, and sometimes, feeling the glassy sheet of Ira's disapproval, she grew numbly, wearily certain that there was no such thing on this earth as real change. You could change husbands, but not the situation. You could change who, but not what. We're all just spinning here, she thought, and she pictured the world as a little blue teacup, revolving like those rides at Kiddie Land where everyone is pinned to his place by centrifugal force."*[1]

The main purpose of this chapter is to investigate social representations of domestic violence in Poland and the cultural background of such representations. This study will focus on male violence against women in the context of conflicts between couples. Physical violence is defined here as one of "the conflict strategies, that is behaviors intended to manage or resolve conflict" (Klein and Johnson 1997). Violence is basically available to the party who is more powerful in the relationship and the decision to use violence is determined by culturally and socially learned cognitive schemata such as gender stereotypes and beliefs about family violence.

## SCOPE OF THE PROBLEM

A 1991 report of the Main Statistics Office claimed that family violence occurred in 30 percent of urban and 40 percent of rural families. A 1993 survey revealed that 8 percent of Polish women had been repeatedly battered by their husbands, and another 8 percent of women reported sporadic beatings. However, as many as 41 percent of divorced women confessed that they had suffered from regular beatings from their ex-husbands, but only 32 percent of female divorcees (and 2 percent of males!) indicated that physical violence was the main cause for divorce. Another survey carried out by the State Agency for Resolving Alcohol Problems reported that about 18 percent of female respondents were battered by their husbands.

With regard to parental disciplining methods a student of mine asked 11- to 13-year-old pupils whether their parents used physical punishment along with other methods. Another question asked which particular kind of physical punishment they had experienced recently. In response to the first question, only 5 percent of the children acknowledged being beaten by their parents. However, indicating a specific method of beating was much easier for them: about 50 percent of the children reported a variety of techniques, ranging from an open-handed slap to being punched with a fist or beaten with a leather belt. Even more telling, when asked if they would beat their own children, about 50 percent of the interviewed children said they would.

It is hard to say how accurately these figures reveal the underlying problem: about 16 percent of randomly selected female respondents are battered by their husbands; a higher number of female victims are in families with alcohol problems; and 50 percent of school-age children are subjected to abusive disciplinary methods. Perhaps the extent of domestic violence is about the same as in other countries, but Poland is unique in its level of denial regarding the existence of such violence, as manifested by the lack of public discussion in the mass-media, the lack of an official policy that addresses these issues, as well as by the lack of professional attention paid by scholars. A Polish proverb says: "One's dirty linen should be washed at home." So, in general, domestic violence is thought of as being confined to the private arena with no access from outside. The other prevalent view is that such behavior happens only in families with alcohol problems. It could be said that the problem is considered a minor nuisance of family life, or an exotic event happening to "Them," not to "Us." Social beliefs about family violence and the leading actors on its stage (i.e. men and women) only recently have become an important issue on the agenda of both sociologists and social psychologists.

## GENDER STEREOTYPES AND CULTURAL TRADITIONS

The basic assumption underlying this study is that gender stereotypes are involved in beliefs about domestic violence and that both are rooted in cultural traditions. In other words, gender stereotypes create a framework within which domestic violence is perceived, interpreted, and then acted upon.

Stereotypes can be thought of as an "individual's set of beliefs about the characteristics or attributes of a group" (Judd and Park 1993: 110). These beliefs serve several functions. They provide specific content and meaning for a given group, for instance, women and men. Second, stereotypes represent a basis for self-definition and are believed to regulate some aspects of social behavior. Moreover, some traditional models of stereotyping argue that beliefs about undesirable characteristics of the target group serve primarily to justify the existing negative affect toward them (Jackson *et al.* 1996).

Gender stereotypes may contain hints, suggestions and prescriptions about how men and women should behave in a particular situation. In fact, beliefs about domestic violence seem to be related to more or less stereotypical views of men and women, especially of the roles they are supposed to perform within families and society. Therefore, it seems reasonable to take a cultural stance when trying to understand the problem of domestic violence in Poland, and explore the cultural traditions that influence gender stereotypes and beliefs about family violence. This view was convincingly expressed by Isabel Marcus, an American scholar, who recently interviewed women in Poland (Marcus 1995). She assumed, in accordance with Polish sociologists, that in Polish society there exist several female and male types and subtypes, which play crucial roles in inspiring aggression toward women, in justifying aggression, and in reacting to aggression.

I will concentrate on three cultural traditions, assumed to be the main forces that shape gender stereotypes in Poland: the Roman Catholic tradition with its Virgin Mary cult, the heroic national past with the martyr "Mother-Pole" as the guardian of national values, and the communist past with its, I would say "fake," egalitarian values, which in essence created another variant of the martyr "Mother-Pole." All of these factors contribute to how people think about domestic violence, that is, to how they think about what is right and wrong in relationships between men and women.

First of all, I must emphasize that gender stereotypes in Poland are deeply rooted in the Christian, Roman Catholic tradition, which stresses family values and the Marian cult. Mary, Mother of God, has a special status in Polish culture. The Polish Catholic church claimed her as the Queen of Poland, and according to a confused mixture of historic and religious beliefs, many times in the history of the nation she has proved herself to be a defender of Polish independence and/or Christian values, which, as Poles believe, are identical with national values. One specific feature of the Virgin Mary cult emphasizes Mary's virtues such as her virginity, her dedicated and painful motherhood and her humility. A female stereotype built upon the Virgin Mary tradition suggests that perfect femaleness means resignation from sexuality, motherhood and passivity. At the same time, Mary represents the "humble people of the Lord" ("the meek who shall inherit the earth"), that is, those who hold the lowest rank at the bottom of the social ladder in this life and who are promised they will be elevated in the afterlife. Roman Catholicism offers a woman, due to her resemblance with the Mother of God, high respect and rewards in her afterlife for the high price of having to suffer, in her mundane life, for her love of "man," who can be either son, husband or father. She must accept everything that life brings her; she must not rebel against man, nor question his rights to be her superior (see also Walczewska 1992). The Judeo-Christian ethic as a whole enhances this picture with general negative attitudes toward females as a source of sin. Therefore, as Frankiewicz (1992) put it, Polish men express great admiration for women in general, but hate any specific woman, and her body in particular.

A second powerful source of prescriptions about how to be a Polish woman can be found in the heroic national history. After the partition of Poland between the three superpowers in the eighteenth century, the family became the only warrantor of the maintenance of a national identity. In addition to their patriotic task of raising children to be Polish patriots and good Catholics, women—especially those of the noble class—took over the estate duties of their absent husbands, who either had been killed in the uprising, or were in jail, or had had to run away from prosecutors. In such times the model of the heroic "Mother-Pole" was created, who supported warriors fighting against oppressors, and sacrificed herself in the name of Fatherland and Family. Thanks to her heroism, she gained high respect within the family and society, which in turn put restrictions on her freedom and narrowed permissible behaviors (Titkow and Domanski 1995). A man paid respect to her as a lady occupying a high position in society, but denied her as an individual with her own needs and rights.

However, the Catholic religion and national history must not be viewed as the only sources of culturally shared beliefs. Gender stereotypes appear to be loaded with values of diverse origin, which very often contradict each other. A well-known fact from contemporary Polish history is that the country had been for many years under the influence of an officially introduced atheism, with values opposite to those rooted in the Catholic faith. But as Anna Titkow says, the Church and the communist system had one thing in common: patriarchal attitudes toward women, ignoring their needs and interests and their right to make their own decisions (Titkow and Domanski 1995). The communist state claimed itself an egalitarian society, with equal rights to work for everybody, including women. Being sensitive to women's special role, the system gave them privileges such as maternity leave, sick leave when their children were ill, and an early retirement age. Not surprisingly, 90 percent of East European women worked outside the home in comparison with 50 percent of women in Western countries (Einhorn 1993). In fact, the right to work turned out to be a duty born of economic necessity, because a husband's wage was not enough to live on. Placing herself in the labor force as an equal to man—and being proud of it—a woman still had to fulfill her commitments to motherhood and everyday chores; alone, with no help from her husband. Such a double or triple burden put enormous pressure on her, but paradoxically, she usually accepted the rules and tried to complete the impossible task of combining all duties smoothly (Domanski 1992). She could not, though, be a perfect mother, a perfect housewife and a perfect employee at the same time. So, being unable to maintain the female ideal she suffered from a constant sense of guilt, therefore becoming a perfect victim, prone to manipulation, and accepting all sorts of punishment from her husband who was unsatisfied with her services. Thus, a woman in the communist system used to think of herself again in terms of the heroic Mother-Pole: full of virtues, such as thriftiness, resourcefulness, energy, and industriousness (Monczka-Ciechomska 1992), and—thanks to the communist state benefits—as a "privileged" full-time working mother and full-time housewife. But at the same time, she was strongly inclined to feel guilty, experiencing a wide gap between the ideal model of Mother-Pole and her actual functioning within this role. Attributing her failure to herself exclusively, she was ready to admit the right of her husband to execute his patriarchal power over her.

It is interesting to see how such confusions about gender might be perceived from a Western perspective. Frances Mallard, a scholar from the University of Portsmouth, observes that

> cultural pressures, including that of the Catholic Church in a strongly religious country, meshed with historical myth and symbols to emphasize and reemphasize the primary notion of woman as child bearer and protector of the hearth. The Marian cult and the nineteenth century patriotic tradition portraying women as destined to raise sons who would in her mundane life die for the Fatherland were two central examples of such symbols. The modern version was reflected in a graffiti on the walls of the Gdansk shipyard in 1980: "Women, don't disturb us! We are fighting for Poland." The view that women

> do and ought to sacrifice themselves for their families remained very strong.
>
> (Mallard 1995: 72)

And another quotation by the same author:

> both the need for a post-communist "cleansing" and the search for new inspiration entailed a rediscovery and reinvention of history, which was and remained "masculine history," heroic and patriotic and richly overlaid with the schizophrenic attitudes to women of the Roman Catholic church.
>
> (Mallard 1995: 61)

For Mallard it is obvious that the actual picture of Polish women is determined by the nation, past and present, which essentially has been founded on masculine values with little room for feminine values.

Summing up, it seems that Marian cult, historical heritage, and communist egalitarianism jointly caught Polish women in a "double bind." On the one side, Polish women indulge themselves in being elevated onto a pedestal and basking in the admiration of Polish men; stepping down from there freely is very hard, for there is too much to lose. On the other side, Polish women accept enormous burdens put on them for being imperfect and sinful, heroic mothers and dutiful housewives, which makes it impossible for them to thoroughly rid themselves of these ordeals; there is no way to escape this "natural" social order.

The female stereotypes rooted in these cultural traditions are the asexual, modest mother who accepts the patriarchal social order, the defender of Polish/Catholic values such as religion, patriotism and courtesy, and the privileged yet hard-working communist woman. Considering the present status of a post-communist country, and all kinds of economic, psychological and sociological changes, I shall, in addition to the forces described above, take into account more recently developed images of women, such as the businesswoman, or the independent woman.

As for male stereotypes, I am going to focus on the "patriarch" as the prevalent male stereotype in Polish culture, the gentleman who knows how to treat a lady, and the partner to an independent woman. These last two are presented as complementary images to female stereotypes.

The study that I am going to describe was designed as exploratory research. The first objective was to identify gender stereotypes and beliefs about family violence and the relationships between them. The second objective was to examine demographic variables that potentially moderate or influence the relationships between gender stereotypes and family violence beliefs such as participants' gender, religiosity and place of residence as well as the length of their own close relationships.

# METHOD

## Sample

The sample consisted of 292 adults (198 women and 94 men), students of a private teacher training college in the relatively poor, northeastern part of Poland. The college offers licencing for unlicenced teachers and educators employed on temporary terms by primary schools and other educational institutions. The mean age was 31.3 years (with a range from 19 to 50 years). All participants had a least a high school degree and most had completed some kind of teacher training at the college level, allowing them to teach in primary schools until finally gaining their teaching licence within a certain period of time.

Only participants indicating that they were in a committed relationship (cohabitating or married) were used for analysis. The average length of these relationships was 9.47 years (with a range from 1 to 25 years). Religiosity was indexed as practicing believers (158 women, 54 men), nonpracticing believers (35 women, 34 men) and nonbelievers (3 women, 4 men). It must be noted that there were only four declared non-Catholics (about 1.3 percent of the sample), but considering the religious diversity in that part of the country (roughly, there are about 20 percent non-Catholics), we can doubt this figure. What prevents many people from disclosing their religion is probably their uneasy minority position, and their suspicion that non-Catholics are not welcome in a predominantly Roman Catholic country (official statistics claim that Catholics constitute 95.5 percent of the whole Polish population). It is clear that there are many more people defining themselves as practicing believers among women than among men. But equally interesting is the fact that among the so-called nonpracticing believers, gender is equally represented.

## Measurement of gender stereotypes and family violence beliefs

Based on the cultural traditions detailed in the preceding section, we generated a preliminary set of questions about images of Polish women and men. The pool of questions about family violence in Poland was based on articles in newspapers and police reports published in the mass media. The first versions of the questionnaires underwent a pilot study with six students. Eventually, three separate questionnaires were developed to examine stereotypes about Polish women, Polish men and beliefs about family violence.

The Polish Women Questionnaire consists of 25 items (Cronbach's Alpha = 0.82) such as "Polish women have the same chance as men to live successfully"; "Polish women get more respect from Polish men than women in other countries get from their men"; and "Polish women have the same access to all public posts as men." The Polish Men Questionnaire has 15 items (Cronbach's Alpha = 0.87) such as "Polish men are sociable, witty, with a sense of humor"; "Polish men, if they use severe punishment, it's only for good reasons"; and "Polish men make the crucial decisions in the family." Finally, the Violence in the Family Questionnaire had 27 items (Cronbach's Alpha = 0.75) including "Domestic violence occurs less often in Poland than in other countries"; "Living in accordance with religious faith is the most effective way of diminishing family violence"; and "A man is aggressive by nature." Participants responded to these statements using five-point scales that ranged from 1—strongly disagree to 5—strongly agree.

## RESULTS

First, I will describe and discuss the factor structure of each questionnaire, then, according to theoretical assumptions concerning the relationships between gender stereotypes and beliefs about domestic violence, I will select those stereotypes that are likely to be important predictors of domestic violence beliefs.

### Female stereotypes

A principal components analysis of the Polish Women Questionnaire yielded seven factors that together accounted for 63.9 percent of the variance in participants' responses. Table 7.1 presents the seven factors along with their defining items and the amount of variance explained by each factor (more technical details of the analysis can be obtained from the author).

The results of the factor analysis show that the image of Polish women is even more complex and diverse than that derived from the cultural traditions presented in the previous section. The most striking finding is that the image of *lady* explains the biggest amount of variance. Apparently, this stereotype expresses some "snobbish" sentiments, perhaps derived from nostalgia for the past, which—in the popular view—is very often equivalent to the past of Polish nobility. Admittedly, in everyday life, there are many social exchanges between the sexes that are based on strict and very formal codes of conduct rooted in the noble tradition. This behavior is especially pronounced between strangers.

Two other stereotypes, *humble and sympathetic* and *Catholic and Polish mother*, relate to values conveyed by the Roman Catholic religion, which—in this country—have a particular nationalistic flavor. As expected, the communist view of women as more privileged than

*Table 7.1* Female stereotypes

| *Factor* | *Factor label and defining items** | *% of variance* |
|---|---|---|
| 1 | *Lady*<br>Good manners // elegant and physically attractive // behaving with dignity // demanding good manners from men | 27.4 |
| 2 | *Humble and sympathetic*<br>Peace-loving // forgiving // taking a back seat // loyal to her man // cheerful, nice and keep warmth at home | 9.7 |
| 3 | *Catholic and Polish Mother*<br>Conveying Christian values to her children // taking care of the religious education of children // keeping up Polish traditions // cultivating national values | 6.7 |
| 4 | *Ambitious*<br>Upwardly mobile // choosing a professional career // free-thinking // resourceful and determined | 6.2 |
| 5 | *Privileged*<br>Having more rights than women in other countries // having more opportunities for self-realization // obtaining more state support | 5.2 |
| 6 | *Man's equal*<br>Having the same chance to be happy as man // having the same access to public posts as men | 4.5 |
| 7 | *Self-centered*<br>Striving toward self-realization // unable to make self-sacrifices for the sake of the family | 4.2 |

*Notes:*
* Items defining factors have loadings higher than 0.50. The // separates the items

women from other (presumably capitalistic) countries also appears; this view is represented in the image of women as *privileged*.

More contemporary times are represented by three factors. Of these three, *ambitious* and *self-centered* relate to activities women may pursue such as choosing a professional career, regardless of whether this is welcomed by their families. *Man's equal* describes a modern view of women as being on the same level and as worthy as men. In contrast to *self-centered*, the image of *Catholic and Polish mother* has a more positive connotation, which may include disapproval of women who are "unable to make sacrifices for the sake of the family."

These female stereotypes may be relevant to domestic violence beliefs in various ways. For instance, positive images such as *lady* or *Catholic and*

*Polish mother* impose on the woman the special role of guardian of national and religious values. It seems that these are highly prescriptive, for, by setting rules, barriers, and limits, they tell a woman how she should behave. If women behave properly, men will reward them by treating them decently; a popular saying goes "Do not hit a lady, not even with a flower." However, in the case of any transgression or betrayal of these stereotypes, a woman deserves punishment. Therefore, those people who hold such stereotypes about women might more easily accept violent acts against "disobedient" women.

The images that emphasize a woman's independence and ability to pursue a career, *ambitious* and *self-centered*, convey a threatening message: the traditionally high status of man at home and in the workplace is at risk. Such stereotypes might facilitate the perception of women as provoking men to be aggressive in defense of their own social position.

The first four factors seem to be most relevant to beliefs about domestic violence; so the following stereotypes will be used as predictors of domestic violence beliefs: *lady*, *humble and sympathetic*, *ambitious* and *Catholic and Polish mother*. The last stereotype, *self-centered*, although theoretically relevant, accounts for too little variance to be taken into consideration.

## Male stereotypes

Factor analyses of the Polish Men Questionnaire yielded four factors that together accounted for 61.1 percent of the variance. Table 7.2 presents the four factors, their defining items, and the amount of variance explained by each factor.

The first factor, *gentleman*, represents a very popular image of Polish men: kissing a lady's hand when greeting, holding the door for a woman, standing up in the presence of a woman, etc. His qualities such as nice manners, charm, and an attentive approach to the weaker sex as well as children, give him the status of a person above any suspicion; indeed, a gentleman never hits a lady, not even with a flower. This reputation of men as civilized and cultured sometimes works as a smokescreen that conceals acts of violence.

The second factor, *partner*, a relatively new category, reflects recent trends in families where the fair division of labor has a high priority. However, the factor's content is not consistent: on the one hand, there is the idea of "sharing duties," probably on equal terms; but, on the other, the focus is on "helping" and "being sympathetic," as if a man does not need to take his share of duties seriously.

The third factor, *respectable father*, is closely related to traditional, Catholic, and conservative family values. In this view, a man has the right to exercise his power, even through violent acts. His wife and chil-

*Table 7.2* Male stereotypes

| *Factor* | *Factor label and defining items** | *% of variance* |
|---|---|---|
| 1 | *Gentleman*<br>sociable // sense of humor // elegant // well-mannered // reliable // being able to work and to have fun // sympathetic // protecting women and children | 35.7 |
| 2 | *Partner*<br>Helping with everyday chores // sharing parental duties // sympathetic // patriot | 10.8 |
| 3 | *Respectable Father*<br>Making crucial decisions for the family // head of the family // punishes wife or children for their own good // aggressive only when drunk | 7.9 |
| 4 | *Good Master*<br>Touchy as regards his honor // defending his possessions (territory) | 6.8 |

*Note:*
* Items defining factors have loadings higher than 0.50. The // separates the items

dren must accept his minor shortcomings, such as his taste for alcohol. The image of *good master* belongs to the same patriarchal culture as the *respectable father* but highlights other aspects of paternalism such as protectiveness and responsibility for others, combined with a strong emphasis on ownership. As Fiske and Glick (1995: 88) say,

> Paternalism is an orientation toward interacting with women as a father dealing with his children. This orientation encompasses not only attitudes of male superiority and dominance over women, but also protectiveness toward women as "the weaker sex."

All factors representing the male stereotypes will be chosen for subsequent analysis.

## Domestic violence beliefs

The factor analysis of the Violence in the Family Questionnaire revealed nine factors that together accounted for 58.2 percent of the variance. Table 7.3 presents the nine factors, their defining items, and the amount of variance explained by each factor.

The first factor, *legitimate orientation*, represents statements indicating that male violence in the family may be legitimate for several reasons.

*Table 7.3* Domestic violence beliefs

| *Factor* | *Factor label and defining items** | *% of variance* |
|---|---|---|
| 1 | *Legitimate orientation*<br>Woman as a victim should come to terms with a violent partner // woman should be more understanding // man hits when he is driven to extremes // shame on the woman who reports to police // man hits because he loves // violent quarrel in the family is private business // man is aggressive by nature // beating as a manner of disciplining an undutiful woman // the woman should accept violence for the sake of children | 19.6 |
| 2 | *Class-based orientation*<br>Violence related to poor economic conditions // in Poland occurs less often than in other countries // violence related to alcoholism | 7.2 |
| 3 | *Wide-range orientation*<br>Majority of women have experienced violence at least once in their lives // women are subjected largely to the violence of men and men are murdered by women sometimes // violence occurs across all classes, levels of education, professions, income, etc. | 5.6 |
| 4 | *Incapable orientation*<br>Physical violence means that man has a weak character // family conflicts are provoked by the interfering in-laws // aggression is a primitive way of family handling | 4.9 |
| 5 | *Disciplinary orientation*<br>Violence as a way of gaining respect // moderate physical violence is the best discipline method | 4.7 |
| 6 | *Social orientation*<br>Violence is more likely to occur in a non-reacting neighborhood // domestic violence reflects general trends in the society | 4.4 |
| 7 | *Religious orientation*<br>Violence takes place in families not following religious rules | 4.1 |
| 8 | *She-likes-it orientation*<br>Physical punishment suits a woman | 3.9 |
| 9 | *Negotiating orientation*<br>There are always more peaceful ways—such as negotiation—of dealing with conflicts than aggression | 3.8 |

*Note:* * Items defining factors have loadings higher than 0.50. The // separates the items

For example, by attributing violent behavior to the man's character or temperament ("a man is aggressive by nature"), to being unable to control himself efficiently ("a man hits when he is driven to extremes"), and to his way of expressing even positive feelings ("a man hits because he loves"). Attributing his violence to his unchangeable nature results in the deflection of responsibility from the man. This factor also includes statements suggesting that the woman "causes" male violence: she "provokes" a man by not fulfilling household duties, and by "not being understanding." Both reasons concern prescriptions of the female gender role, i.e. how to be a good housewife, and how to be a caring and nice woman. This kind of attribution implies that a woman "deserves" punishment for bad or careless behavior that is not suitable to her gender role. This interpretation of domestic violence as understandable male behavior ("boys will be boys") that is enacted for "good reasons" (e.g. to reprimand an imperfect woman) leads to the conclusion that a woman should accept the assaults, and not take any action against a violent partner, for the sake of family and children.

The second factor, *class-based orientation*, represents the belief that acts of violence are restricted to particular social groups, those in poor economic conditions and those who abuse alcohol. No doubt, alcohol abuse and poverty create many problems. This is especially true in Poland, where the level of alcoholism is exceptionally high. "The poor" or "alcoholics" are easy targets to identify to do "something about." What is more, it seems that such an opinion allows one to see Poland in general as a country relatively free from violence ("In Poland violence occurs less often than in other countries"). But confining the problem to certain social groups may prevent people from recognizing the violence in other groups, and, again, this approach removes responsibility from those who are neither poor nor alcoholic.

The third factor, *wide-range orientation*, represents a belief opposite to violence as class based. Statements reflected in the third factor assume that domestic violence occurs regardless of social class, level of education and economic conditions, and that most women have this kind of experience.

The next factor, *incapable*, represents beliefs that link violence to certain types of personality such as lack of character ("weakness") and intellectual deficits ("primitiveness"), but also failure of keeping interfering third parties (i.e. in-laws) out of the family. Such an attitude confines domestic violence to the incidental violent act, committed by rather primitive men, not by "normal" or "decent" men.

Of the last five factors I would like to mention only the notion that violence is related to religious beliefs; defined solely by one item ("violence takes place in families not following religious rules").

The ideas described above represent views on causes, types, and occurrence of domestic violence in Poland as they were endorsed in our sample. The factor explaining most of the variance represents violence as a legitimate means. Other accepted views minimize violence by connecting violent acts to certain groups (*class based*), or certain types of people (*incapable*, and *she-likes-it*, i.e. "masochistic women"). These approaches toward domestic violence might explain to some extent why it is so difficult to resolve the problem on the social and psychological level. First, people do not consider domestic violence as a problem of the entire society, and second, they are likely to justify the "rare" incidents of violence as understandable and provoked by victims.

It will be interesting to see what kind of stereotypical thinking is behind such ideas, and how women and men differ in this regard. These questions will be addressed in the following sections.

**Predicting domestic violence beliefs from gender stereotypes**

In the analysis presented in this section, gender stereotypes will serve as predictors for specific beliefs about domestic violence. To examine which gender stereotype contributes to a particular domestic violence belief I selected the following set of variables. For female stereotypes, *lady, humble and sympathetic, Catholic and Polish mother* and *ambitious*. For male stereotypes, *gentleman, partner, respectable father* and *good master*. Demographic variables included gender, religiosity, place of residence, and length of own close relationship. Results of a multiple regression analysis for the entire sample are presented in Table 7.4.

Looking at Table 7.4, we can see that domestic violence beliefs are not dependent on the predictors in the same way. First, there are some beliefs about violence that seem not to relate to any gender stereotype. These are wide-range orientation, social orientation, and negotiating orientation. Disciplinary orientation could also be included in this set, as it has only one nonstereotypical predictor, gender. What these orientations have in common is their wider social perspective on the issue of violence. Probably, one needs to give up rigid ways of thinking in terms of gender stereotypes in order to see how domestic violence is spread across the social classes, how many women are subjected to the violence, how domestic violence mirrors general trends in the society and how to resolve conflict with methods other than aggression.

Second, the amount of variance predicted varies for different beliefs. For example, gender stereotypes predicted relatively high amounts of the variance of class-based (20.6 percent) and religious orientation (14.7 percent). Third, the most powerful gender stereotypes seem to be those of *respectable father* and *Polish and Catholic mother*. These stereotypes appear as predictors of factors I, II, IV, VII and VIII. Nevertheless, the patterns of relationships between independent and dependent variables

*Table 7.4* Predicting domestic violence beliefs from gender stereotypes

| *Belief* | *Stereotype* | *AdjRsq* | *B* | *SE B* | *Beta* | *T* | *SigT* |
|---|---|---|---|---|---|---|---|
| Legitimate | Respectable father | 0.04 | 0.19 | 0.06 | 0.20 | 3.06 | 0.002 |
| Class-based | Lady | 0.08 | 0.20 | 0.06 | 0.28 | 3.13 | 0.002 |
| | Catholic and Polish mother | 0.13 | 0.18 | 0.07 | 0.23 | 2.75 | 0.006 |
| | Respectable father | 0.16 | 0.22 | 0.07 | 0.19 | 3.40 | 0.001 |
| | Gentleman | 0.21 | 0.22 | 0.07 | 0.21 | 3.41 | 0.001 |
| Wide-range | No predictors | | | | | | |
| Incapable | Catholic and Polish mother | 0.03 | 0.20 | 0.07 | 0.18 | 2.92 | 0.004 |
| | Religiosity* | 0.07 | 0.33 | 0.11 | 0.18 | 2.36 | 0.019 |
| | Good master | 0.09 | 0.15 | 0.06 | 0.15 | 2.87 | 0.005 |
| Disciplinary | Gender** | 0.02 | -0.15 | 0.07 | -0.15 | -2.24 | 0.026 |
| Social | No predictors | | | | | | |
| Religious | Religiosity | 0.06 | -0.42 | 0.11 | -0.24 | -3.67 | 0.000 |
| | Duration of relationship | 0.09 | 0.02 | 0.01 | 0.18 | 2.18 | 0.030 |
| | Residence*** | 0.11 | 0.17 | 0.08 | 0.15 | 2.18 | 0.030 |
| | Respectable father | 0.13 | 0.15 | 0.07 | 0.13 | 2.32 | 0.021 |
| | Ambitious | 0.15 | 0.14 | 0.06 | 0.14 | 2.17 | 0.031 |
| She-likes-it | Catholic and Polish mother | 0.03 | -0.14 | 0.07 | -0.16 | -2.11 | 0.036 |
| | Religiosity | 0.04 | 0.22 | 0.11 | 0.13 | 1.98 | 0.049 |
| Negotiating | No predictors | | | | | | |

*Note:*
* 1—Practicing believers, 2—Non-practicing believers
** 1—Women, 2—Men
*** 1—Town, 2—Small town, 3—Village

vary as regards the specific orientation toward domestic violence. How can we explain this?

## *Legitimate orientation*

The *respectable father* stereotype is the only predictor of the legitimate orientation toward family violence. Those who adhere to this image of a man are more likely to justify domestic violence in terms of man's right to exercise his power over a woman, and more likely to demand that a woman be silent and passive. This pattern of relationship is rooted in patriarchal ideology.

*Class-based orientation*

A combination of female and male stereotypes is responsible for this orientation. The perception of women as ladies and mothers, and the perception of men as gentlemen and fathers, makes people think that violence is present only where there are no ladies or gentlemen, and no good mothers or good fathers. Thus, it is easy to find violence only among people of the lower social classes who live in poor conditions, and among drunkards and their wives. It seems that this pattern relates to the snobbish heritage of the noble class in Poland.

*Incapable orientation*

This pattern does not have much consistency. Each predictor seems to work in a different way. Holders of the female stereotype *Catholic and Polish mother* are more likely to attribute violence to one's weakness. Perhaps a good mother is one who forgives "minor misbehavior." On the other hand, results show that the less religious a person is, the more likely he or she will be to adopt this orientation, as if one's higher religiosity does not allow her or him to tolerate somebody's weakness. Assuming that the mother image is of a religious origin, these two views on violence taken together are not compatible.

*Discipline orientation*

Women are more likely to perceive domestic violence as a way of handling the family. It shows that these women have probably internalized authoritarian methods of exerting power.

*Religious orientation*

There are five predictors for this orientation. It is quite obvious that the more religious a person is, the more likely she or he is to perceive the world from a religious perspective. The duration of a relationship is a good predictor as well, because long-term commitments (in this sample, mostly marriages) are usually based on a religious foundation. The next predictor, *respectable father*, nicely fits into the model for its strong connections with the Catholic religion. But the appearance of the last predictor, the female stereotype *ambitious*, is rather confusing. Taking into consideration the entire set of predictors, it might be said that a religious orientation is more characteristic for practicing believers, for long-term couples, for residents of small towns and villages, for holders of the traditional *respectable father* male stereotype, and for holders of a modern *ambitious* female stereotype. To some extent, it could be explained this way: Since this stereotype contradicts the traditional female role, it is likely that acceptance of the ambitious woman makes one feel guilty, therefore she or he seems to turn to religion for comfort.

*She-likes-it orientation*

This approach assumes that there are some masochistic women who seek out violent men. Those who think that way are not likely to perceive women as mothers (the *Catholic and Polish mother* stereotype correlates negatively), and they are less religious. It seems that this is one case where religion works against the cynical views of domestic violence victims.

## Gender differences in beliefs about domestic violence

However, the most important question is that about gender differences in perceiving domestic violence. This is for two reasons. First, women are more likely to adopt the perspective of a victim, whereas men prefer the perspective of perpetrator, which might account for differences between their views of domestic violence. Second, in-group stereotypes for one gender (e.g. for males) become out-group stereotypes for the other gender (e.g. for females), so these might work differently as predictors of domestic violence beliefs. Therefore, in this section the sample will be split into two subgroups according to gender to see which variables predict domestic violence beliefs for women and for men.

Table 7.5 displays the mean regression factor scores for domestic violence beliefs for women and men. Considering that the numbers of women and men are unequal in this sample, the comparison results should be interpreted cautiously.

It turns out that there is no difference between women and men as regards *social orientation*, *she-likes-it orientation*, and *negotiating orientation*. This means that both women and men approve to the same degree such approaches to violence. Compared with men, women got higher factor scores on *wide-range*, *discipline*, and *religious orientations*. On the other hand, men had higher scores concerning *class-based* and *incapable orientation*.

The configuration of differences between women and men conveys the message that men marginalize the problem by restricting domestic violence to special groups and/or to certain individuals. Women are in a more difficult position. As potential victims, they do not consider domestic violence as legitimate behavior, but they accept authoritarian and religious rules which shape both domestic life and relations between wife and husband.

Multiple regression analyses were performed for women and men separately, in order to find specific patterns of relationships between the examined variables. I will focus only on three types of beliefs about

*Table 7.5* Regression factor mean scores of domestic violence beliefs by gender

| *Beliefs about domestic violence* | *Mean scores* | | | |
|---|---|---|---|---|
| | *Women (n=198)* | *Men (n=95)* | *T* | *SigT* |
| Legitimate | -0.07 | 0.14 | -1.69 | 0.091 |
| Class-based | -0.13 | 0.26 | -3.13 | 0.002 |
| Wide-range | 0.08 | -0.17 | 1.97 | 0.050 |
| Incapable | -0.08 | 0.16 | -1.93 | 0.055 |
| Disciplinary | 0.09 | -0.20 | 2.35 | 0.020 |
| Social | 0.06 | -0.12 | 1.37 | n.s. |
| Religious | 0.08 | -0.17 | 2.04 | 0.042 |
| She-likes-it | -0.05 | 0.11 | -1.30 | n.s. |
| Negotiating | 0.06 | 0.12 | -1.39 | n.s. |

*Table 7.6* Predicting *legitimate orientation* for women and men (multiple regression, stepwise method)

| *Gender* | *Stereotype* | *AdjRsq* | *B* | *SE B* | *Beta* | *T* | *SigT* |
|---|---|---|---|---|---|---|---|
| Women (n=148) | Respectable father | 0.06 | 0.19 | 0.07 | 0.23 | 2.85 | 0.005 |
| | Religiosity* | 0.08 | -0.29 | 0.15 | -0.17 | -2.15 | 0.037 |
| Men (n=95) | Catholic and Polish mother | 0.06 | -0.25 | 0.11 | 0.25 | -2.19 | 0.032 |

*Note:*
* 1—Practicing believers, 2—Nonpracticing believers

domestic violence: *legitimate orientation*, *class-based orientation* and *religious orientation*.

Results of regression analyses for *legitimate orientation* show that predictors are different for women and men (see Table 7.6). It appears that women who are more likely to adopt a *legitimate orientation*, tend to adhere to the view of the *respectable father*. It seems that holding the traditional stereotype of man as father along with their higher religiosity makes women think that domestic violence is acceptable. For men, the female image of the Catholic and Polish mother appears to be the only predictor of the *legitimate orientation*. The stronger the stereotype of the *Catholic and Polish mother*, the less likely men were to endorse violence as legitimate. Or, the more men endorse a *legitimate orientation*, the less

*Table 7.7* Predicting *class-based orientation* for women and men (multiple regression, stepwise method)

| *Gender* | *Stereotype* | *AdjRsq* | *B* | *SE B* | *Beta* | *T* | *SigT* |
|---|---|---|---|---|---|---|---|
| Women (*n*=198) | Respectable father | 0.06 | 0.22 | 0.07 | 0.25 | 3.10 | 0.002 |
| | Gentleman | 0.12 | 0.17 | 0.06 | 0.23 | 2.36 | 0.020 |
| | Partner | 0.15 | 0.23 | 0.07 | 0.18 | 3.41 | 0.001 |
| Men (*n*=95) | Lady | 0.13 | 0.14 | 0.06 | 0.36 | 2.11 | 0.038 |
| | Good master | 0.20 | 0.20 | 0.10 | 0.28 | 2.02 | 0.047 |
| | Duration* | 0.29 | 0.06 | 0.02 | 0.31 | 2.88 | 0.005 |
| | Catholic and Polish mother | 0.33 | 0.20 | 0.08 | 0.20 | 3.03 | 0.003 |

*Note:*
* Duration of own relationship

likely they are to perceive women as Catholic and Polish mothers. Therefore, for men, the traditional view of a woman as mother who protects Catholic and national values serves as a buffer against endorsing a *legitimate orientation* toward violence.

To predict *class-based orientation* endorsed by women, the following male stereotypes ought to be considered: *respectable father, gentleman* and *partner* (see Table 7.7). So, if women enjoy a "positive" and coherent image of men, with a father as a leading figure, they are more likely to think of domestic violence as confined to some groups of poor people with alcohol problems. Behind the *class-based orientation* displayed by men there is a more complex configuration of female and male stereotypes and duration of the relationship. Almost 20 percent of the variance is explained by two predictors, i.e. by the *lady* stereotype, and the *good master* stereotype. If men think of women as well-behaved ladies, and consider themselves to be good masters who care about their "stock" (household), definitely, they distance the incidents of violence from their own lives and locate them in remote places. These two stereotypes are supported by the experience of long-term relationships (a wife has proved to be "good enough" for such a long time, thus, there is no need to punish her), then sealed by the *Catholic and Polish mother* stereotype.

For *religious orientation* endorsed by women, the place of residence, and the male stereotype of *partner* are the significant predictors (see Table 7.8). It is interesting that the religiosity variable, significant in the model estimated for the whole sample (see Table 7.4), disappeared for the female subgroup. It seems that for women, place of residence (i.e. small towns and villages) and religiosity are confounded, so that place of residence is

*Table 7.8* Predicting *religious orientation* for women and men (multiple regression, stepwise method)

| *Gender* | *Stereotype* | *AdjRsq* | *B* | *SE B* | *Beta* | *T* | *SigT* |
|---|---|---|---|---|---|---|---|
| Females (n=198) | Residence* | 0.07 | 0.23 | 0.08 | 0.26 | 2.77 | 0.006 |
| | Partner | 0.11 | 0.19 | 0.07 | 0.22 | 2.93 | 0.004 |
| Males (n=95) | Duration | 0.08 | 0.28 | 0.12 | 0.28 | 2.15 | 0.034 |
| | Ambitious | 0.14 | 0.28 | 0.11 | 0.24 | 2.76 | 0.007 |

*Note:*
* 1—Town, 2—Small town, 3—Village

sufficient to predict the religious orientation of women. The *partner* stereotype, which contributes further to the variance, probably reinforces the religious approach by sharing the same views. What makes men think about domestic violence in terms of religious orientation is their commitment to a relationship, and perceiving women as ambitious. So, the interpretation given in the previous section, that the discrepancy between traditional female role and this unfeminine stereotype makes people seek comfort in religion, seems to refer exclusively to men.

## DISCUSSION

At least two limitations of this study should be mentioned. The first limitation concerns the suspicion that the sample is not fully representative of the Polish population. The quality of the research may suffer from the disadvantages created by the specific characteristics of this sample. First of all, in the teacher job (a "pink collar job") men are outnumbered by women, which may create some "minority–majority" problems. So it is hard to guess which values of which gender are dominant. On the one hand, owing to the effects of simple numbers, female views may overcome male views. On the other hand, a powerful minority, as men can be, may easily impose their values on a weaker majority. For instance, the consequence of the uneven proportion of men and women in our sample might be that, given the stronger religious commitment among Polish women than men, religiosity could be overrepresented in this sample. Therefore, the question remains open as to whether such beliefs may be generalized to other groups where proportions of men and women are the same as in the general population. This is one reason why generalizing the reported findings should be done very cautiously. Moreover, an important feature of this group is the fact that teachers, especially those employed in primary schools, are the most underpaid category among professionals in this country. This produces a lot of frustration, anger, and perhaps various coping strategies, such as seeking comfort in family life, or in religion, which may influence their cognitive representations of social life. Finally, a relatively equal level of education across the sample does not allow us to test hypotheses concerning the impact of education on values in contemporary Poland. According to recent studies (Reykowski 1994), education seems to explain the vast majority of social phenomena in this country.

Despite these shortcomings, one needs to consider the positive implications of the teacher sample. Teachers' thinking about social phenomena represents a model system of values operating during a given time across the society. There is strong pressure from society on teachers to make them obedient deliverers of the "correct" system of values. So, they become quite a reliable barometer of the actual state of the Polish mind. Hence, the study sample chosen from people of this profession appears to be the proper group for examining popular beliefs concerning social problems. Nevertheless, future research should avoid the limitations mentioned above.

The second limitation of the study concerns the fact that the questionnaire items were selected—to some extent—arbitrarily, according to theoretical assumptions rather than being derived empirically. It has to be stated that a certain bias in the research concerning gender stereotypes is not unimaginable. For instance, the author, as a woman, might bring into the methodology in-group/out-group effects, such as a more homogeneous perception of the other sex. That may be why the Polish Men Questionnaire was shorter, and fewer factors were revealed. An implicit feminist stance might have cast a shadow on the pool of items assessing domestic violence. In further research, questionnaire items should cover a wider range of attitudes toward violence.

As mentioned before, the study had no ambition to test precise hypotheses but was planned so as to get some insight into representations of domestic violence in Poland. The data collected among a sample of teachers in northeastern Poland produced several important results.

1 Beliefs about domestic violence represent a variety of orientations toward family violence, its occurrence, causes, social and psychological explanations, etc. such as "legitimate orientation toward domestic violence" and "class-based orientation." The first orientation reflects a widespread view Isabel Marcus (1995) refers to as the "local folklore validating a connection among love, violence and marriage." In this study, holders of the *legitimate orientation* seem to connect domestic violence to the natural aggressiveness of man, and to his "right" to administer justice. So, what he is doing is legitimized by nature and by common law. A woman must be aware of the "biological" side of her partner (e.g. don't tease the beast), and accept good and bad from

him submissively, especially when the welfare of innocent children is at stake. It appears that both parties accept the rules, and nothing can be done to change this situation.

*Class-based orientation* focuses attention on the lower classes as the site of violence. Such an orientation has a psychological function, because the attribution of domestic violence to alcoholics, the uneducated and the poor allows the distancing of oneself from difficult problems, and consequently maintaining respect for oneself. On the social level, a *class-based orientation* has substantial consequences: acts of violence committed by people from other social groups (i.e. non-alcoholics, of higher education, etc.) makes the aggression unrecognizable, thus difficult to accept as real.

2 Gender stereotypes are relevant to some beliefs about domestic violence, but to other beliefs they are not. There is a cluster of beliefs about domestic violence, to which gender stereotypes are irrelevant. These beliefs are based rather on everyday observations of other people's lives, observations made with a good deal of common sense.

However, gender stereotypes are involved in the majority of exposed beliefs. Therefore, on the basis of stereotypes held by people, one can predict which particular orientation toward violence they will likely adopt. The most powerful stereotypes related to violence beliefs are those rooted in the patriarchal order of the world, i.e. the image of Father which must be complemented by the image of Mother. Both stereotypes are connected to Polish culture, with many links to the Roman Catholic religion, and the heritage of Polish nobility. The problem is that perceptions and actions based on stereotypical thinking are not easy to modify. So, if we want to influence how people deal with domestic violence, we should first work on gender stereotypes and their cultural background.

3 There are differences between men and women as to what they think about domestic violence, and how their beliefs are determined by stereotypes and other factors. Men tend to minimize the problem of domestic violence by confining it to certain groups or individuals. Also, men are more likely to justify violence. Women put violence in a wider social perspective, and are less ready to justify violence as a legitimate behavior.

But the most important finding provided by this study is that women and men come to the same beliefs from different positions. For instance, a *legitimate orientation* among women can be explained by their embracing the image of the *Respectable father*, and their strong religiosity. So, what keeps women's minds on the proper path is subordination to the Master as confirmed by religious laws. As for men, the *legitimate orientation* relates to the image of the *Catholic and Polish mother*. It seems that they accept violence as a legitimate means for punishing women who deviate from the role society has imposed on them. Different patterns were found for men and women also as regards *class-based orientation* and *religious orientation*. It is worth noting that for women, it is only male stereotypes which govern their views on violence. But for men, both male *and* female stereotypes are relevant.

Finally, it might be concluded that male stereotypes seem to play more important roles in how people think about violence. Male stereotypes turn out to be better predictors of domestic violence beliefs than female stereotypes, both for men and women. Such a conclusion contradicts the widespread opinion that female stereotypes facilitate violence. On the contrary, the image of Mother to some extent works against adopting the legitimate orientation.

## FINAL REMARKS

This research demonstrates how complicated the problem of domestic violence is when one wants to explore its cognitive aspects. The results highlighted the involvement of gender stereotypes in thinking about violence, particularly stereotypes concerning men. If this connection proves valid, then in order to make any changes in how people deal with domestic violence, we should first change the generally accepted image of Polish men. The question is, how can this be accomplished in a patriarchal society?

## NOTE

1 I am grateful to Kirk Palmer for his enlightening support with the English language. I am also grateful to the travel grant from the Association of Universities and Colleges of Canada and the Canadian International Development Agency that allowed me to present this research at the 8th International Conference on Personal Relationships, August 1996, in Banff, Canada.

## BIBLIOGRAPHY

Domanski, H. (1992) *Zadowolony niewolnik? nietownosciach miedzy mezczyznami i kobiaetmi w Polsce* [Happy slave? Study on inequalities between men and women in Poland], Warszawa: IFIS PAN.

Einhorn, B. (1993) *Cinderella goes to market: Citizenship, gender and women's movement in East Central Europe*, London: Verso.

Fiske, S.T. and Glick, P. (1995) "Ambivalence and stereotypes cause sexual harassment: A theory with implications for organizational change," *Journal of Social Issues* 51: 97–115.

Frankiewicz, M. (1992) "Kobieta jako zrodlo grzechu" [Woman as a source of sin], in S. Walczewska (ed.) *Glos maja kobiety* [Women have a voice], Krakow: Convivium.

Jackson, L.A., Sullivan, L.A., and Hodge, C.N. (1996) "Stereotype effects on attributions, predictions, and evaluations: No two social judgements are quite alike," *Journal of Personality and Social Psychology* 65: 69–84.

Judd, C.M. and Park, B. (1993) "Definition and assessment of accuracy in social stereotypes," *Psychological Review* 100: 109–128.

Klein, R. and Johnson, M.P. (1997) "Strategies of couple conflict," in S. Duck *et al.* (eds) *Handbook of personal relationships* (2nd edn), Chichester: Wiley.

Linville, P. and Carlston, D.E. (1994) "Social cognition of the self," in P.G. Devine *et al.* (eds) *Social cognition: Impact on social psychology*, San Diego, CA: Academic Press.

Marcus, I. (1995) "Dark numbers: Domestic violence in Poland," unpublished manuscript.

Mallard, F. (1995) "Women in Poland: The impact of post-communist transformation," *Journal of Area Studies* 6: 60–73.

Monczka-Ciechomska, M. (1992) "Mit kobiety w polskiej kulturze" [The myth of woman in Polish culture], in S. Walczewska (ed.) *Glos maja kobiety* [Women have a voice], Krakow: Convivium.

Reykowski, J. (1994) "Collectivism and individualism as dimensions of social change," in U. Kim *et al.* (eds) *Individualism and collectivism: Theory, method, and applications*, London: Sage.

Tajfel, H. (1972) "La catégorisation sociale," in S. Moscovici (ed.) *Introduction à la psychologie sociale* (vol.1), Paris: Larousse.

Titkow, A. and Domanski, H. (1995) *Co to znaczy byc kobieta w Polsce*? [What does it mean to be a woman in Poland?], Warszawa: IFIS PAN.

Walczewska, S. (ed.) (1992) *Glos maja kobiety: Teksty feministyczne* [Women have a voice: Feminist texts], Krakow: Convivium.

Chapter 8

# Explanations for wife beating in Greenland

Bo Wagner Sørensen

Bo Wagner Sørensen received his B.A. in eskimology in 1978 from the Institute of Eskimology, University of Copenhagen, Denmark and his M.A. (1985) and Ph.D. (1993) in anthropology from the Institute of Anthropology, University of Copenhagen.

*The focus on wife beating in my Ph.D. dissertation was not intended from the start, but rather sprang from fieldwork experiences in Nuuk, Greenland, in 1988 and 1989. (I happened to have a neighbor who beat his wife. Soon I also heard many stories about wife beating and got involved in actual cases concerning friends and acquaintances.) My interest in wife beating and interpersonal violence may be seen as a case of reality encroaching on the scholarly mind. Before I began publishing on wife beating in 1990, however, I was interested in gender studies in general and I have taught courses in gender studies at the Institute of Anthropology.*

*Doing research in a particular region of the world, one inevitably relates to the existing body of literature. On the whole, the literature on the Arctic seems marked by an often implicit functionalist approach which, again, influences the way that scholars deal with social phenomena and problems. Wife beating is thus often cast as a symptom of society out of balance, which, I think, obscures the fact that people are social actors with embodied motivation rather than automatons or cultural dopes who simply react unwillingly to structural conditions and changes.*

*Greenlanders and Inuit are often treated as homogeneous populations who suffer from historical injustice. Correspondingly, wife beaters tend to be seen as victims on a par with the actual victims of violence. While I do not mean to neglect the aspect of historical suffering, I think that too narrow a focus on this aspect obscures more than illuminates our understanding of the use of violence in today's society. Instead, I suggest focusing on the aspect of social agency and the relationship between violence, power, gender, personhood, and self-representation.*

*What I would like the reader to take home from my chapter is to question and rethink the popular idea that wife beating is an act of powerlessness. My field experience tells me that often it can be characterized as an habitual act, or simply, a "habit." Trying to understand the use of violence, I would stress the aspect of using violence "in order to" as this approach seems capable of accounting for the relationship between a motivated and tactical use of violence and the individual male self-understanding and self-representation.*

*I would also like the reader to question and rethink our tendency to separate mind/reason and emotion. Instead, I argue in favor of an integrated perspective. "Embodied motivation" is a concept that encompasses both reason and emotion at the same time.*

*And finally, I would like the reader to question and rethink the idea that people are creatures that simply react unwillingly to societal restraints and changes. Instead, I focus on people as social actors or agents who act within society according to ideas about Self and Other.*

*As one Greenlandic woman, age 50, said: "There are also many men, perhaps most men, who beat to show that they are stronger than she is, without any other particular motive."*

In this chapter I discuss wife beating in Nuuk, Greenland, from two different perspectives. I will contrast a symptom approach to wife beating with an approach based on social agency. After explicating both approaches, I will introduce the phenomenon of wife beating in Greenland and present local perspectives on wife beating and their implications. Along the way I will draw on my own fieldwork in Nuuk as well as on the literature on Greenland, Canada, and Alaska. My fieldwork took place during the periods of 1988 to 1989 and 1992 to 1995. Nuuk is the capital of Greenland, with a population of 12,482 as of January 1994 (Grønland 1994: 378). The town comprises 22.5 percent of the total population in Greenland.

## SYMPTOM VERSUS AGENCY: TWO THEORETICAL PERSPECTIVES

Although wife beating is a widespread social phenomenon it has not caught the interest of many anthropologists so far. One of the reasons may be that wife beating represents the so-called dark side of culture (Counts 1992: xi). Probing into the silent domains of social life may thus leave the anthropologist in an awkward relationship with the local population, or perhaps rather with a part of this population. Another reason for the reluctance to deal with violence may be that research into this specific phenomenon is perceived as a feminist enterprise rather than part of mainstream anthropology (cf. Strathern 1987). Even so, more and more anthropological literature on wife beating and the relationship between sex, gender and violence has been published in recent years.[1]

Wife beating in Greenland and elsewhere tends to be seen by professionals and researchers alike as a deviance from normal orderly life rather than as part of normal life.[2] This means that the phenomenon is often perceived as a symptom of disorder in society at large. As Henrietta Moore has recently put it in an inspiring article on the problem of explaining violence in the social sciences, we generally imagine interpersonal violence as a breakdown in the social order—something gone wrong in society (Moore 1994: 154). From this "health model" perspective, violence is an irrational, emotional response to certain objective structural conditions—a symptom of social anomie.

The focus on deviance may be justified from a moral point of view, but from an analytical point of view it seems rather futile because it directs our gaze toward an abstract entity called society instead of focusing on individual perpetrators of violence and their motives for beating. Though individuals are located in a specific society and cultural reality that mark them in certain ways, this does not mean that they act as mere automatons or "cultural dopes." There is still room for individual agency based on rational choices, embodied motivation, interpretations and life perspectives. However, the social sciences have difficulty resolving the duality of individual and society and the conventional solution has been to derive the first from the second (Cohen and Rapport 1994: 2). Since the 1980s, a growing interest within anthropology in social practice and agency has questioned this crude determinism thoroughly (cf. Ortner 1984).

While I suggest focusing on individual agency and motives for beating, I do not argue in favor of a symptom approach on the individual rather than the societal level. Both seem to be based on underlying functionalist and idealistic assumptions that leave no room for violence except as deviance from the stable, healthy and well-functioning rule. To the extent that many professionals and researchers are inclined to perceive male use of violence against women as an irrational act that is way out of bounds, we are prone to ask "Why do men beat their wives?" instead of asking "Why not?" Assuming that there must be deep, underlying reasons for wife beating, we often search for causal relationships between childhood experiences and wife beating, socioeconomic conditions and wife beating, personal/cultural identity and wife beating, etc. Explanations for wife beating thus tend to revolve around aspects of "because" rather than "in order to" (Sørensen 1994). The search for the roots of violent behavior often results in a typification of the violent man who is, for instance, characterized by "low self-esteem and poor impulse control" (Frieze 1987:118). The very search for the roots of violence may also be seen as a tradition in European scholarship, "where causes have generally been identified as antecedents" (Hastrup 1992: 6). The question then is: How far do we have to go back in individual male biography to account for present violent behavior and does this backward look make much sense? It is a fact that men sometimes beat their wives to forestall future actions on the part of the wives, in which case the conventional idea of causation is turned upside down.

The symptom approach to violence against women often takes for granted that the use of violence is ultimately a cry for help. Perpetrators of violence are thus sometimes depicted as the true victims, whereas the victims of violence, even though they are recognized as victims of concrete violent episodes, are nevertheless depicted as the mentally stronger of the two parties. It follows from this perspective that male perpetrators of violence need help, professional and therapeutic, to overcome their violent outbursts as they are not able to control themselves and need to engage in a dialogue with their inner feelings in order to come out as new and improved, well-balanced, self-confident, and thus nonviolent men.

I do not mean to discard altogether the workings of counseling and therapy, but a theoretical perspective that tends to construe aggressors as the true victims seems to turn things upside down and also to be somewhat naive as to the intimate relationship between gender, violence, and power. Men are certainly not all-powerful *vis-à-vis* women as power is a relational, situational, and contested matter. At the same time, it is worth holding on to the fact that most people, males or females, do not engage in violent acts at random. Instead they evaluate the situation and the relative physical strength and social power between themselves and their opponents before they actually strike out. Men in general have the advantage of being physically stronger than women and quite a few men are also more experienced in the field of physical combat, which means that they may strike out against their wives without much risk of immediate physical retaliation. Moreover, if wife beating, as is often the case, is seen by society at large as a phenomenon belonging to the sphere of privacy, this adds to the likelihood that men will beat their wives if they feel like it, often thinking that they are well within their rights to do so.

To construe wife beating as a symptom of deep-seated male problems is questionable as it obscures agency, power, instrumentality, and individual choice as central elements of violence. Instead, I agree with David Riches (1986: 12) who suggests that we treat violence as a strategically, consciously employed resource (see also Klein and Johnson 1997 on the concept of strategic choice) and with Moore who suggests seeing violence as "the sign of a struggle for the maintenance of certain fantasies of identity and power" (Moore 1994: 154). Riches' suggestion, however, appears to be inspired by interest theory and it may assume too much reflection and rationality on the part of the actors, whereas Moore's approach is more in line with strain theory which may be better suited to account for actors' motives, shaped by certain ideas of personhood and the possibilities and restraints to take up these ideas in social life (cf. Ortner 1984:

151–52; Geertz 1973). Instead of separating reason and emotion, which is part of Western traditional thinking, we should integrate them as "no reason can be given for an act or decision that does not also involve the actor's emotions, however weak or strong. There is no conflict between reason and emotion" (Parkin 1985: 139; see also Wikan 1991).

## THE PHENOMENON

It is not possible to give exact figures on wife beating in Nuuk, but this is a general problem with statistics on violence against women (cf. The World's Women 1995: 158). Most beatings go on unnoticed except by family, friends, and neighbors, who are either told about it later or detect the physical marks or just happen to overhear the episode. The police are sometimes involved when the going gets tough and neighbors call police in order to make them stop the noise. Episodes like these are registered as "domestic disputes," a term that covers a whole range of phenomena and therefore tends to neglect and belittle wife beating as a phenomenon *per se*. Altogether, female victims of male violence make up a vulnerable category when it comes to the practice of the rule of law in Greenland (Jensen 1989).

Only the more serious incidents of wife beating lead to treatment in the emergency room or to hospitalization. The hospital practice is geared toward diagnosing and treating injuries; the hospital does not take statistics of injuries resulting from wife beating. However, a medical research project that was carried out in 1983, covering registered injuries due to accidents and violence treated in the hospitals of Greenland during a two-month period, estimated the rate of violence against women to be about twenty times higher in Greenland than in Denmark (Jørgensen *et al.* 1984). The findings also showed the injuries to be often more serious than those reported in similar research findings from Denmark. The perpetrators of violence were primarily younger men who had been drinking alcohol and most of the victims were women aged 20 to 29. The violence had usually taken place in the couples' own homes.

My own experiences may give a hint of how widespread a practice wife beating in Nuuk may be. In the apartment building that I lived in during fieldwork in 1988–89, the next-door neighbor regularly beat his wife. The next time I stayed in Nuuk, I once again happened to have a neighbor who beat his wife, only this time he lived in the flat below. Visiting and talking to friends and acquaintances in town, I also heard their stories about neighbors who beat their wives occasionally or on a regular basis. These stories usually came up accidentally and I did not have to probe for them. Now and then, some of my friends would be involved in actual cases of wife beating, in which they were confidants of the battered women or their husbands.

During my fieldwork in 1989, I sent out a questionnaire covering a wide range of themes: among others, wife beating.[3] Fifty-seven percent of the respondents answered affirmatively to a question about whether women in their close circle of family or friends had been subject to violence from husbands or lovers, 36 percent answered "no" and 7 percent did not answer the question at all (cf. Sørensen 1994: 79). In order to find out how local people perceived the relationship between violence and responsibility, I also asked to what degree, if any, female victims of violence "bring it on themselves." Eighty-eight percent of the female and 75 percent of the male respondents answered that women bring it on themselves sometimes, whereas 8 percent of the female and 12 percent of the male respondents answered that women never bring it on themselves.

These answers seem to indicate that most people perceive male use of violence as an unfortunate, and yet understandable, act, or as a way out of certain situations. One reason for this perspective may be that people tend to think of violence as involving two equally responsible parties. Thus, wife beating often is referred to in terms of "they fight" and "it takes two," and many people seem to believe that responsible women do not engage in situations in which they may encounter violence. The responsible and clever wife would not give her husband any reason to beat her in contrast to the irresponsible and sloppy wife who neglects her duties, her children and her husband, being too focused instead on going out, having a good time and, perhaps, drinking. An elderly woman pointed out that in her opinion the problem of wife beating really began when women turned to drinking, too. The statement is quite interesting as it indicates that the sober and responsible woman is expected to tackle her drunk husband in a sensible way, whereas the woman who encroaches on male prerogatives by drinking on a par with her husband is likely to ask for trouble.

Most people in Nuuk are also familiar with women whose personality and behavior they tend to characterize as "bitchy," and such personal experiences may likely enter their perception of violence against women in such a way that they refrain from taking a firm stand on the issue in general. Instead, they tend to evaluate each specific episode involving individuals they know. Most people in Nuuk thus do not take sharp issue with male use of violence on grounds of principle. Interestingly, this even holds true for some of the women who have been exposed to violence themselves.

As David Riches (1986: 3) points out, the concept of violence carries certain connotations of illegitimacy that make it all the more important for researchers not to apply the concept uncritically to those social actions and acts that may be interpreted differently from a local point of view. When people in Nuuk say "they fight," this may indicate that, in their conception, the aspect of illegitimacy is downplayed or perhaps even irrelevant. However, the notion of violence as illegitimate was sometimes invoked in actual cases of wife beating, especially by younger women, which may be suggestive of a historical turning point in Greenlandic views on the subject (cf. Sørensen 1990: 93).

It is worth keeping in mind that violence is a contested concept and matter, which means that there is not just one local perspective or interpretation of actual cases of inflicted physical hurt. Riches (1986: 8) also stresses the political aspects of violence, suggesting that we focus on "the basic triangle of violence"—that is, the interrelationship between the perpetrator, the victim, and the eventual witness(es) who may have different interpretations of the event. Although in most instances of wife beating there are no witnesses, except perhaps the couple's own children, we may think of other, indirect, witnesses such as the general public as well as individuals who become implicated in cases of wife beating as relatives or friends.

Although wife beating sometimes is seen as an understandable act, it is not glorified or approved of in general. Rather, people tend to see it as an outcome of a certain way of life characterized by partying and drinking that may lead to accusations of infidelity, arguments, and fights. People in general also tend to distinguish between individuals or families leading a proper, nonabusive daily life and those who lead a life characterized by heavy abuse and lack of control, thus dissociating themselves from the latter. However, this distinction does not cover the actual occurrence of wife beating which cannot be placed squarely in one category. Wife beating is not always associated with alcohol and one kind of abuse does not necessarily imply or lead to another.

Upper- and middle-class thinking on wife beating tends to cast the phenomenon as a problem of the working class. Even if the concept of class is not part of the everyday vocabulary in Greenland, the concept of lifestyle serves a similar purpose. Working-class lifestyle is depicted as a life from hand to mouth, indicating a certain casual attitude toward life in general.

However, wife beating in Greenland is also a widespread phenomenon among male members of the cultural and political elite and it is an open secret among the inhabitants of Nuuk which high-ranking officials and politicians beat their wives. The tendency to conflate wife beating and class position may be due to ideas about violence as primitive and uncivilized, which again accounts for a process of "othering" that places violence and abuse apart from oneself.

For many people in Nuuk, the weekends herald a time of pleasure, parties and drinking, and Friday afternoons are often characterized by a frenzy of hectic activity and excited expectations filling the air. Times when Fridays are also pay days can be inferred from the tremendous activity in town and from police reports as well. When people drink they often get more reckless than usual; this goes for men as well as women. Drunk people often become more daring and talkative and drunk talk often leads to quarrels, confrontations, challenges, and ultimately fights and beatings. Part of the violence thus seems to be connected with certain lifestyles and drinking patterns of the wife beater or of both husband and wife. It should be pointed out, however, that women do not have to "make excesses" to be beaten by their husbands. Sometimes, it happens and there need not be any reason other than the husband's own capricious reasoning.

In 1983, a crisis center for battered women was established in Nuuk on the initiative of a group of local women. The center is run by a couple of employees and a body of volunteers; the working expenses are paid by the municipality of Nuuk and the Greenland Home Rule (state aid). Since then, other centers have been established in some of the other Greenlandic towns, but their exact numbers have varied over the years as some have been closed down for some time due to lack of municipal funding and/or local initiative. Anyway, the very establishment and visibility of these institutions are likely to have had an effect on the local population in general in the sense that more people are aware of the problem of wife beating.

On International Women's Day, March 8, 1996, the crisis centers in Nuuk, Aasiaat and Narsaq planned and carried out demonstrations against violence against women. Despite rather stormy weather, about 200 inhabitants of Nuuk, mostly women, joined the demonstration that started at the crisis center and ended at the town hall (Atuagagdliutit 1996b: 6). Among the slogans on the signboards were: "Violence is unacceptable," "We demand better legislation for the victims of violence" and "Remember the children" (Atuagagdliutit 1996a: 5). The demonstrations were followed by speeches and radio interviews with women working in the association of crisis centers in Greenland. Altogether, the demonstrations indicate local awareness of violence against women which is part of a local discourse on gender relations in general. However, it is also worth noting that wife beating tends to be seen as a "family problem" rather than a problem of male violence against women. This family problem perspective is characteristic of most women working within the crisis center organization in Greenland.

## VIOLENCE AND IDENTITY

Even if wife beating and other forms of interpersonal violence are widespread (Larsen 1991: 77–78), Greenlanders in general do not see violence as part of Greenlandic identity, culture, and social practice. This idea is very much in line with the popular, reified conception of culture according to which culture is something one "has," preferably in large amounts and something one can be proud of (cf. Handler 1985). Violence, even if it is a social fact, does not fit in here, but may rather be seen to represent the negation of Greenlandic culture. In general, neither battered Greenlandic women nor women who have had personal experiences with violence at some point seem to identify themselves as victims of violence. In comparison with, for example, Indian women from the Bolivian and Peruvian highlands—who according to Harris (1994) and Harvey (1994) seem to accept, though not whole-heartedly, that wife beating is the married woman's lot and who accordingly identify with the hardships of womanhood—Greenlandic women in general do not expect physical abuse to be part of married life. Instead, violence is imagined as "imported," and as originating elsewhere. It is often seen as one of many so-called social problems arising, or at least spreading, in the wake of modernization of Greenland in the 1950s and 1960s and the ensuing "culture clash," which is a popular, condensed expression of historical development. The literature on Greenland also tends to conflate very different phenomena by placing them under the concept of social problems and connecting them rather directly to the modernization process (cf. From *et al.* 1975; Kleivan 1984a: 705; Larsen 1994: 199; Lynge 1995). As a result, very different social phenomena even today tend to be read as symptoms of structural changes, leaving individual agency out of consideration.[4]

The idea that violence is not really of native Greenlandic origin has striking parallels to other Inuit populations. Ann Fienup-Riordan comments upon violence in her book *Eskimo Essays* (1990: 149) in which she writes: "Today in Alaska, non-natives all too often continue to consider violence in rural Alaska as without precedent in traditional non-violent Eskimo society and therefore as being 'introduced,' a product of 'culture contact'." But this view is not restricted to non-natives as Fienup-Riordan shows: "Perhaps more significant, some Alaska Eskimos agree with this interpretation. At the 1988 annual meeting of the Eskimo sovereignty group, the Yupiit Nation, Yup'ik elders were almost unanimous in their denial that violence and warfare had existed in traditional Yup'ik society" (*ibid.*). Fienup-Riordan (1990: 149–150) points to the importance of cultural politics in understanding such denial:

> [Such statements] reflect a powerful current political attempt to represent Eskimo history and culture as distinct from and superior to its non-native counterpart. Although non-natives deny Eskimo violence out of ignorance, the native denial represents a decision to emphasize one part of their history rather than another.

Fienup-Riordan further explains how acts of violence described in several of the early sources were most often viewed as the "natural consequences" of a society constrained by a harsh environment and lacking formal mechanisms of social control. In general, the conventional literature on Inuit populations has a distinctive eco-functionalist bent (Sørensen 1994: 125–30). Riches (1990: 78) also speaks of an empiricist functionalist tradition within the field.

In Greenland, the issue of wife beating also tends to be highly politicized, implying that the actual phenomenon is often belittled and explained away, whereas ethnopolitics come to the front. Even female Greenlanders inspired by feminist thinking sometimes seem to trivialize the problem when they argue that wife beating in Greenland is not more widespread than in Denmark, only more visible. Such statements often invoke different cultural personalities in that Greenlanders are represented as more "honest," and violence in Greenland thus more public.

To sum up, there is a tendency among both scholars and the native populations of the Arctic to assume that violence is not really part of traditional native life. Today's violence in the local communities is therefore often represented as a symptom of disintegration of traditional ways and values, originating in colonial and neocolonial policy. As a result, violence is externalized. When Danish and other scholars externalize the responsibility for violent behavior, their reasons may be based on a "don't blame the victim" perspective in that they tend to cast both perpetrators and victims of violence as victims of modernization, but even if their intentions are good, they seem to reproduce a paternalistic attitude toward whole populations who are denied agency and who are all lumped together in spite of internal social differentiation, different interests and perspectives. People are seen as reacting to external impingements rather than acting within a certain structural framework (cf. Ortner 1984: 159).

Studies on contemporary Inuit tend to be based on a tradition–modernization dichotomy implying a focus on how people adapt to so-called modern life. The very concept of adaptation tends to fixate the Inuit in a world frozen in time, whereas Euro-Americans, for example, do not adapt to a changing world, but are rather part of it. It is moreover sometimes taken for granted that the Inuit have to start from point zero as their traditional way of life has been disrupted completely. Edmund Carpenter is illustrative in this regard when he writes about historical change among Canadian Inuit:

> Then, suddenly and powerfully, came a massive intrusion of Western culture, with results so inevitable they cannot be charged to the mistakes of men. The newcomers could not see the patterns of Eskimo life; they smashed into them as innocently as men walk through

> cobwebs. And so the Eskimos lost all of those essential, invisible things which give people unity, confidence, self-respect and the habits, so hard to restore, of a disciplined social life. What they were offered, apart from the higher substitutes of free enterprise and Christianity . . . were material goods and medicine, entertainment and alcohol and a bitter sense of having lost some indefinable but precious thing.
>
> (Carpenter 1982: 81)

It is a fact that historical changes in the Arctic have been drastic. However, the emotional picture drawn by Carpenter seems too general, historically unspecific and a child of its time, the 1960s to early 1980s. The same picture sometimes is drawn of Greenland in both popular and scholarly writings, even if Greenland has been a Danish colony since 1721, which means that historical change has not come overnight (cf. Gad 1984; Kleivan 1984b; Nuttall 1994; Thuesen 1988).[5] Underlying a good part of the literature on the Arctic is a diehard organic and functionalist conception of culture which fits nicely with James Clifford's general description and critique of the concept of culture:

> A powerful structure of feeling continues to see culture, wherever it is found, as a coherent *body* that lives and dies. Culture is enduring, traditional, structural (rather than contingent, syncretic, historical). Culture is a process of ordering, not of disruption. It changes and develops like a living organism. It does not normally "survive" abrupt alterations.
>
> (Clifford 1994: 235)

The polar concepts of tradition and modernity cast the Inuit as trapped between times and contrasting, incompatible ways of living. Their entrapment, in turn, accounts for images of cultural disruption, decay, perplexity and insecurity, which are hardships that they have to face and deal with in order to come out as new, modern individuals. Rather than treating tradition and modernity as exemplifying two different objective times and entities, they should be treated as concepts in use, that is, concepts which both researchers and local people make use of when ordering and making sense of reality (Sørensen, 1997). Even if 1950 has been canonized as the historical turning point from tradition to modernization in the literature on Greenland, Greenlanders themselves often use the concepts of tradition and modernity in a much more nuanced way in everyday discourse. Some tend to place traditional Greenland in the last century, whereas others speak of the 1970s as representing traditional culture. The dividing line between tradition and modernity is likely to remain on the move in the years to come.

The contrast between traditional ways and modern life is imbued with explanatory power to justify as seemingly self-evident the notion of a direct causality between modernization of the Arctic and so-called social problems of all kinds. However, the early historical sources on Greenland also comment on wife beating (Sørensen 1990: 104–105). Deriving individual social acts directly from major historical changes is problematic, not the least when it comes to explaining contemporary acts of violence against women.

It should also be mentioned that the Greenland Home Rule was established in 1979, with the explicit intention of creating a society based on Greenlandic premises. Yet, wife beating does not appear to be on the wane. In principle, Greenland is ruled by Greenlanders. However, due to the small population and the lack of educated people and specialists in certain fields, Greenland still has to rely on imported contract workers and professionals, especially from Denmark. A good part of the employees in the home rule administration are thus of Danish origin; some of them stay for a three-year contract period while others tend to stay on.[6] It should be pointed out that even though Greenlanders and Danes are held apart conceptually, in real life they live together, intermarry and have children.[7]

## EVERYDAY VERSUS "DEEP" EXPLANATIONS

During my fieldwork I encountered many different explanations for wife beating. In these, a certain pattern stood out clearly, showing that whenever people referred to a concrete episode involving family, friends, or acquaintances, their explanations centered on individual personality traits, drinking habits, or the way of life in general. The personality traits spoken of would usually be jealousy or bitchiness and "mad behavior when drunk." When people were asked to explain wife beating in Greenland in general, a dramatic explanatory shift took place in that they tended to invoke certain master narratives (cf. Bruner 1986) dealing with the rapid historical change and its implications. I should mention that most of those who did try to explain the general phenomenon of wife beating belonged to the upper middle class and that some of them were public figures with a nationalistic bent.

Anyway, people seemed to make use of two explanatory approaches; one focusing on individual agency when dealing with concrete cases and another focusing on structural forces when dealing abstractly with the level of violence in general. Whereas the agency approach seemed to be an immediate response to everyday life experiences, the structural or symptom approach seemed to be of a more conscious nature and more closely connected with public statements. Accordingly, this approach is the one embraced in the media.

Whereas the first approach is placed squarely in everyday local politics, the latter is part of an ethnopolitical discourse. As it is, the two perspectives have different implications as regards personal responsibility for violence. Focusing on individual behavior, personality, and way of life, the agency perspective seems to distinguish between different kinds of local people, that is, those who are responsible and well-behaved as opposed to those who are not. The symptom perspective, on the other hand, is based on a cultural opposition at another level, namely the opposition between Greenlandic and Danish culture which according to the dominant cultural discourse are rather incompatible entities. Often invoked, "culture clash" is an expression based on a personification of culture, according agency to culture itself (Strathern 1992: 51).

Whatever explanation is adopted, it is somehow based on social experience. Causality is a construction based on experience and different experiences contribute to different causal models. Everyday experiences in Nuuk seem to contribute to ideas about a causal relationship between drinking and violence, jealousy and violence, and "bitchy" behavior and violence. In turn, historical experiences and the way ideas about history and culture are implicated in everyday social practice generate ideas about a causal relationship between foreign (Danish) dominance, modernization based on foreign cultural premises, and violence. Which explanation people prefer seems to be a matter of individual choice based on experience, while at the same time individual explanations tend to be situational, that is, based on context. This also means that whatever explanation is emphasized, it has different political implications.

In everyday life in Nuuk, violence seems to be dealt with as a matter of course. Violent episodes that involve people whom one knows are sometimes retold to others as good stories without much dramatizing. Being unfamiliar with violence myself, I was pretty shaken by the stories and my immediate reaction was to ask why it had happened. However, from the reactions to my "whys" and my insistence on a detailed description of the precise words and acts that led to the incident, I concluded that they were considered beside the point, not interesting or worth thinking about. Violence just happens occasionally. One of the incidents I was told involved a group of friends in their late twenties who were out together. One of the young women was with her boyfriend, but she happened to make up to another man who was actually a rather close friend of her boyfriend. Later that evening her boyfriend beat up the other man. Whether he beat up his girlfriend, too, I never found out. Anyway, the story I heard was presented in a slightly humorous fashion and the boyfriend's use of violence was not questioned because his friend "had asked for it."

One night I was sitting in a bar in Nuuk when a fist fight suddenly broke out between two men at a nearby table. It was a fierce fight with blood running down their faces and soon tables were turned and bottles and glasses broken. People around the two men just seemed to move away a bit to watch the fight from a safe distance: live performance at close range. I was horrified and went to the bar counter to make the staff do something about it and call the police. When I later discussed the episode with friends in Nuuk, I realized that my reaction had been way out of line and pretty amusing. I had been overreacting according to local ways of dealing with such episodes. Violent public episodes involving a man and his wife are not treated differently.

By these examples I do not mean to say that people in Nuuk are insensitive toward one another. Rather, the examples indicate that most people are used to observe violence and perhaps are personally involved occasionally. "Ordinary" violent incidents are thus not dramatized or taken very seriously, unless if one's closest family or friends are the victims of violence of a nonroutine kind. Wife beating among neighbors is usually commented on with a shrug of the shoulders—"this is their way of life, their choice." People also do not pity perpetrators of violence by seeing them as victims of strong, external forces in this everyday life discourse on violence, which has a remarkable matter of course ring to it. Violence seems natural.

## VIOLENCE AND EMOTIONS

Most scholars dealing with interpersonal violence and other social problems in contemporary Greenland (see, for instance, Larsen 1991, 1995; Lynge 1995) are inspired by Jean L. Briggs who has published extensively on "traditional" Central Canadian Inuit emotions and handling of emotions, especially in relation to socialization (Briggs 1970, 1985, 1991). It is therefore worth while to make a short introduction to Briggs's approach.[8]

Even though Briggs emphasizes the ambiguities in the socialization process, her framework seems to be based on the idea that emotional control is a must given the unpredictable and dangerous life under harsh climatic conditions. People thus have to be sensitive toward one another's emotional state and they have to overcome problematic emotions that may threaten the vital cooperation and mutual trust (Briggs 1991). Inuit socialization inculcates emotional control as a cardinal virtue in the children. Owing to both personal repression and social control mechanisms, people appear to be "never in anger," which does not mean, however, that this dangerous emotion is not felt by individuals. In circumstances of less social control and less vital interdependence between Inuit individuals, a situation characterizing Inuit living in towns rather than on the land, such dangerous emotions are sometimes expressed with all the more force (Briggs 1985: 49).

Briggs is silent on the aspects of gender and power and their relations to the cultural ideal of emotional control; rather the ideal is presented in general, gender neutral terms. Briggs (1987) seems indebted to the psychoanalytic approach to emotions: they may be successfully repressed for some time, but if the control mechanisms fail, emotions may become explosive. Underlying her approach is a psychological orthodoxy on emotions, the hydraulic model, that has been debated and criticized in recent anthropological literature in which emotions are dealt with as social constructs invoked in discourse and politics (cf. Abu-Lughod and Lutz 1990; Heelas 1982; Lutz and White 1986; Solomon 1984).

Inspired by Briggs's perspective, Breinholt Larsen focuses on a supposedly traditional Inuit behavior characterized by emotional control and conflict avoidance. He writes that

> it is my hypothesis that the high prevalence of violence in Greenland today is caused by an adverse interaction between salient features in traditional conflict behavior still a vigorous part of contemporary Inuit culture and new elements in the social life of the Greenlanders brought about by the rapid social change during the past few decades.
>
> (Larsen 1991: 77)

The supposed traditional conflict behavior thus seems to account for a certain non-confrontational personality type that is contrasted with a Western personality type characterized by direct verbal confrontation.

However, it is questionable to attribute a certain conflict behavior and personality to a whole population, disregarding important factors such as social status, age, gender and power. Breinholt Larsen seems to argue that conflict-avoiding behavior is inappropriate in today's society in that it leads to repression and pent-up emotions that may explode during alcohol consumption when people loosen up and take "time off" from ordinary social norms. He thus suggests that Greenlanders develop new skills in conflict resolution by starting to verbalize conflict matters and emotions (*ibid.*: 85). Once again, we are presented with the hydraulic model of emotions and the idea that words can replace physical violence. However, this idea is highly questionable and I doubt that wife beating men are not aware that the use of physical violence is more persuading and effective than mere words.

Writings on contemporary social problems in Greenland are imbued with emotions, not the least writings on interpersonal violence. However, emotions and emotional expressions are more often than not taken at face value rather than treated analytically. Men are thus often believed not to be able to control their emotions in actual cases of wife beating. Consequently, according to the hydraulic model of emotions, emotions are believed to take control of the otherwise rational individual subject who is replaced by an automatic pilot and wife beating is cast as an irrational act. Lila Abu-Lughod and Catherine Lutz (1990) show, however, how emotions are invoked in social communication and are also deeply embedded in power. Emotions are powerful means that can be used by certain people to legitimate certain acts. The man who regrets that he has to beat (discipline) his wife in order to keep the family together, is a case in point.

## GENDER, SOCIALIZATION, AND VIOLENCE

When gender is invoked in local explanations of wife beating it is mostly in connection with socialization and the historical development, which is often imagined to have resulted in changing gender relations that have been detrimental to Greenlandic men in general. Accordingly, wife beating is seen as a symptom of male powerlessness rather than an act of power.

The focus on socialization seems to highlight the different treatment and expectations of boys and girls and the final outcome of an allegedly widespread practice of spoiling boys who learn not to take no for an answer. The emphasis is thus on maternal agency as a form of local social practice. However, the agency perspective stops at the mothers who are believed to be mainly responsible for the end product of this practice: the adult man who is used to being served and obeyed. Upbringing is seen as destiny, implying that the adult man himself is not to blame for his eventual violent outbursts as his mother made him what he is once and for all. This idea has a familiar ring to it. As Rayna Rapp (1995: 79) writes in a recent article on heredity:

> Maternal health practices are frequently discussed in the language of epidemiology, substance abuse and lifestyle choices, but they also engage a much older and enduring morality play. As feminist anthropologists have pointed out, women in many cultures, especially Euro-American cultures, are held, and hold themselves, responsible for nurturance. When something "goes wrong," that too is powerfully pictured as a failure of female responsibility. In our folk models of reproduction the "quality control" of children is construed as women's domain.

The Greenlandic discourse on maternal responsibility thus does not seem very different from the Euro-American one in its tendency to depict men as victims of maternal "outdated" upbringing, which serves as an implicit excuse of male violence.

Explanations for male violence based on the child rearing and maternal responsibility often intersect with a popular discourse on changing gender relations and hence changing power relations, in Greenlandic society. The picture presented sometimes tends to be one of female winners and male losers in a historical perspective as women are believed to have maintained their traditional key position within the family in addition to participating in modern wage work, whereas men are believed to suffer from being ousted by women and Danish men on the labor market, which, in turn, have affected both their position within the family and their self-esteem. Different sources from Greenland, Canada, and Alaska also seem to embrace the idea that women may be in a better position to "live in both worlds" due to a historical development that in some respects has been more favorable to women than to men (Dybbroe 1988; Lennert and Thomsen 1991; McElroy 1975; Fogel-Chance 1993).[9]

However, the picture presented in the popular discourse seems to be based on implicit ideas of a "natural" male authority that has been lost and should be regained for the sake of male health and society. It also tends to treat men and women as ahistorical, generalized categories in the sense that different generations of men and women are not distinguished. One therefore gets the impression that all Greenlandic men and women have experienced the same hardships and gains during the period of transition from tradition to modernization.

In today's Greenland, for the most part, both men and women are wage earners (62 percent) employed in the public sector, while about one-third (31 percent) are either unemployed, retired, students, or housewives (Bjerregaard *et al.* 1995: 39). Few Greenlandic men are full-time hunters and fishermen (7 percent of the population engaged in active employment). Most Greenlandic politicians and persons in positions of power are men, even if more and more women are coming to the fore. Also, motherhood can hardly be characterized as having more historical continuity than fatherhood. The biological aspect notwithstanding, both concepts and their contents have changed with time.

In light of the current popularity of the "strong women" and "weak men" perspective, which is also well-known in Euro-American discourse on gender relations and the purported male identity crisis (cf. Fitzgerald 1993: 109–134), it is no wonder that many people tend to perceive male acts of violence as compensatory acts stemming from frustration, maladjustment and insecurity.[10] Lynge states, for instance, that today's Greenlandic men have difficulty "in finding natural ways of feeling important" (Peqqinnissaq 1994: 10). Altogether, this mental picture of men out of balance seems to imply a symptom approach to violence.

## MALE WEAKNESS?

The very idea that Greenlandic men in general are less prepared for modern life than women seems to be based on popular psychology according to which an "unthinkable act" such as wife beating is readily cast as a symptom of male insecurity. However, it is worth looking closer into the precise meanings of the concept of insecurity and how it is related to agency.

First, men are not all-powerful *vis-à-vis* women and wife beating may be interpreted as a sign that male authority is under attack, but this is certainly not the same as arguing that men are weak or powerless. Second, if a man's masculinity is indeed hinged upon control of his wife, this makes him vulnerable to the wife's actions and attitudes (cf. Stølen 1991: 96–97). Although there are many different and competing discourses of masculinity in today's Greenland, it still seems that the dominant masculine identity is based on the idea that a man is the family head and the main breadwinner, even if this "ideal" often does not correspond with reality. It follows that the maintenance of a family position, as well as "proper" gender behavior and attitudes by husband and wife are central to male identity and public status and thus to male self-representation.

Henrietta Moore (1994: 151) introduces the concept of "thwarting" to account for the fact that some men turn to violence against their wives: "Thwarting can be understood as the inability to sustain or properly take up a gendered subject position, resulting in a crisis, real or imagined, of self-representation and/or social evaluation" (cf. Lindisfarne 1994: 87). Even if Moore speaks of a male "crisis," it should be pointed out that her analytic focus is on the individual, subjective male point of view, which in turn is intimately related to social discourses and other people's evaluations. Although her approach therefore differs from a simplistic symptom approach to male violence, the concept of "crisis" may become insipid by being used in this general way.

The analytic concept of thwarting seems to make good sense in many Greenlandic cases of wife beating where men turn to violence when they feel that their social position and self-representation is threatened from either the inside or the outside or both (cf. Sørensen 1990: 107). Quite a few Greenlandic men, who do not beat their wives on a regular basis, turn to wife beating in situations in which their wives are about to leave them or if they suspect that their wives are unfaithful or disloyal. Other men, who routinely engage in wife beating, seem to react violently to whatever they perceive as female challenges to their own sense of masculinity. These perceived challenges often revolve around seemingly trivial matters such as who speaks up when, who gets the last word, who decides when to go out, go home, etc. Yet, such trivial matters can be thwarting the masculine sense of self which may be reconfirmed and reassured by disciplining the wife who by crossing proper gender lines has asked for it herself. The wife is also often the victim of so-called displaced violence, in which other people's behavior and attitudes threaten the husband's self-representation, as she is the only person that he can control and she is the one who confirms her husband's masculinity by the proper adoption of the feminine subject position (Moore 1994: 153–154). Violence thus makes sense as a strategically, consciously employed resource that restores "the proper balance" and serves to maintain fantasies of identity, power, and control. No matter how heated and emotional the act of wife beating may seem, it can still be seen as a rational act from the individual male perspective. In this act, the aspect of "in order to" can be seen to encompass the aspect of "because"—that is, the man beats his wife in order to punish her or shut her up, while at the same time his depressed masculine self-representation is bolstered and reassured.

## A REASON FOR VIOLENCE?

It seems futile to search for the objective reason(s) for violence. Still, the individual perpetrator of violence may have good reasons for beating according to his own view and fantasies and usually he believes he has a right to do so. Even though the individual perpetrator of violence may think and explain that he was carried away by his emotions, I believe that the aspects of rational choice and embodied motivation are worth emphasizing. Just as some men may choose to use physical violence to enforce their will and thus reconfirm their masculinity, others may choose not to and they may even find the use of physical force unthinkable and conflicting with their personal sense of masculinity. Yet, for some men the use of violence seems to be the obvious and most likely solution to their representational "crises," and it seems to work for them, at least in the short run. So, why not?

When people in Nuuk are directly confronted with the general issue of wife beating, they tend to think that there must be a "deep" reason. Accordingly they tend to invoke certain master narratives such as the culture clash, male psychological insecurity due to historical change, maternal upbringing, etc. These explanations seem to be based on a search for the exact point of time when things went wrong, whether in history and society or individual male biography. The explanations are retrospective and not capable to account for the "here and now" character of female challenges, male "crises" and wife beating. In contrast, in everyday life, people tend to see wife beating as a matter-of-course phenomenon, as if it was a natural, rather than a social event. Another ambiguity concerns the question of responsibility for violence, which tends to be externalized in the master narratives, whereas the everyday life explanations engage both husband and wife as equally responsible parties. The gender-related significance of wife beating surfaces in a peculiar ambiguity of both scholars and lay people when they consider the use of violence in general incomprehensible, but nevertheless do not question the "naturalness" of male violence against women. It is more often than not taken for granted that violent men are under great pressure and hence cannot be held fully responsible. Presumably, they react "because of" rather than "in order to." All these ambiguities are quite interesting and may contribute to the fact that wife beating is very much alive and thriving, even though the implications of discourse for social practice seldom are recognized among local people themselves.[11]

## NOTES

1 See, for instance, Counts *et al.* (1992); Harvey and Gow (1994); Sørensen (1990, 1994, 1995); Stølen (1991). The references are not at all exhaustive.

2 The term "professionals" refers to a whole range of people who deal with violence as part of their jobs such as, for instance, women working at crisis centers, social workers, policemen, etc.

3 The questionnaire survey involved a random selection of the inhabitants of Nuuk, aged 18 to 80 years and born in Greenland. A total of 208 questionnaires (43 percent), comprising 101 male and 107 female respondents, were filled in and subsequently handled.

4 This is characteristic for literature on Inuit on the whole. See, for instance, Richard G. Condon (1982) on Canadian Inuit.

5 In 1953, Greenland's colonial status was changed and Greenland became an integral part of Denmark. In 1979, Greenland Home Rule was established.

6 About 3,243 persons living in Nuuk are born outside Greenland. For the whole of Greenland, about 7,390 persons are born outside Greenland. Most of these people are Danes, but not exclusively. It is not a one-way traffic from Denmark to Greenland, however, as just about as many Greenlanders live in Denmark as Danes in Greenland for a shorter period or on a permanent basis (Sørensen 1993: 34–35). The exact figures for Greenlanders in Denmark are nonexistent, but a census taken in 1985 stated a total number of about 6,000 (Grønland 1986: 25–26). However, cultural identities are not always clear-cut when it comes to children of mixed couples living in Denmark.

7 My own questionnaire survey indicates that 16 percent of the married or cohabiting male respondents had a Danish spouse; the corresponding figures for female respondents were 28 percent (Sørensen 1994: 46). See also note 3.

8 This short introduction may be doing some violence to Briggs's perspective and framework as nuances are necessarily lost.

9 The authors referred to differ considerably in their exact approaches and explications of the relationship between gender and continuity and change, but space does not allow me to go into details.

10 See, for instance, LaPrairie (1987) on Canadian Indians.

11 Often they are not recognized by scholars dealing with interpersonal violence and other contemporary social issues in Greenland (and the Arctic) either.

## BIBLIOGRAPHY


Abu-Lughod, L. and Lutz, C.A. (1990) "Introduction: Emotion, discourse and the politics of everyday life," in C.A. Lutz and L. Abu-Lughod (eds) *Language and the politics of emotion*, Cambridge: Cambridge University Press.

Atuagagdliutit/Grønlandsposten [Greenlandic newspaper] (1996a) "Det er så yndigt at følges ad . . . " (KK), p. 5.

—— (1996b) "Demonstrationer for kampen mod vold mod kvinder" (PM), p. 6.

Bjerregaard, P., Senderovitz, F. and Ramlau-Hansen, L. (1995) *Mennesker og sundhed i Grønland*, København and Nuuk: DIKE and Landsstyreområdet for Sundhed, Miljø og Forskning.

Briggs, J.L. (1970) *Never in anger: Portrait of an Eskimo family*, Cambridge, MA: Harvard University Press.

—— (1985) "Socialization, family conflicts and responses to culture change among Canadian Inuit," *Arctic Medical Research* 40: 40–52.

—— (1987) "In search of emotional meaning," *Ethos* 15: 8–15.

—— (1991) "Expecting the unexpected: Canadian Inuit training for an experimental lifestyle," *Ethos* 19: 259–287.

Bruner, E.M. (1986) "Ethnography as narrative," in V.W. Turner and E.M. Bruner (eds) *The anthropology of experience*, Urbana, IL and Chicago, IL: University of Illinois Press.

Carpenter, E. (1982) "Sedna's challenge," *Dialectical Anthropology* 7: 81–89.

Clifford, J. (1994) *The predicament of culture: Twentieth century ethnography, literature and art*, Cambridge, MA, and London: Harvard University Press.

Cohen, A.P. and Rapport, N. (1994) "The very idea," *Anthropology Today* 10: 1–2.

Condon, R. G. (1982) "Seasonal variation and interpersonal conflict in the Central Canadian Arctic," *Ethnology* 21: 151–164.

Counts, D.A. (1992) "Preface," in D.A. Counts, J.K. Brown and J.C. Campbell (eds) *Sanctions and sanctuary: Cultural perspectives on the beating of wives*, Boulder: Westview Press.

Counts, D.A., Brown, J.K. and Campbell, J.C. (eds) (1992) *Sanctions and sanctuary: Cultural perspectives on the beating of wives*, Boulder: Westview Press.

Dybbroe, S. (1988) "Participation and control: Issues in the debate on women and development—A Greenlandic example," *Folk* 30: 111–132.

Fienup-Riordan, A. (1990) *Eskimo essays: Yup'ik lives and how we see them*, New Brunswick and London: Rutgers University Press.

Fitzgerald, T. K. (1993) *Metaphors of identity: A culture–communication dialogue*, Albany: State University of New York Press.

Fogel-Chance, N. (1993) "Living in both worlds: 'Modernity' and 'tradition' among North Slope Inupiat women in Anchorage," *Arctic Anthropology* 30: 94–108.

Frieze, I. H. (1987) "The female victim: Rape, wife battering and incest," in G.R. VandenBos and B.K. Bryant (eds) *Cataclysms, crises and catastrophes: Psychology in action*, Washington, DC: American Psychological Association.

From, A., Jensen, K.J., Friis, P. and Kjær, A. (1975) *Sociale problemer i Grønland*, København: Socialforskningsinstituttet, Publikation 64.

Gad, F. (1984) "History of colonial Greenland," in D. Damas (ed.) *Handbook of North American Indians*, vol. 5: *Arctic*, Washington: Smithsonian Institution.

Geertz, C. (1973) "Ideology as a cultural system," in C. Geertz, *The interpretation of cultures*, New York: Basic Books.

Grønland (1986) *Årbog*, København 1987: Ministeriet for Grønland.

—— (1994) *Statistisk Årbog*, Nuuk: Grønlands Statistiske Kontor, Grønlands Hjemmestyre & Atuakkiorfik.

Handler, R. (1985) "On having a culture: Nationalism and the preservation of Quebec's patrimoine," in G.W. Stocking, Jr. (ed.) *Objects and others: Essays on museums and material culture*, Wisconsin: University of Wisconsin Press.
Harris, O. (1994) "Condor and bull: The ambiguities of masculinity in Northern Potosi," in P. Harvey and P. Gow (eds) *Sex and violence: Issues in representation and experience*, London: Routledge.
Harvey, P. (1994) "Domestic violence in the Peruvian Andes," in P. Harvey and P. Gow (eds) *Sex and violence: Issues in representation and experience*, London: Routledge.
Harvey, P. and Gow, P. (eds) (1994) *Sex and violence: Issues in representation and experience*, London: Routledge.
Hastrup, K. (1992) "Introduction," in K. Hastrup (ed.) *Other histories*, London and New York: Routledge.
Heelas, P. (1982) "Anthropology, violence and catharsis," in P. Marsh and A. Campbell (eds) *Aggression and violence*, Oxford: Basil Blackwell.
Jensen, H.G. (1989) "Den grønlandske kriminallov og kriminalpolitik i dag," *Nordisk Tidsskrift for Kriminalvidenskab* 4: 276–289.
Jørgensen, B. *et al.* (1984) "Voldsulykker i Grønland," *Ugeskrift for Læger* 145: 3398–3401.
Klein, R.C.A. and Johnson, M.P. (1997) "Strategies of couple conflict," in S. Duck, K. Dindia, B. Ickes, B. Milardo, R. Mills and B. Sarason (eds) *Handbook of personal relationships* (2nd edn), Chichester: Wiley.
Kleivan, H. (1984a) "Contemporary Greenlanders," in D. Damas (ed.) *Handbook of North American Indians*, vol. 5: *Arctic*, Washington: Smithsonian Institution.
Kleivan, I. (1984b) "West Greenland before 1950," in D. Damas (ed.) *Handbook of North American Indians*, vol. 5: *Arctic*, Washington: Smithsonian Institution.
LaPrairie, C. (1987) "Native women and crime: A theoretical model," *The Canadian Journal of Native Studies* 7: 121–137.
Larsen, F.B. (1991) "Interpersonal violence among Greenlandic Inuit: Causes and remedies," in P. Kern and T. Cordtz (eds) *NUNA MED '91: En grønlandsmedicinsk konference*, Nuuk: Nuna Med.
—— (1994) "The quiet life of a revolution: Greenlandic home rule 1979–92," in T. Greiffenberg (ed.) *Sustainability in the Arctic: Proceedings from Nordic Arctic research forum symposium 1993*, Aalborg: Aalborg University Press.
—— (1995) "Voldelige situationer," in P. Kern and P. Bjerregaard (eds) *NUNA MED '94: En grønlandsmedicinsk konference*, Nuuk: Nuna Med.
Lennert, L.S. and Thomsen, M.L. (eds) (1991) *Kvinder i Grønland: Sammen og hver for sig*, Nuuk: Atuakkiorfik.
Lindisfarne, N. (1994) "Variant masculinities, variant virginities: Rethinking 'honour and shame'," in A. Cornwall and N. Lindisfarne (eds) *Dislocating masculinity: Comparative ethnographies*, London and New York: Routledge.
Lutz, C. and White, G.M. (1986) "The anthropology of emotions," *Annual Review of Anthropology* 1: 405–436.
Lynge, I. (1995) "Vold og selvmord i Grønland: Er der en fællesnævner?," in P. Kern and P. Bjerregaard (eds) *NUNA MED '94: En grønlandsmedicinsk konference*, Nuuk: Nuna Med.
McElroy, A. (1975) "Canadian Arctic modernization and change in female Inuit role identification," *American Ethnologist* 2: 662–686.
Moore, H. (1994) "The problem of explaining violence in the social sciences," in P. Harvey and P. Gow (eds) *Sex and violence: Issues in representation and experience*, London and New York: Routledge.
Nuttall, M. (1994) "Greenland: Emergence of an Inuit homeland," in Minority

Rights Group (ed.) *Polar peoples: Self-determination and development*, London: Monority Rights Publications.
Ortner, S.B. (1984) "Theory in anthropology since the sixties," *Comparative Studies in Society and History* 26: 126–166.
Parkin, D. (1985) "Reason, emotion and the embodiment of power," in J. Overing (ed.) *Reason and morality*, London: Tavistock.
Peqqinnissaq (1994) "Vi skal kunne rumme alt det nye," Interview med psykiater Inge Lynge, *Peqqinnissaq* 4: 10, Direktoratet for Sundhed og Miljø, Nuuk.
Rapp, R. (1995) "Heredity, or: Revising the facts of life," in S. Yanagisako and C. Delaney (eds) *Naturalizing power: Essays in feminist cultural analysis*, New York and London: Routledge.
Riches, D. (1986) "The phenomenon of violence," in D. Riches (ed.) *The anthropology of violence*, Oxford: Blackwell.
—— (1990) "The force of tradition in eskimology," in R. Fardon (ed.) *Localizing strategies: Regional traditions of ethnographic writing*, Edinburgh and Washington: Scottish Academic Press and Smithsonian Institution Press.
Solomon, R.C. (1984) "Getting angry: The Jamesian theory of emotion in anthropology," in R.A. Shweder and R.A. LeVine (eds) *Culture theory: Essays on mind, self and emotion*, Cambridge: Cambridge University Press.
Sørensen, B.W. (1990) "Folk models of wife-beating in Nuuk, Greenland," *Folk* 32: 93–115.
—— (1993) "Bevægelser mellem Grønland og Danmark: Etnicitet, følelser og rationalitet i migrationen [Movements between Greenland and Denmark: Ethnicity, emotions and rationality in migration]," *Tidsskriftet Antropologi* 28: 31–46.
—— (1994) *Magt eller afmagt? Køn, følelser og vold i Grønland* [Power or powerlessness? Gender, emotions and violence in Greenland], København: Akademisk Forlag.
—— (1995) "La violence conjugale: Simple symptôme ou geste planifié dans l'ordre social?," *Service Social* 44: 165–180.
—— (1997) "Contested culture: Trifles of importance," in C. Buijs and J. Oosten (eds) *Braving the cold: Continuity and change in Arctic clothing*, Leiden: Research School CNWS.
Stølen, K.A. (1991) "Gender, sexuality and violence in Ecuador," *Ethnos* 56: 82–100.
Strathern, M. (1987) "An awkward relationship: The case of feminism and anthropology," *Signs* 12: 276–292.
—— (1992) *Reproducing the future: Essays on anthropology, kinship and the new reproductive technologies*, Manchester: Manchester University Press.
Thuesen, S.T. (1988) *Fremad, opad: Kampen for en moderne grønlandsk identitet*, København: Rhodos.
Wikan, U. (1991) "Toward an experience-near anthropology," *Cultural Anthropology* 6: 285–305.
World's Women (The) (1995) *Trends and Statistics*, New York: United Nations.

Chapter 9

# Violence without end?

## Some reflections on achievements, contradictions, and perspectives of the feminist movement in Germany

Carol Hagemann-White

*I began college (Radcliffe) with a major in Math and Physics, then switched to Medieval History for my B.A. I went to Germany for graduate study in Philosophy (doctorate at the Free University of Berlin, 1970), then began as teaching assistant in the sociology department there; I got my second post-graduate degree (*habilitation/venia legendi*) in Sociology in Berlin as well. My first professorial position was in political science; I now have a chair in educational theory and women's studies.*

*My first empirical study ever and my first area of feminist "praxis" was the evaluation of the first German shelter for battered women (1977–1980), during which I also spent a year and a half doing counseling and practical support. I have been reinvolved in policy-oriented research close to the feminist projects on violence against women repeatedly since then and am probably one of the three most popular speakers on the topic in Germany. This gives me not only a long-standing interest in the topic, but also a sense of responsibility—I am part of the story I am trying to reflect on. Violence against women, once a radical feminist issue, has entered the mainstream of women's politics in Germany. No area of feminist concern has been so successful in defining both the problem and the mode of social response; with shifting accents the issue has remained in the public eye. Feminist institutionalization has its own problems and contradictions; the short-term nature of shelters and hotlines fails to meet basic claims of the victims on society; there has been a shift from solidarity to individualization. More descriptive analysis of feminist movements in context is needed for comparative study and to understand the dynamic and contradictory nature of these developments.*

*What I want the reader to take home from this chapter is the realization that feminist activism, by changing consciousness and language, also changes reality, although not necessarily in the direction of its own goals and that conceptual frameworks can become a dead end if they don't change as well.*

Violence against women within the family surfaced as a widespread problem through feminist activism. In particular, the first shelters for battered women were demanded and created in the mid-1970s, nearly simultaneously in North America, Europe and Australia, by initiatives emerging from the new women's movement. Throughout, these activities met with similar responses: denial, anger, and ridicule. Women who chose male violence as a defining issue of feminism were perceived, and saw themselves, as radicals. This has changed profoundly, but as of yet we have little analysis of the various "careers" that the topics of physical and sexual violence against women have traversed. Existing comparative studies have been restricted to the English-speaking countries of Canada, the USA, and Great Britain (Dobash and Dobash 1992; Walker 1990). The example of Germany to be examined here is instructive in several ways, both in respect to the significant influence of feminist positions and to their institutionalization and its consequences. The following discussion will trace changes since the early feminist struggles and try to identify what has been achieved and what has been lost relative to those programmatic goals. Limitations of space preclude more than an occasional comparative remark; but as the young feminist rebellion was international in its thinking, so the final sections of this chapter will try to describe elements implicit in the confrontation with violence which may constitute some common ground for the future.

## FROM RADICAL ACTIVISM INTO THE MAINSTREAM

In the German social democratic welfare state of the early 1970s, calling attention to the plight of a disadvantaged group was neither new nor unusual. Yet the feminist way of naming violence against women and proclaiming solidarity with its victims constituted at the time both a clear provocation and a denouncement of existing political, religious, or welfare organizations as implicated in making such violence possible. Looking back it seems that the German women's movement was able to play on the theme of collective guilt with unique effectiveness (the more so because the repetition of the postwar re-education theme was fully unconscious). Yet the rebellious quality of advocacy for victims of violence derived from a deeper contradiction. After all, it would have made political sense in terms of government policy at that time to fund services for women who have the misfortune to be battered or raped, just as other disadvantaged groups were to be reintegrated into the welfare society. Support and services were offered because these groups were seen as less fortunate than the great majority, because their situation was the exception and their suffering seemed unfair. Indeed, it was precisely this logic that persuaded government agencies to finance the first shelters for battered women.

The feminist provocation was its reversal of the relationship of exception and rule. The concept "violence against women" stood for the view that rape and battering are not caused by individual personality or behavior patterns, but are rooted in a patriarchal society. Their violence negates the individuality of the victim and reduces her to the fact of being female and as such violable: it is this that hurts all women in attacking one. Violence against women does not arise on the dark edges of a largely civilized society, but in its center; it does not controvert the norm so much as extend it to its logical consequence.

Over the past twenty years in Germany, the concept of violence against women has moved into the mainstream of public discourse. High-level politicians, administrative officials, union representatives, theologians, or community leaders now use the term—particularly if they are themselves women—without hesitation and discuss the problem not in terms of individual misfortune but of social injustice (Janshen 1991). There is widespread awareness that, in all walks of life, men inflict sexual, emotional, and physical injuries on women, and that society is responsible for offering safety and resources to the women so injured.

The mainstreaming of what had seemed an inherently oppositional concept accentuates what has been, in Germany, a gender division of discourse. And indeed, the publication of private violence has done much to raise the collective political consciousness of women as a group. It is a woman-identified and sensitizing issue which has become publicly acceptable, but to which men rarely speak at all. (The silence even of men deeply opposed to violence corresponds to feminist intimations of collective guilt, an accusation to which there is no defense.) Against this background, a considerable number of activities, projects, centers and networks for women and girls have emerged, and many have gained temporary or permanent public funding. In Germany, with a population of about 81 million, there are now over 375 shelters for battered women. In lesser numbers, we also have a wide variety of other projects: feminist counseling centers, hotlines on sexual violence, publicly subsidized "night taxis" for women's safety, informative television programs. Services and crisis centers for sexually abused girls (or for girls and boys) are becoming more frequent; municipal governments and local newspapers discuss the safety of parking garages and the effects of city planning on women's sense of personal security as serious political issues.

No area of feminist concern has been so dramatically successful, both in defining the problem and in generating acceptance for its approach to intervention: The early feminist projects have put their stamp on the whole field. It is generally agreed that counselors should act as advocates for the victims of violence. Shelters and social work services alike agree that space for women to talk with and receive support from women only is a necessary feature of helping systems; they agree on the central importance of empowering women and girls as well as of stressing the societal causes of sexual and domestic violence and the commonality of victimization. Shelters try to approximate an open-door policy, to protect anonymity, place no administrative limit on the duration of a stay or the number of returns and aim to respect the way a woman handles her life (Brandau *et al.* 1990; Berliner Frauenhaus 1978; Hagemann-White et al 1981; Steinert and Straub 1988).

In 1991, my research group surveyed all of the projects, shelters and counseling agencies in the state of Lower Saxony offering services to women or to children who become victims of battering, rape, sexual abuse, forced prostitution, or other forms of gendered violence. The organizations surveyed varied in their commitment to a general philosophy and in their structure; they included the Catholic and Lutheran church organizations, the "Workers' Welfare" and other traditional social welfare organizations, the Child Protection League and a variety of local feminist and grass-roots groups. Frequently, these organizations have engaged in heated controversy over questions of principle in public debate. However, on the level of actual counseling and crisis support, we found among those who do the work—almost all of them women—considerable agreement in their understanding of violence as well as in their philosophy of services and self-help (Hagemann-White *et al.* 1992). Such a consensus would have seemed quite improbable in earlier years.

There is, of course, controversy and competition between organizations; as in other countries, funding is usually insufficient, often unreliable or discontinuous. Yet it is also true that persistent funding problems are hardly specific to women's projects as such. The relative success of the feminist philosophy in this field raises more fundamental questions. For how should we interpret the broad agreement on women's advocacy and empowerment in confronting male violence? Does it imply that such violence is a permanent feature of society? Are shelters accepted like safety belts, a means of limiting the extent of damages, needed because not even the most circumspect driver can be certain of avoiding a car crash? Battering, we would have to conclude—as our grandmothers did—is just one more thing that can happen to women if they live with men; therefore we need hotlines, shelters, and social services for women because that is what men are like. To demand supervision and better lighting of dark city corners and garages, taxis, and escort services at night defines as an inalterable fact of life that, when men get an opportunity to rape, they will use it. The implication of all these activities and services is that naming the violence has unwittingly normalized it. Yet the goal of the movement was quite different: to put an end to men's violence and victimization of women.

## WHAT HAS CHANGED AND HOW?

In retrospect, the most striking fact is that the issue of violence against women has been kept on the political agenda, in one form or another, for nearly twenty years. Given the general tendency of public interest in emotionally charged issues to exhaust itself, this is really quite remarkable. There has been a price, of course: public concern has been reawakened again and again by shifting media attention to other forms of violence, new victims, new types of abuse, often before sufficient services for the previous group could be established. These shifts create the illusion that each new wave of attention discovers something terrible that had been hidden, kept secret, silenced until just now. And this is indeed true for each individual woman, each adolescent or child who finally speaks out. Nonetheless, the revelation is not really "news" to those working in the field and often all too familiar. The feminist movement has been a reluctant participant in sensational journalism, but has kept the issue on the table.

The second major accomplishment is conceptual and it was so rapid and complete that it is easy to lose sight of its importance. A glance back at the literature before 1970 illuminates what has changed. It is not strictly true that gender-related and sexual violence were non-existent for social services, the law, psychology, or sociology. It is rather that violent acts were perceived as part of a problem with another name and melted into that background. Thus, when men beat their wives, this was but one example of marital conflict, or perhaps one aspect of family breakdown, alongside alcoholism, child neglect, and divorce; and indeed the term "violent couple" could suppress entirely the question of who beat whom. Rape turned up as a particularly piquant form of aberrant sexuality, or as a special case of deviant or criminal behavior, inviting comparison between different types of criminals. Sexual abuse of children lurked under the surface of discussions of incest, whose traditional concern seems to have been what keeps adolescent sons from possessing their mothers, with a—not incidental—tendency to ignore both issues of age and issues of consent altogether. Different as they were, in each context the act of violence remained diffuse, because it was not, in itself, conceptualized as the problem. This has changed profoundly, resulting at least in Germany in a genuinely new consciousness of gendered violence as problematic, which might be called a reversal of figure and ground. Political and academic discussions today usually presuppose a clear distinction between the prior situation, whatever its tensions and difficulties and the eruption of masculine violence. One sign of this change in focus is the virtual disappearance of questions that used to be typical, epitomized in the classic "What did she do to provoke him?" (still implied in Gayford 1983). They have been replaced by questions pointing to violence as morally unacceptable: "Why do men resort to violence?" And although its implications are debatable, even the question "Why does she stay?" (Gelles 1976; cf. Okun 1988) implies a perception of violence as crossing a vital line.

The focus on violence as a distinct problem has its correlate in the conceptual frameworks referred to. Neither sweeping theories of patriarchal domination by threat of rape and battering (Brownmiller 1975), nor the concept of structural violence more popular in European feminism (Frauenhaus Köln 1980) has proved a lasting orientation for practical and political work with women who have been attacked and violated. Although these theories have proved enlightening on symbolic and historical interconnections, they also tend to obscure the difference between social pressure and physical injury, between watching television and being raped, between being discouraged from looking for a job and being battered if you try. In pointing out the ways in which all women are affected by the underpinnings of violence in male domination/hegemony, they implicitly place all women in the role of a victim from birth and convict all men of collaboration by virtue of their masculinity.

For practical work against violence and in support of women, it has been vital to separate violence from its background in traditions, customs, socialization, personality, or the unconscious, and to perceive it as an action or series of actions chosen by an individual who could have chosen otherwise and who can be held accountable for committing it. Only a concept of violence as "action" provides a framework in which to name and describe the injury resulting to each specific woman from what specific men have done to her. Implied in this approach is some degree of responsibility of others—including the woman herself—for their own actions in the face of violence and its repetition.

Although violent acts must be interpreted in context, they must also be named as they are felt, as violations—of the body, the will, the sense of self. To do so presumes the (potential) ability of each woman (and each child) to delineate her personal boundaries and to reclaim them; only from this premise can it make sense to expect that men learn non-violent ways of interacting with women. Such a demand requires seeing batterers or rapists as actors and thereby insisting that whatever the pressures, conflicts and aggressive feelings behind it, an act of physical or sexual violence is chosen in the face of alternatives.

Especially during the past ten years, a common understanding of the interrelated forms of sexual violence and battering has crystallized. The triad of masculinity, sexuality, and physical injury characterizes a "continuum of violence" (Kelly 1988) which affects different victims in different ways (Hagemann-White *et al.* 1992). The phrase "violence against women," while still widely used, has come to seem inadequate; as awareness has grown that children of both sexes are sexually abused.

And very similar patterns of violence emerge between men as well, for example in prison, where men suspected of homosexuality, or considered weak or inferior, are raped and thereby degraded to being "women" for the dominant men.

We are confronting a web in which heterosexuality is interwoven with violence. Within it, the role of physical damage is more subtle than was initially realized. In the early stages of the movement, violation of women's bodies was theorized as making patriarchal domination in all of its other forms possible (Brownmiller 1975). Bodily injury and forced penetration, actual or potential, were placed at the center of public discussion: shelters and hotlines documented the brutality of abuse as proof of women's oppression as well as of the need for services. With increasing knowledge about the various forms of violence an awareness has grown that sexual abuse may not require threats of other violence: children can be exploited with the aid of their trust and adult authority and abuse can occur without medically identifiable injury and without even touching the child's body. Sexual harassment on the job does not have to draw on physical intimidation: economic power is effective as well.

Yet although looks and words can violate sexually just as they can humiliate and batter, injury to the body is still central to the concept of gendered violence. On the one hand, the body is the home of the sexual self that is violated, if only by exposure to pornographic images and thought; and it is often the body's ability to experience release—in love or sleep—that is permanently crippled by violent heterosexual acts. And on the other hand, physical battering, although it primarily tends to bruise and break, is predicated on the assumption of a continuing sexual relationship, or intended to enforce one. These interconnections explain why the emerging consciousness of a continuum of violence as society's problem has developed cumulatively, rather than being fragmented by the multiple issues that have been brought to the fore.

## SUCCESSIVE WAVES OF AWARENESS

The broadened awareness emerged in successive waves of public discourse on violence. In Germany, the first issue in this discussion was battering. Galvanized by the International Tribunal on Crimes Against Women in Brussels in 1974, feminist activists fought for and gained funding for shelters in Berlin and Cologne. Both the controversy surrounding their woman-centered philosophy and the publicity that these shelters (and initiatives in other towns) gave to the facts of woman-battering contributed to spreading awareness of domestic violence as a major social problem.

Rape hotlines, on the other hand, remained volunteer projects working from the self-financed "women's centers" in which consciousness-raising and activist groups of the new women's movement met. The hotline groups were less willing to involve themselves in state funding with its bureaucratic procedures and social work implications, and were also less successful in gaining the political impact necessary to be funded. In the decade that followed, sexual harassment at work and rape in marriage emerged as issues of public debate, although in both cases the results in terms of policy or services were meager.

More recently concern and outrage have been generated on sexual abuse of children, and especially of girls. On this issue, a highly active, often passionate and clearly practical grass-roots movement has emerged. As in the shelter movement of the 1970s, women's groups and feminist projects were pivotal in the beginning, yet very soon a strong involvement of social workers, child care and school teachers and women in related professions became visible. The demand for information and professional training outstrips that for immediate services and intervention. This reverses the pattern of the emerging shelter movement, when the majority of social work professionals hesitated to accept the new approach, while hundreds of battered women were seeking safety and help. The kinds of projects arising in the 1990s are, as a consequence, more varied, while the shelters have tended to adhere to a widely shared concept whose basic tenets are seldom debated publicly.

Sexual violence to children seems to mobilize a unique potential for outrage and pressure for action. The realization that it often continues for years in seemingly "normal" families is a shock and the response is usually a call for active intervention. The reverse side of the medal is, of course, that girls (or boys) still encounter disbelief, precisely because recognition of sexual violence demands involvement or action. Thus, the issue itself is experienced at a high level of emotional turmoil. The tension is exacerbated by court cases in which the intervention of professionals or of feminist projects has been contested, with considerable publicity and issues of suggestive questioning or overinterpretation raised. For some writers, the discussion of sexual violence to children seems to have been the final straw: largely silent during the early phases of the debate on sexual violence, they are now very vocal in suggesting that feminist activists exaggerate the incidence of sexual abuse and are motivated by denial and repression of children's sexuality (Rutschky and Wolff 1994). This first real backlash to the movement against violence against women is fairly recent and certainly less influential than its counterpart in the USA; it is too early to say whether it prefigures a broader change of sentiment. However, there are signs of increasing hesitancy toward intervention among teachers, social workers, child carers, and the concerned public in general.

In the main, the pattern of recurring waves of concern for "new" aspects of gendered violence seems to continue: The trade in women from Third World countries and from Eastern Europe has received more attention, and more recently, "ethnic" rape in the wars in former Yugoslavia moved to center stage. At the same time, the issue of domestic sexual violence to girls proved critical in another way, as a crystallization point for the growth of feminist and public consciousness. Battered women's shelters and rape hotline groups increasingly began to deal with women's past experience of sexual violence in childhood and youth. Working with and learning to understand sexually abused girls (or boys) also tends to awaken in both feminist activists and social work or teaching professionals (primarily women) submerged memories of their own past experiences of sexual domination or violence. The result of this crystallization seems to be a desire to move beyond creating shelters and supportive agencies for each separate form of violence and beyond caring for the victims while ignoring the perpetrators (Hagemann-White *et al.* 1992). There has been a growing sense of impatience among shelter workers at the prospect of generations of refugees from domestic violence; increasingly, the question is being asked "Why should the victims—rather than the assailants—be expected to leave?" (Hoff 1990). At the same time, this proves a frightening question for some of those heavily invested in shelter work, who doubt profoundly that any other approach could be reconciled with advocacy for women. Apprehensive of possible shifts in the flow of scant funds, some of the feminist shelters have become entrenched opponents of any new approach.

At present, society offers assistance—if at all—in escaping from immediate threat. This is vital: providing personal safety in a crisis can interrupt the ongoing, seemingly inescapable violence and the woman, girl, or boy can at least realize the possibility of having choices and perhaps begin to act. Yet the reality of only temporary shelter, the emphasis on hotlines and self-help, feminist taboos on any notion of deficiency in the victims which could be construed as a fault, also contain messages to the victim: that she ought to be able to pick up the pieces and begin to function as soon as the violence ceases; and that, not being at fault, she could not have suffered lasting damage. These implicit messages are very close to the line beyond which the real impact of violence disappears from view. When the effects cannot be ignored, when women are not able to "function" after rape or battering, psychological counseling may be considered. This is a foreshortening of intimate violence, viewing it from the demands it makes on coping ability. In fact, there is both a specific element of trauma involved due to the intimacy of the violation, as well as an element of betrayal of social trust: the former tends to be underestimated and the latter overseen in short-term women's advocacy counseling.

## WHAT HAS BEEN FORGOTTEN AND HOW DID IT HAPPEN?

Victims of gendered violence—and similarly, of racist violence—have not one, but two fundamental claims on a humane society. The claim to assistance in seeking personal safety, in escaping violence and starting anew is one. The other is a claim to justice, to some kind of confirmation of a moral community which stigmatizes the violence and not its victim.

Recognition of these basic claims is not to be confused with a naive belief in their present reality. Neither one nor the other can be guaranteed for any woman, whether in a shelter or outside it, as long as violence against women permeates society. No promise of safety or of secure community can be made; the task at hand is rather to articulate these claims as legitimate and to create safe spaces and symbolic events which have experiential validity in expressing a concrete vision.

In the course of institutionalization, the German feminist movement against violence to women has increasingly emphasized individual change and independence, separation from the violent man, and building economic and social self-sufficiency. This push toward individualization is no longer in balance with the perspective of solidarity, whose central expression in the early stages of the movement was the word "we." Solidarity is a political concept, not to be conflated with empathy; its referent is a community, not the individual. It was implicit in the work of groups and projects of the women's movement, whose political energy derived both from shared pain and from a vision of community. Workers in projects have often felt disappointed, even betrayed by women who, as victims of physical violence, remained reluctant to break with norms and leave familiar ways, who despite counseling returned to a batterer and to a violent home. Yet these women, in their own context, also expressed what may be the same need for continuity and community that moved feminists to take up their work. Less able to make a public statement, they may withdraw from counseling after receiving the individualist message: "Take care of yourself, find your own life." Safety, support and the healing of injuries rarely succeed in isolation; they presuppose an experience of belonging and of being able to turn to others. Concepts of individual autonomy, emotional self-sufficiency, self-fulfillment, and free choice of roles and relationships cannot address the deep need to restore trust in a dependable, nonthreatening community. Violence in intimate relationships may, of all experiences, be the one most apt to mobilize this need.

Given the relative success of an activist feminist approach to the issue of violence in Germany, an explanation is called for: How could the dimension of solidarity, so central to the early feminist movement, be gradually muted and replaced by an emphasis on validating women's individuality? The answer may lie in the ways in which ideas were woven with practices. In the German women's movement, the idea of solidarity was closely tied to the vision of an autonomous women's culture. Rediscovering matriarchy, learning to print and circulate our own literature, our own music, creating bookstores, art galleries, retreats and courses of study exclusively for women and celebrating women's parties—these were closely interrelated with the work against violence. The answer to patriarchal violent domination was sought in creating autonomous space for women and a counter-culture with new images and values.

Yet the implementation of shelters, hotlines, and counseling brought activists into close contact with the most brutal and intimidating forms of male sexism and violence. The sheer number of victims and the devastating extent of their suffering was usually a shock, even for feminists theoretically convinced of a violence-ridden patriarchy. Many shelter workers found themselves having nightmares as a consequence of meeting an unbroken stream of women, each with a life history of pain, but also due to the constant threat of batterers' attacks on the shelter and the indifference of authorities to the threats on women's lives. Moreover, the women seeking escape and support had no lasting interest in creating a counter-culture of women. The work left little time or energy for imagining, much less creating, an alternative cultural reality.

Meanwhile, the day-to-day work in shelters had to become dominated by counseling and practical social work: helping women through dozens of bureaucratic procedures, collecting belongings with police protection if possible, looking for housing, handling changes of schools and day care. The shelter worker was most frequently involved when a woman was not able to deal with one of these problems herself, when mutual aid did not suffice and professional skills became relevant. As a result, feminist activists were seeing the victims of violence primarily in the light of what they could not do on their own. Thus, practical work with victimized women frequently involved a subtle temptation to develop rescue fantasies and a tendency to alternate between idealization and disappointment (Brückner 1983). Beginning in the early 1980s, influential literature and informal discussions in the shelter movement focused increasingly on the ways in which societal as well as personal ideals of femininity and motherhood predispose women to accept male violence and to cast themselves as rescuers.

The political framework of feminist activism included a conscious decision to work with women as their advocates; this was based both on conviction of the need for a counter-weight to the support and sympathy that men find in most of society, as well as on a conviction of the commonality of women's oppression. Yet in the daily work of shelters and related projects, the violence hung like lead weights on our feet and effectively hindered flights of creative cultural change: in these circumstances, to work solely with the women and their experience of violence directed all energy toward changing the woman's involvement in her own victimization. In the activist literature there is increasing discussion of what keeps women from leaving a violent man; why mothers do not act more energetically to protect their daughters from sexual abuse; why women so frequently return to a batterer after staying in a shelter and even after finding new housing and a new job; why indeed women marry men whom they know to be violent in the first place. In the theories that emerged during these discussions, violence increasingly took the shape of a relationship problem.

In actual fact, networks, projects, and agencies are most developed and effective for victims of family violence, or of violence within the context of a personal intimate relationship. Women, girls, and boys are helped to escape further injury, usually by giving up their homes, their neighborhood, their schools, and many of their personal possessions. Counseling serves to loosen the emotional and practical bonds holding the victim to the violent relationship. And, indeed, this is what professionals in social work and psychology have learned to do well. Thus the "success" of the feminist approach also facilitated a professionalization process in the political movement against violence against women and within its projects.

In emphasizing breaking away and starting anew, this approach tends to play down the violence itself, after going through a first cathartic speaking-out, because the perspective of individualization has few resources for coming to terms with crippling injury and lasting pain, particularly in a country in which psychotherapy is not widely popular. Furthermore, the approach is scarcely helpful in dealing with types of masculine violence that do not rest on an intimate relationship or on emotional dependency of the victim. The global traffic in women—for marriage or prostitution—, or rape of street prostitutes, for example, does not call for a more independent individual able to leave an unhappy relationship, nor does this apply to stranger and near-stranger rape or to the pornography trade. The emphasis on understanding and supporting women in conjunction with the gradual professionalization of feminist projects has led to a one-sided cultivation of "separation skills."

While the support of individualization has been, and remains, helpful in addressing the traps in the traditional female role, in de-legitimizing male domination and possession of women, the concept of solidarity seems more useful for confronting the violence itself. Both for the feminist activists, with their high risk of burnout and for the women facing years of violence with their high risk of resignation and return, it seems vital to experience some signs of hope that an end of the violence is conceivable and the hurt and damage may heal. Healing, wholeness, is not really an individual process.

This may be the fundamental reason why women working in the field increasingly articulate a demand for change in the response of the legal system—which in Germany has only recently gained impetus as a political issue. Throughout the 1980s, feminist activists were largely skeptical of legal intervention, accepting the state only as administrator of public moneys. Although it soon became evident that shelters and safe places for women are not enough, the movement was slow to engage with the idea that violent men be called to account, made to answer for their actions and that the issue is not primarily to see assailants and abusers punished but to restore to women some sense of a (potential) community which could reject abuse unconditionally. With much soul-searching and controversy, the law is being recognized as one possible vehicle of a symbolic community in this sense: a far from perfect vehicle, no doubt, but better than none.

## RE-CREATING A VISION

The philosophy of the shelter movement implied two profound convictions. One was the belief that violence did not arise out of special characteristics of the victims or the assailants, but out of the structure of patriarchal society; therefore all women are threatened and hurt by every incidence of sexist violence, because all women are potentially victims. It could happen to any woman at any time. The second conviction, equal in importance and expressed in the vast energy invested into shelter work as well as in the organization of the shelters, was that, here and now, women do have the option of not living in a violent relationship and do not have to resign themselves to being victimized. Activists could not have done their work without this second conviction.

These two convictions are not, perhaps, the contradiction they may seem. To focus clearly on violence as, itself, the problem, one must have a concept of nonviolence. And if the critique of violence was not directed to individuals, neither could the idea of nonviolence. Implied in feminist activism, albeit unrecognized, was the vision of a community of women and men in which violence is to be neither expected nor tolerated.

Naming the violence patriarchal, thus a problem of society and not of individuals, framed the issue as the social permission accorded men, their privilege and liberty to exercise violence and to grasp sexual satisfaction against the will of women. The critique pointed to society's failure to make men accountable for such violent acts as they may—from whatever motives—choose to carry out, as long as the victim is a "legitimate target": "his" woman, an "available" woman, in fact any woman, since the success of the attempt can be tantamount to proof of her guilt.

This critique makes sense only against the backdrop of moral standards for a society in which common decency and respect between women and men would be the norm.

Looking too closely at women's entrapment into violence has led into a morass in which issues of the quality of individual relationships are confounded with issues of the moral quality of a community. This has crippled both discourses, that on gendered violence and that on the ways women and men can shape close relationships, on relearning affection and friendship and reinventing love. German feminism has not found a way to articulate women's advocacy and women's identification with love of, and respect for, other women while opening this view to include a positive, active role of men, and the vision of a nonsexist, nonviolent community that could be anticipated in our words and actions today. Projects in which men confront male violence are alternately lionized and attacked as a threat to feminism: what would it be like to treat them as self-evident, as if there ought to be hundreds of them? Critiques of the legal system and its treatment of violence against women tend to end with feminist "closure," demonstrating that nothing better was to be expected: what would it mean to take shelters as the starting point for presenting to the public, again and again, a clear and present political expectation that violence be treated as a punishable offense—that rapists, batterers, and sexual abusers be made responsible for their actions and that they, rather than the victims, suffer the consequences?

A certain constitutional pessimism is associated with the strong tradition of critical social theory in Germany (and its very weak tradition of social change from the bottom up), which no doubt have influenced feminism as well. There seems to be a sense of powerlessness behind the hesitation to express, or even to form, expectations that the community might sanction violence in earnest. It is underscored by reluctance to be placed in the position of moralizing. Both have some roots in German history, but they also relate profoundly to the cultural construction of the female as inferior, since women have carried the burden of community and morality in the most difficult of times, while being ridiculed for doing so. There could be no more appropriate issue than violence against women to reverse these values, but perhaps for this very reason it continues to be difficult.

The paradox of mainstreaming reaches beyond the issue of violence and seems inherent to feminist movements in a modern society. Feminism gains social and political legitimacy when issues resonate with a broader public, yet each "success" generates ambivalence among those closest to the realities of the problem and their typical response of emphasizing patriarchal oppression may end in confirming what the movement intended to change. The dynamic potential of such developments is often all but invisible to the activists in concrete locations: in this respect, interaction of research and practical work can prove valuable for both sides.

A closer look at what has happened to the concrete issue of violence may also tell us a great deal about the commonalities and differences between cultures and societies. For example, there may indeed be the affinity that Gillian Walker (1990) suggests between a radical feminist definition of the problem as "violence against women" (as opposed to "family violence") and a preference for criminal justice intervention strategies. Yet the German historical–cultural background has (understandably) led feminists to avoid such cooperation. Conversely, the popularity of a therapeutic approach in the USA may not be attributable to the definition of the problem as much as to the powerful American tradition of individual solutions to socially produced problems (Dobash and Dobash 1992). These interactions point to the need for more concrete descriptive analysis of specified movements and their contradictions.

## BIBLIOGRAPHY

Berliner Frauenhaus für mißhandelte Frauen (1978) *Frauen gegen Männergewalt*, Berlin: Frauenselbstverlag.

Brandau, H., Hagemann-White, C., Haep, M. and Del Mestre, A. (1990) *Wege aus Mißhandlungsbeziehungen: Unterstützung für Frauen und ihre Kinder vor und nach dem Aufenthalt im Frauenhaus*, Pfaffenweiler: Centaurus.

Brownmiller, S. (1975) *Against our will: Men, women and rape*, Toronto, New York and London.

Brückner, M. (1983) *Die Liebe der Frauen: Über Weiblichkeit und Mißhandlung*, Frankfurt am Main: Verlag Neue Kritik.

Buzawa, E.S. and Buzawa, C.G. (1990) *Domestic violence: The criminal justice response*, Newbury Park, London and New Delhi: Sage.

Dobash, R.E. and Dobash, R.P. (1992) *Women, violence and social change*, London and New York: Routledge.

Frauenhaus Köln (1980) *Nachrichten aus dem Ghetto Liebe: Gewalt gegen Frauen, Ursachen, Auswirkungen, Bewältigungsstrategien*, Frankfurt am Main: Verlag Jugend und Politik.

Gayford, J.J. (1983) "Battered wives," in R.J. Gelles and C.P. Cornell (eds) *International perspectives on family violence*, Lexington and Toronto: D.C.Heath.

Gelles, R.J. (1976) "Abused wives: Why do they stay?," *Journal of Marriage and the Family* 38: 659–668.

Hagemann-White, C., Kavemann, B., Kootz, J., Weinmann, U., Wildt, C.C., Burgard, R. and Scheu, U. (1981) *Hilfen fur mißhandelte Frauen: Abschlußbericht der wissenschaftlichen Begleitung des Modellprojekts Frauenhaus Berlin* (Schriftenreihe des Bundesministers für Jugend, Familie und Gesundheit 124), Stuttgart, Berlin, Koln and Mainz: Kohlhammer.

Hagemann-White, C. with Lang, H., Lübbert, J. and Rennefeld, B. (1992) *Strategien gegen Gewalt im Geschlechterverhältnis: Bestandsanalyse und Perspektiven*, Forschungsberichte des BIS 4, Pfaffenweiler: Centaurus.

Hoff, L.A. (1990) *Battered women as survivors*, London, New York: Routledge.

Janshen, D. (ed.) (1991) *Sexuelle Gewalt: Die alltägliche Menschenrechtsverletzung*, Frankfurt am Main: Zweitausendeins.

Kelly, L. (1988) *Surviving sexual violence*, Minneapolis: University of Minnesota.
Loseke, D.R. (1992) *The battered woman and shelters: The social construction of wife abuse*, Albany: State University of New York.
Okun, L. (1988) "Termination or resumption of cohabitation in woman battering relationships: A statistical study," in G. Hotaling, D. Finkelhor, J.T. Kirkpatrick and M.A. Straus (eds) *Coping with family violence: Research and policy perspectives*, Beverly Hills, London and New Delhi: Sage
Rutschky, K. and Wolff, R. (ed.) (1994) *Handbuch sexueller Mißbrauch*, Hamburg: Ingrid Klein.
Steinert, E. and Straub, U. (1988) *Interaktionsort Frauenhaus: Möglichkeiten und Grenzen eines feministischen Projekts*, Heidelberg: Wunderhorn.
Walker, G.A. (1990) *Family violence and the women's movement: The conceptual politics of struggle*, Toronto, Buffalo and London: University of Toronto.

# Part IV

# Commentaries

# Chapter 10

# Family violence

## Leonardo, roots, rose-colored glasses, and other observations

Frank D. Fincham

Frank Fincham received his academic training in developmental psychology at the University of Witwatersrand (South Africa), in social psychology at the University of Oxford (UK), and in clinical psychology at the State University of New York at Stony Brook (USA).

*I have a research program on conflict and cognition in marriage and one on the impact of interparental conflict on children. My point in this chapter*[1] *is that no discipline or research perspective can provide a complete understanding of family violence and that theoretical analysis is critical to advancing empirical work on this topic.*

"In the temple of Science are many mansions."

(Albert Einstein)[2]

The professional response to family violence is diverse, reflecting not only the complexity of the phenomena studied but also a variety of established and emerging traditions in the social sciences. This volume not only offers a slice of this diversity but also extends its boundaries. Faced by such diversity it is easy to feel overwhelmed. The purpose of this commentary is to offer an alternative response and, in doing so, to highlight some of the challenges the volume poses for understanding family violence.

## ABANDONING LEONARDESQUE ASPIRATIONS

No discipline or research perspective can provide a complete understanding of family violence. One response to this circumstance is for scholars to aspire to become modern-day Leonardos competent in more than one discipline. In an incisive analysis of interdisciplinary research, Campbell (1969: 328) warns against such "Leonardesque" aspirations, reminding us that knowledge is a collective social product best realized through "a continuous texture of narrow specialties which overlap with other narrow specialties." Accordingly, the goal of the individual researcher should be to enrich his or her narrow specialty rather than to aspire to competence across disciplines.

From this perspective, the heterogeneity represented in the present volume is but a sample from the "texture of narrow specialties" that defines the field of family violence and poses the question of how each contribution might enrich our own unique perspective. By keeping their chapters remarkably jargon free, the contributors have aided in the accessibility and potential usefulness of their analyses. It is inevitable that as we move from overlapping to nonoverlapping perspectives and specializations, direct translation of ideas across disciplinary and subdisciplinary boundaries may prove difficult and in some cases impossible. However, the intellectual benefit of looking beyond the boundaries of our particular perspective can be profound.

## RETURNING TO ROOTS: PARTICULARS VERSUS UNIVERSALS

Although research on spouse abuse and shelters for battered women in Europe predate their counterparts in North America (Pagelow 1984), the literature on family violence has been dominated by studies conducted in the USA. This volume provides a timely reminder to professionals that family violence is not an "American" phenomenon. At the same time, it challenges us to examine whether we can extend the findings of North American researchers to the European context.

The analysis of philotimo in Greek family conflict and the importance of historically based master narratives for understanding wife beating in Greenland, to pick only two striking examples in this book, alert us to the importance of culturally specific factors in researching family violence. At the same time, the study of coercive interactions in Spanish families builds on and extends the important work of Patterson, Wahler and colleagues with North American families. Such juxtapositions challenge us to examine whether there are factors underlying culturally specific aspects of family violence that have universal application.

In the case of the Greek and Greenland examples it is relatively easy to translate the content of the explanations offered into a few underlying causal attribution dimensions (e.g. causal locus, stability) that appear to have universal application. For these examples the exercise is post hoc and therefore a product of scholarly analysis. However, it need not necessarily be so as such dimensions can also be identified by respondents themselves when data are collected—both analytic methods are appropriate and need not yield the same information to be useful. Can other analyses offered in this volume similarly be translated into more universal terms?

Whatever the answer to the above question, the present volume also serves the important function of reminding us about a natural laboratory, Europe. For example, the status of family violence in post-communist Poland contrasts with that found in some Western European countries and provides fertile ground for exploring the emergence of such awareness in understanding and addressing the problem of family violence. Similarly, the social forces in Germany that have influenced the feminist movement are different to those in countries such as Britain, and comparative analyses have the potential to illuminate societal factors important for understanding family violence and societal responses to it. If nothing else, this volume challenges us to consider the implications that cultural and national factors have for the phenomena studied and for our research.

## VIOLENCE IS NOT VIOLENCE IS NOT VIOLENCE

Few researchers dispute that family violence is a widespread problem. However, consensus quickly breaks down around the issue of how widespread it is. One reason for this is that the word "violence" has different referents for different scholars. Some prefer to restrict the term to severe acts of physical aggression to emphasize, in part, the urgent need to respond to the problem of family violence. Others adopt a broader definition that includes any act of physical aggression between family members. Some analyses of family violence, like the present volume, also include discussion of nonphysical conflicts between family members.

The goal in drawing attention to the various referents for "family violence" is not to identify which is most appropriate but rather to emphasize the variety of phenomena referred to by this single term. All the phenomena are relevant to understanding the perpetration of harm among family members. For example, among spouses psychological aggression often precedes physical aggression (Murphy and O'Leary 1989) and low levels of physical aggression typically precede more severe ones (O'Leary and Jacobson, forthcoming). However, whether it is optimal to use the same term to refer to these related phenomena is open to question: this variety increases the potential for confusion, especially when the referent for the term is not clear or when statements made about one referent are generalized inappropriately to another.

Although seemingly terminological, the challenge is a conceptual one. How is the core construct of family violence (and allied constructs) to be defined? Is violence simply a more extreme form of aggression or is it qualitatively different? And if there is consensus on a core construct (or set of constructs) what theory will we use to translate the construct into measurement operations? Can a single construct be applied equally well to what happens between parent and child, adult children and elderly parents, child siblings, and spouses? Alternatively, do we need a family of related constructs for what is currently captured under the umbrella of family violence? Although one could argue whether these are the best questions to ask, there is little doubt that fundamental questions like them need to be addressed. Even erroneous, but clear, answers can further our understanding, for knowledge is advanced more by error than by confusion.

## IS THERE A PLACE FOR ROSE-COLORED GLASSES?

The inclusion of so many phenomena under the umbrella of family violence gives rise to a further, but easily avoided, problem. Few would dispute that severe physical aggression in families represents the darker side of human existence. It is difficult, if not impossible, to view physical harm done to children, elderly parents, or a spouse by a family member through anything other than dark glasses. But not all the phenomena included in this volume represent pathology.

In his chapter on family conflict in France, Le Gall draws on Simmel's work to remind us that conflict is a form of socialization. And, one must hasten to add, socialization experiences can result in adaptive or maladaptive outcomes. Too often we view conflict as negative, if not pathological. Yet conflict is normative in families. Children learn how to deal with divergent, incompatible interests through observation of conflict among family members and through their own direct involvement in such conflict. Many, if not most, learn adaptive conflict resolution skills. Family conflict can be a powerful, positive force as well as a destructive, negative one. What makes the difference?

Some of the variability in child outcome is governed by the parameters of the conflict (e.g. intensity, lack of resolution) and there is some evidence to support the intergenerational transmission of family violence (see Cummings and Davies 1994). However, not all children exposed to destructive forms of family conflict and violence grow up to be violent. Scholars of family violence might profit from adopting the perspective of developmental psychopathology, an interdisciplinary endeavour in which the study of adaptive functioning is viewed as integral to understanding maladaptive functioning (Cicchetti and Cohen 1995). The interest in mechanisms and processes that moderate the outcome of risk lends itself well to the study of family violence.

Conceptualizing conflict as a potentially healthy process also allows us to gain a fresh perspective on the diversity of contributions to this volume. In research, as in society, it is often through the conflict of differing perspectives that fresh, more useful approaches to problems emerge (Pruitt and Rubin 1986).

## THE UBIQUITOUS PROBLEM OF LEVELS OF ANALYSIS

Also closely allied to concerns about the construct of family violence is the level of analysis. This can be applied to the unit analyzed and the level of explanation offered.

### Unit of analysis

Most research on family violence has focused on dyads, usually the marital dyad or the parent–child dyad. However, as the analysis of conflict in French and Greek families reminds us, conflict occurs in larger units than dyads that can include extended family members. As one moves from dyadic to triadic and larger units of analysis, it behoves one to recognize properties that emerge at different levels of analytic unit. For example, coalitions between individuals may be an important element of understanding violence within triadic or larger units, an element that, by definition, cannot enter into the study of violence in dyads. Again, it is important to be clear about the analytic unit referred to in any statement about family violence.

### Level of explanation

As indicated above, some levels of explanation may be unique to the analytic unit studied. However, a more complete understanding of family violence is likely to entail various levels of explanation. Bronfenbrenner's (1979) ecological model has recently been used to summarize explanations for family violence (e.g. Belsky 1993; Emery and Billings, forthcoming). It identifies four levels of analysis, individual characteristics (e.g. personality factors, age, alcohol problems), the immediate context (existence of stressors, family size), the broader ecological context (e.g. social isolation versus support, availability of services, poverty) and the societal or cultural context (e.g. beliefs about violence, family privacy). One level of explanation (e.g. cultural) does not preclude any other (e.g. individual), nor is it reducible to another. While the study of each is important, it is the interplay among them that is likely to prove critical and which, as the present volume shows, is most in need of attention.

## "TELLING MORE THAN WE CAN KNOW"

Another issue in need of further attention is emphasized by perhaps the most consistent theme in this volume, namely, individual and collective understanding and explanation of family conflict and violence. This is an important topic and the chapter on British women's accounts of family stress and conflict in their lives demonstrates the kind of rich insights that can be gained from such analysis. It is hard to imagine that such understanding is irrelevant to how individuals and groups respond to family conflict and violence. It is equally difficult to imagine that such understanding is all, or perhaps even mainly, what determines behavior.

In an influential paper whose title comprises the subheading of this section, Nisbett and Wilson (1977) initiated a line of research that documents the limits of our understanding of what determines how we feel and behave. To be sure, we have strong, and often elaborate, views of why we feel and behave as we do but these views are not always accurate. It seems quite likely that in the heated context of family conflict and violence people act "mindlessly" and exhibit overlearned behaviors. Indeed, Cerezo (this volume), citing Crittenden, notes that the mental models built up through attachment experiences and the patterns of behavior to which they give rise, are not assumed to be consciously available to the individual. If this is the case, then the understanding and accounts given for conflict and violence must, in part, represent post hoc constructions that draw upon cultural knowledge of how people react to and deal with such situations. In this case, they may tell us more about cultural knowledge or social representations than individual functioning. As stated, such cultural knowledge is undoubtedly one factor that influences individual functioning but it is not the only one.

Research on family violence has ignored the role of cognitive processing that occurs outside of conscious awareness. In this respect it is not much different from the broader field of personal relationships within which it can be situated. However, there is research emerging in this broader field that illustrates the value of exploring nonconscious processes. For example, Fincham *et al.* (1997) have shown that the ease with which spouses make evaluative judgements of the partner (measured in milliseconds) moderates the stability of their marital satisfaction over 6-month, 12-month and 18-month periods; spouses who are quicker in making such judgements (whose evaluations are "chronically primed" or whose attitude to the partner is highly "accessible" and activated in the presence of the partner) apparently are less open to new data about the partner and hence have more stable levels of marital satisfaction over time.

## RESEARCH, ACTION AND ACTION-RESEARCH

Some of the statements made in the prior section about the "mindless" or nonconscious antecedents of behavior may be disturbing to some readers, especially those whose approach to family violence is action oriented. Such an approach has considerable precedent in this field. Indeed, the field would not have come into being when it did were it not for the efforts of activists like Erin Pizzey who helped raise public consciousness about spouse abuse in Britain and establish in 1971 one of the first shelters for battered women. Up until this time, mental health professionals were conspicuous by their absence and did little to address the problem of spouse abuse or even alert the public to its existence. Fortunately, activists, many of whom identify themselves as feminists, continue the important work started by people like Pizzey.

A critical axiom among activists is that there is no excuse for family violence and that perpetrators must be held responsible for their actions. This essential element to addressing the problem of family violence does not, however, necessitate that the origin of such violence must always rest in mindful, conscious cognitive processes. To believe that the causes and treatments of a problem must reflect the same underlying factor is a logical error; depression that has an underlying biological cause can be treated successfully with cognitive therapy and depression rooted in social causes can be treated successfully with antidepressant medication.

There is no contradiction in holding people fully responsible for their behavior even if it reflects the operation of nonconscious cognitive processes. Awareness, intentionality and control are separate and orthogonal qualities of cognitive processes (Bargh 1992) and the existence of nonconscious, cognitive antecedents to violent behavior certainly does not mean that the behavior is unintentional. That consequating violent behavior helps both the perpetrator and the victim appears to be increasingly well established. However, this leaves unexamined the mechanism by which this effect is produced. Attention to the mindlessness of much violent behavior may lead to ways of further potentiating the positive effects of consequating violent behavior and perhaps to the identification of alternative pathways to violence that are suitable targets for primary prevention.

As the above paragraph suggests, the field of family violence is still fraught with a tension between activism and scholarly inquiry. Some manage to address the need for both action and scholarship by doing action-research where the research itself constitutes an intervention. Unfortunately, when this tension is not dealt with constructively the biggest losers are the people whose lives we seek to improve either through direct activism/intervention or through generating a more complete understanding of family violence. Just as activism is critical, so too is inquiry into difficult, uncomfortable questions. For example, is our response to child sexual abuse so dominated by the needs of the professionals involved that it unwittingly perpetrates the harm to children—an action that we all seek to avoid (cf. Fincham *et al.* 1994)? It is too easy to denigrate analysis of such questions as a "backlash" rather than to take them seriously. Yet our emotional revulsion to child sexual abuse must not preclude dispassionate appraisal of such issues. Similarly, "dispassionate" scholars need to be more mindful of the ideological implications of their research and guard against the inappropriate uses to which it can be put.

## MAINTAINING PERSPECTIVE

The field of family violence is not unique in challenging us to maintain our perspective in addressing an important social problem but it is one that makes great demands in this regard. This volume reminds us of the scope of the challenge in representing the diversity of perspectives that are appropriately brought to bear on the problem and to the fact that family violence does not respect national boundaries. There is no doubt room for constructive conflict in the field; indeed the present analysis suggests that such conflict is critical in advancing our efforts. But the efforts are ours collectively for it is only through collective efforts that embrace the diversity represented in this volume that we shall advance understanding of family violence and thereby act optimally to improve the lives of those touched by this important social problem.

## NOTES

1 This chapter was prepared while the author was a Social Science Research Fellow of the Nuffield Foundation and supported by a grant from the Economic and Social Research Council.
2 Albert Einstein, *Essays in Science*, New York: Philosophical Library, p. 1.

## BIBLIOGRAPHY

Bargh, J.A. (1992) "The ecology of automaticity: Toward establishing the conditions needed to produce automatic processing effects," *American Journal of Psychology* 105: 181–199.

Belsky, J. (1993) "Etiology of child maltreatment: A developmental–ecological analysis," *Psychological Bulletin* 114: 413–434.

Bronfenbrenner, U. (1979) *The ecology of human behavior*, Cambridge, MA: Harvard University Press.

Cicchetti, D. and Cohen, D.J. (1995) "Perspectives on developmental psychopathology," in D. Cicchetti and D.J. Cohen (eds) *Developmental psychopathology, Vol. 1: Theory and methods*, New York: Wiley.

Campbell, D.T. (1969) "Ethnocentrism of disciplines and the fish-scale model of omniscience," in M. Sherif and C.W. Sherif (eds) *Interdisciplinary relationships in the social sciences*, Chicago: Aldine.

Cummings, E.M. and Davies, P. (1994) *Children and marital conflict*, New York: Guilford.

Emery, R.E. and Billings, L.L. (forthcoming) "Family violence," *American Psychologist*.

Fincham, F.D., Beach, S.R., Moore, T. and Diener, C. (1994) "The professional response to child sexual abuse: Whose interests are served?" *Family Relations* 43: 244–254.

Fincham, F.D., Beach, S.R.H. and Kemp-Fincham, S.I. (1997) "Marital quality: A new theoretical perspective," in R.J. Sternberg and M. Hojjat (eds) *Satisfaction in close relationships*, New York: Guilford.

Murphy, C.M. and O'Leary, K.D. (1989) "Psychological aggression predicts physical aggression in early marriage," *Journal of Consulting and Clinical Psychology* 57: 579–582.

Nisbett, R.E. and Wilson, T.D. (1977) "Telling more than we can know: Verbal reports on mental processes," *Psychological Review* 84: 231–259.

O'Leary, K.D. and Jacobson, N.S. (forthcoming) "Partner relational problems with physical abuse," in *DSM IV: Sourcebook*, Washington, D.C.: American Psychiatric Association.

Pagelow, M.D. (1984) *Family violence*, New York: Praeger.

Pruitt, D.G. and Rubin, J.Z. (1986) *Social conflict: Escalation, stalemate, and settlement*, New York: McGraw-Hill.

Chapter 11

# Social responsibility and the production of knowledge about interpersonal violence

*Rebekah Bradley and Keith Davis*

Rebekah G. Bradley has an M.A. in psychology from Wesleyan University and is a doctoral candidate in clinical psychology with a focus on women's studies at the University of South Carolina. Her research interests are in the area of interpersonal violence. Keith E. Davis (Ph.D., social psychology, Duke University) works on personal relationships, particularly pathologies of romantic love such as stalking and abuse.

*We would like to emphasize that writing and researching in the area of interpersonal violence requires the researcher to be clear about the implications of the research findings with respect to his or her sociocultural context and personal values.*

If I am not for myself, who will be for me? And if I am only for myself, what am I? And if not now, when?

(Hillel, *Pirkei Avot*)

Renate Klein is to be congratulated for bringing together a very diverse group of scholars—diverse conceptually, empirically, in their academic disciplines, and in their local cultures within the broad European geographical area. Looking at research related to interpersonal violence from such a wide array of cultures and theoretical formulations tends to draw a reader's mind (at least momentarily) away from the results presented in each chapter to questions about how the knowledge presented in each chapter might be influenced by how it was created (both in terms of location and method). For example, how is it that such different views of battering in intimate relationships were presented by Kwiatkowska writing from Poland about Poland and by Sørensen writing from Denmark about Greenland?

Thus, this volume provides the service of encouraging the audience to step back from the text and ask questions about its creation. Is it possible (or desirable) for the members of one culture, operating in general or in the role of social scientist, to give characterizations of another culture that are not ethnocentric? Or are we all inevitably doomed to perceive others only through our own "culturally tinted [distorted] lenses"? And, what are the implications of looking through these lenses? Examining the roles of power, ideology, distribution of family work, and explanations for violence within the family or between dating partners raises the above issues about the creation of knowledge. In commenting on these contributions, we have identified a pair of related questions to address. First, how, in the study of interpersonal violence, can we balance concerns about "objectivity" with concerns for social justice? Second, given these concerns, what are the aspects of a valuable integrative approach for creating knowledge about interpersonal violence?

## BALANCING CONCERNS ABOUT "OBJECTIVITY" WITH CONCERNS FOR SOCIAL JUSTICE

To set the stage for answering this question, we would like to place research on interpersonal violence into a historical perspective. The second wave of feminism in the United States set the stage for understandings of interpersonal/family violence upon which many of the contributions to this volume build. During the early 1970s, the feminist movement in the United States transformed our understanding of interpersonal violence. They named rape, violence in intimate relationships, and child abuse as cultural, political phenomena rather than as incidences of personal misfortune. This shift allowed (feminist) social scientists to begin to explore interpersonal violence. The chapter by Croghan and Miell (this volume) draws on a feminist perspective and shows how difficult it is for women who are dealing with striking inequalities in family workload associated with the birth of their first child not to be overcome by the rhetoric of the normal "family." Croghan and Miell demonstrate the power of a culturally constructed view of the "family" through quotations in which the women excuse partners who seem to do almost nothing to help with the newborns.

The feminist attention to interpersonal violence provided a new perspective and opened the door for increased investigation of interpersonal violence by social scientists from many perspectives. Some social scientists have looked at interpersonal violence from a micro perspective, analyzing the interactions of family members as related to child abuse (e.g. Cerezo, this volume) or looking at the narratives of women with newborn babies (e.g. Croghan and Miell, this volume). Others have taken a macro perspective, looking at cultural beliefs and attitudes (e.g. Theodossopoulou-Papalois and Theodossopoulou, this volume). Further, some have looked at interpersonal violence from the level of individual behavior and beliefs, while others looked from the level of cultural norms and practices. These different perspectives created debate within and across disciplines.

Some researchers suggest that those who take a cultural norms perspective are too political in their work and do not use proper scientific methods, while others suggest that the scientific researchers have reinscribed interpersonal violence as an individual misfortune. These contrasting suggestions become a debate about who has the authority to create knowledge about interpersonal violence. The debate is not merely acrimonious; instead it holds the potential to confer the power to identify what is violence and what is not, to specify which discourses are valid for discussing violence and which are not, and with whom to lay responsibility, or lack thereof, for interpersonal violence.

The recognition that the research of social scientists who look at interpersonal violence (and the editors and tenure review boards who influence which research is presented to the public) has the above powers goes beyond the positivistic idea of social scientists as objective explorers who sort the systematic variance in order to reveal already existing truths. Feminist theorists (among others) have challenged this positivistic appeal to essential truths, reductionism, and belief that the social position and values of a given researcher can be rendered irrelevant by an objective scientific method. These theorists include social constructionists, postmodernists, and descriptive psychologists who have provided powerful critiques of traditional epistemologies.

Unfortunately, out of this debate over what science ought to look like, a dialectic setting scientific authority against experience emerges. As with most dialectics, innovative and useful knowledge is created by the tension between the two opposing positions in this debate rather than by resolving the debate. Social scientists, then, must walk a tightrope between empirical laws and personal experience. Therefore, we need to determine when tools used to describe universal truths serve our goals and when tools used to describe local truths serve our goals. Elizabeth Minnich writes:

> Our goal is not necessarily to undo all universals and the very idea of universals. It is to particularize accurately, to demystify the functions of power and hierarchy. It is not, after all, universalization itself, or abstraction itself, that is necessarily harmful; it is false universals, faulty and mystified abstractions, that concern us. And they concern us because they mask the possibility of approaching, at least, visions and concepts and commitments that could inspire us all.
>
> (Minnich 1990: 181).

We need to be clear about our goals and clear about our methods as well as the relationship between the two. This begs the question of our goals. If the goal is not to simply identify an already existing truth, then what should a social scientist seek? One answer to this question, the one for which we will argue here, is social justice.

## A FRAMEWORK FOR CREATING KNOWLEDGE ABOUT INTERPERSONAL VIOLENCE

In the following sections, we shall discuss some key distinctions and methodological approaches that appear to hold genuine promise for our enterprise. These theoretical works share some important features with the philosophical traditions that have challenged a positivistic approach to science. They involve keeping one's eye on behavior and behavioral worlds. They require a formal representation of behavior that adequately describes its complexity and structural relationships including phenomena such as social practices, social institutions, cultures, or ways of life. Descriptive psychology has applied such an approach to the issues of multicultural contact and relationships (Ossorio 1983). "Descriptive psychology is a set of distinctions designed to get at all of the possibilities or sets of facts about people and their behavior" (Ossorio 1995: 255). The most distinctive feature of descriptive psychology, when set against the positivistic social science approach, is its insistence on viewing the person as a responsible agent capable of understanding complex systems, and placing her or him at the center of its conception of science. This means that a descriptive psychologist is aware of the process through which she creates knowledge and is aware that subjects are active participants in the creation of knowledge, not merely objects. Descriptive psychologists insist on local theorizing about behaviors based on "thick" descriptive data and conceptually rich formats so that the possibility of generalizing from individual cases to larger social units is not thrown away. Thus, descriptive psychology strives to make possible generalized statements about contrasting descriptions of interpersonal violence such as those presented in this volume without giving up the meaning conferred on each description by the environments from which each was written.

A key component of this approach is understanding a behavior's significance by placing the behavior within broader social practices and institutions of a culture. This expands the parameters through which data is interpreted. With regard to interpersonal violence, it means not only looking at standard research parameters (e.g. how many slaps or kicks have occurred, by whom, toward whom) but placing these behaviors within a meaningful context.

For descriptive psychologists, the crucial diagnostic question for significance or meaning is "What is he or she doing by doing that?" Answers to such questions take the form of a movement up a ladder of significance. Cultural anthropologists like Geertz (1973, 1983) use a parallel procedure to make the "foreign" and "exotic" intelligible.

It is perhaps easiest to imagine this process as a dialogue in which a person familiar with an environment is asked by a visitor to explain a local custom. Suppose that we, as outsiders, were to ask Römkens and Mastenbroek about their chapter in this volume using a descriptive psychology approach. Our dialogue might go as follows:

OUTSIDER What are the young Dutch men doing by showering their new found girlfriends with attention?"

INSIDER They are taking the first steps in the social process of "romantic love."

OUTSIDER What are they doing by doing that?

INSIDER In this case, they are using the appearance of caring and vulnerability to seduce the girls into a relationship where they are able to control them by exploiting their feelings of romantic love toward the men.

Central to the Römkens and Mastenbroek chapter is a switch from a relationship of equals in which both persons' feelings and wishes count, e.g. romantic love, to a relationship of domination and control in which the ideology of romantic love is used as a tool for personal gratification by the young men and results in the exploitation of the young women. An analysis that focuses on meaning exposes the switch for what it is: a counterfeit of romantic love.

If each question represents a move up a ladder of significance, the goal is to arrive at an answer about the significance of a behavior from within its context that nonetheless speaks to issues which have meaning across contexts. The chapter by Römkens and Mastenbroek raises questions about the role of social practices like "romantic love" in maintaining abusive inequalities in relationships. To the extent that "romantic love" is implicated in relationships of inequality how might that provide information for corrective social action (do we ban Valentine's day? How do we talk to our daughters about Disney movie romances and romantic pulp fiction?). The fact that a central and meaningful social practice, such as romantic love, can be used in a counterfeit manner does not imply that the entire practice must be eradicated; rather, it implies that we are responsible for enacting the social practice in a careful manner. Even well-meaning practices can easily transform into unethical ones if we do not consistently evaluate the meaning(s) of our behaviors in their current context(s).

Hagemann-White's chapter (this volume) raises the question of how the significance of the social issue of violence against women has changed as it moved from the context of radical feminist politics to that of the mainstream. Although the types of social responses, activities, projects, centers and networks for serving women and girls look the same, they take on different meaning in each context. In the context of radical feminist politics these activities were responses to a systematically unequal social system. In the context of mainstream society they are directed toward the psychological wellbeing of individuals. Without looking at the purpose of activities such as rape crisis centers *in context*, as did Hagemann-White, it would be difficult to recognize that perhaps activities which were originally intended to challenge a victim-blaming culture may now be supporting such a culture.

Another framework for the production of social justice-oriented research comes from the work of feminist social scientists. Out of the tension between the objecting voice of feminism and the "objective" voice of science some formulations of a feminist social science have emerged. Drawing from a wide range of feminist writers (Fine 1992; Hekman 1997; Haraway 1991; Harding 1991; Collins 1990; Williams 1991) we have summarized three basic elements we see in a feminist epistemology.

1 Feminists do not take the position of disengaged knower who can be separated from what is known through a "scientific method" or other algorithms for validity. Instead, we seek validity through a reflexive analysis of the relationship between knower, process for knowing, and known.
2 Feminist research rejects knowledge that is separated from its socio-historical and political contexts.
3 Feminist research is produced as part of a community struggle, an alliance, against racism, sexism, classism, or any other set of beliefs which justifies depriving others of "equal access to the valued resources of society" (Lorber 1994: 294).

Meeting each of these criteria is likely to lead to research in which the author of knowledge takes responsibility for its creation and its implications. For example, Cerezo (this volume) acknowledges that her research is part of an effort to create programs that will prevent physical child abuse. Le Gall (this volume) traces the role of social and historical understandings of "family" in order to make sense of conflict within families from the perspective of teenagers. And Sørensen (this volume) challenges the social construction of violence that does not hold males accountable for committing domestic violence just because they can get away with it.

This volume brings together research from many cultures on the topic of interpersonal violence and reminds us that science is not simply discovering, describing or explaining what is "out there." Social science is itself a social practice which, like other social practices, needs to be addressed with questions such as "What are we doing by doing science?" and "Does social science practice strive to be a part of an alliance against injustice?" This means that we need to go beyond asking if our research projects are ethical in the sense of not violating the basic rights of research participants. We ought to be conceiving our work as contributing to social justice.

When the intrinsic social practices of a community or culture are systematically exploited so that their inherent potential benefits are available only to a subset of the community, that constitutes an ethical violation. And, as social scientists we do not benefit ourselves or our communities by documenting the ethical violation without naming the evil as such. In the area of interpersonal conflict/violence, we need to do more than documenting that it does exist and documenting the practices that maintain it. We need to point out the precise actors and roles that commit the violence. Otherwise we are tempted to remain stuck in the position of naming general occurrences or practices as the problem without specifying the exact nature of the ethical violation that has occurred. For example, we may notice that in social relationships where people are interdependent not all persons are granted the benefit of safety and security. If, however, we make statements such as, "women are frequently abused by their husbands," or "girls are often raped by their boyfriends," not only have we not really explained the phenomena but we leave ourselves open to charges such as that of being "hysterical man-haters." We may try to defend ourselves by making other observations such as, "well, women hit men also" or "the couples where this occurs have poor communication skills." While both statements may also be documented, the nature of the ethical violation has still not been named. We need to explain what types of gender roles and social powers grant and even encourage some men to make the choice to rape or hit women. We need to explicate the interpersonal and social dynamics which explain the link between communication skills and violence and we need to identify the circumstances in which women may also hit men and the needs that are being fulfilled. In short, when social practices have become vehicles for abuse we need to highlight how and by whom they are being used so that we can mount a forceful challenge to the abuses observed. If we do not, we, ourselves, have become part of a social practice, social science, which systematically uses its social role in a manner complicit with abuses of power.

## BIBLIOGRAPHY

Collins, P.H. (1990) *Black feminist thought: Knowledge, consciousness, and the politics of empowerment*, New York: Routledge.
Fine, M. (1992) *Disruptive voices*, Ann Arbor: University of Michigan Press.
Geertz, C. (1973) *The interpretation of cultures*, New York: Basic Books.
—— (1983) *Local knowledge*, New York: Basic Books.
Haraway, D. (1991) *Simians, cyborgs, and women*, New York: Routledge.
Harding, S. (1991) *Whose science? Whose knowledge? Thinking from women's lives*, Ithaca, NY: Cornell University Press.
Hekman, S. (1997) "Truth and method: Feminist standpoint theory revisited," *Signs: Journal of Women in Culture and Society* 22: 341–365.
Lorber, J. (1994) *Paradoxes of gender*, New Haven: Yale University Press.

Minnich, E.K. (1990) *Transforming knowledge*, Philadelphia: Temple University Press.

Ossorio, P.G. (1983) "A multicultural psychology," in K.E. Davis and R.M. Bergner (eds) *Advance in descriptive psychology*, Greenwich, CT: JAI Press.

—— (1995) "Persons," in A. Putman (ed.) *The Collected works of Peter Ossorio*, vol. 1. Ann Arbor, MI: Descriptive Psychology Press. (Originally published in 1966 by Linguistic Research Institute, Boulder, CO.)

Williams, P. (1991) *The alchemy of race and rights: Diary of a law professor*, Cambridge: Harvard University Press.

Chapter 12

# Complexities of family violence and the need for belongingness

*Ileana Arias*

*I received my doctorate in clinical psychology at the State University of New York at Stony Brook. My program of research is devoted to elucidating the individual and relationship antecedents and consequences of domestic violence in order to facilitate prediction and, consequently, control of domestic violence among American dating, cohabiting, and married dyads, and its destructive impact on individuals, families, and society. The ability to reduce the incidence and negative impact of domestic violence depends on the extent to which we understand what leads an individual to aggress physically against his or her spouse and what determines an individual's willingness to remain in abusive relationships. To that end, my work has been devoted to examining potential psychological causal variables in three major areas: individual abuser characteristics, individual victim characteristics, and relationship characteristics. Additionally, I have focused on coping with and consequences of battering among women and their children.*

*My point is that family functioning and family violence are influenced by variables from various levels (e.g. micro- and macrosystems); when we address family conflict, we need to be mindful of what we take away from families and family members in addition to what we may provide for them.*

The sociopolitical contexts in which families exist are in continual flux. Changes in such contexts have implications for the definition, structure, and functions of a "family," and the roles that compose this fundamental unit. Families are continuously challenged by change and can only ensure their survival and stability by adjusting to external demands. Pressure to redefine the family and family roles provokes conflict of interests between families and the sociopolitical context, and among family members occupying various family roles. As in other interpersonal relationships, conflicts of interest then are inevitable occurrences among families (Coser 1956, 1967; Simmel 1955) and trigger normal processes of accommodation and assimilation through which families change and develop (Sprey 1969, 1974). As such, conflict *per se* does not threaten the health or functioning of families. Rather, tactics employed by family members in the processes of accommodation and assimilation determine family functioning and health. Methods of conflict resolution may range from: (1) adaptive tactics such as rational discussion, reasoning, and negotiation; (2) to more destructive ones such as threats, insults, humiliation, intimidation, and coercion, herein referred to as psychological abuse; and (3) to more extreme measures such as physical force and violence, herein referred to as physical abuse (Straus 1979). Conflict theorists predict that individuals will engage in destructive tactics such as physical violence when more adaptive measures such as discussion and negotiation have been ineffectively used to resolve conflicts of interests (Sprey 1974).

Traditionally, family researchers across disciplines have been concerned with prediction and explanation of family members' choice of less adaptive conflict resolution tactics such as physical abuse, and to a lesser extent psychological abuse, as exemplified by the chapters in this volume. Consistent with conflict theory, the use of less adaptive measures is occasioned by failure to resolve conflicts of interest with more adaptive ones. Hence, families characterized by abuse may be victims of greater external pressures for change, may not have access to adaptive strategies, or are limited in the effective application of adaptive strategies, or some combination thereof. By definition, families consisting of members who choose psychologically and physically abusive tactics for resolving conflict are dysfunctional and worthy of professional attention. Additionally, focus on abusive forms of conflict resolution is in response to their destructive impact and the incongruence between the occurrence of abuse and the expectation of provision of a "safe haven" by the nuclear (and to some extent, the extended) family.

Physical violence has been shown to have a significant destructive impact on individual and family functioning (cf. Arias and Pape 1994). Besides the obvious physical injuries, women victimized by intimate partner physical violence are at high risk for psychological disorders and malfunctioning, suicide and homicide, and a wide range of chronic and acute physical illnesses. The destructive impact of physical abuse of children and their exposure to violence among other family subunits also has been well documented. More recently, American researchers have begun to focus on determinants and impact of psychological abuse. Psychological abuse has been found to be associated with low self-esteem (Aguilar and Nightingale 1994), anxiety, depression, and fear of the partner (Follingstad *et al.* 1990), alcohol abuse (Arias *et al.* 1996), physical illness (Marshall 1996) and post-traumatic stress disorder (Arias and Pape, forthcoming; Astin *et al.* 1993; Cascardi *et al.* 1995; Kemp *et al.* 1991). Children of psychologically abused women have been found to be characterized by higher levels of depressive symptomatology and lower self-esteem (Arias and Street 1996).

Researchers have attempted to identify intrapersonal, interpersonal, and contextual variables that can guide the development of primary, secondary, and tertiary family violence prevention programs. Unfortunately, researchers and theoreticians in the United States (and Europe as well, as evidenced by the chapters in this volume) primarily have examined and speculated about family violence within the confines of their respective disciplines. The complexity of the determinants of family violence, and the interrelationships among these determinants, has not been fully appreciated, hampering the potential impact of intervention measures. For example, to what extent will communication skills training reduce spouses' propensity to use psychologically and physically abusive conflict resolution tactics in the context of communities that value family maintenance above all else? While researchers cannot be expected to develop expertise in various disciplines or to examine all aspects of family violence, they can recognize and address the implications of other systems for their work. Felson and Tedeschi (1993) offer a heuristic for guiding and informing family violence research: the social interactionist perspective. The social interactionist perspective is based on four principles: (1) aggression and violence are instrumental behaviors and so we must consider the costs of inhibiting aggression and violence; (2) aggressive behavior is a normal consequence of human interaction, a response to a perceived injustice or norm violation, or to achieve another's compliance; (3) aggression is largely influenced by interpersonal and situational variables, including third parties in addition to the perpetrator and immediate victim; and (4) the values and expectations of the perpetrator are significant determinants of evaluations of alternative conflict resolution strategies.

Family violence scholars primarily have addressed the first two assumptions and to a lesser extent the fourth assumption of the social interactionist perspective. For example, research and intervention focus on providing skills to facilitate the use of nonviolent forms of conflict resolution, changing family and societal contingencies impinging upon the use of violence, and restructuring perpetrators' attributions and perceptions of family members and the impact of their violence (cf. Edleson and Tolman 1992; Vivian and Heyman 1996). However, the third assumption has been largely ignored. Cessation of family violence is considered to be dependent upon changes in the characteristics of the perpetrator or, at best, changes in the interaction between the perpetrator and victim(s). Rarely, are characteristics of "third parties" such as neighbors, churches, local communities and respective organizations, agencies and personnel considered. Thus for example, while interventions focus on the provision of alternative methods of conflict resolution or on changing family rules and expectations, little attention is devoted to the implications for accomplishing and maintaining these changes in the context of communities that may not value and therefore not support such changes. In communities where maintaining families intact is of high priority, victims of family violence may not be likely to avail themselves of potentially effective measures such as assertiveness skills and legal prosecution of the batterer.

These frequently recommended strategies may be perceived by the victim's community as contrary to maintaining family relationships intact. Consequently, the victim is in a position of protecting him/herself by enacting strategies that will not be supported and may even lead to some degree of ostracism (e.g. "she is a bad wife"). The chapters in this volume by Cerezo, by Theodossopoulou-Papalois and Theodossopoulou, and by Sørensen are excellent illustrations of the importance of understanding the community (extended family or beyond) in explicating the boundaries of family conflict and violence, and involving the community's support in attempting to eliminate conflict and violence effectively.

Theoreticians adopting a feminist perspective have come closest to including the community's perspective and involvement in their approach to family violence. Feminist theoreticians and researchers assume that family violence is the result of the subordinate positions that women and children occupy in families relative to men (Bograd 1988). Family ideology of the Western system of institutions (including religious, political, and economic) are thought to specify, maintain, and reinforce the dominating and controlling position of men that facilitates abuse of women and less powerful family members (Dobash and Dobash 1979). Accordingly, feminist perspectives call for empowering women and children by changing the hierarchical nature of family organization (Dobash and Dobash 1979; Bograd 1988). Such attempts have primarily focused on mobilizing legal intervention and mandating that family violence be treated as other forms of criminal violence. Mandatory arrest and subsequent prosecution are thought to protect victims of family violence and to elevate the position of women and children relative to men. However, feminist theoreticians and researchers have failed to consider that the extent to which mandatory arrest laws and prosecution will be enacted, and subsequently effective, may depend largely upon the extent to which enacting such measures are consistent with the community's (including extended family, neighbors and coworkers, church, and society) family ideology. To the extent that the community's ideology consisting of the hierarchical nature of family organization does not change, attempts to eliminate family violence by increasing women's and children's positions within the family to equal men's will fail. Perhaps attempts to empower women by changing family ideology must be done directly rather than indirectly. Families struggle with the conflict between traditional specifications of family structure and functioning in the context of a changing communal environment. Unfortunately, relative to families, communities themselves may not be as sensitive to contextual changes that necessitate corresponding changes in family ideology. Communities may need to acknowledge and incorporate contextual changes in order to empower families to effectively and adaptively respond to conflict. In her chapter in this volume, Hagemann-White clearly illustrates the potential contradictions in community action and emerging family ideology. To be sure, while society and other immediate communities need to develop and change family ideology, the changes must result in a family structure that, convincingly, can meet individual and community needs currently thought to be met by traditional family structures. Community resistance to changes in family ideology typically are the result of the fear of eroding family structure *per se*. Thus, potential changes must be presented as a change in structure to meet contextual demands and not a replacement or elimination of the "family."

Interestingly, resistance to family ideology change is seen at the individual as well as the group level. As is characteristic of American dating and married samples, participants in the work of Croghan and Miell, Kwiatkowska, and Le Gall (in this volume) historically and presently excuse their partners' abusive behavior in various ways all in the service of maintaining family ties. The narratives of adolescent women in the chapter by Römkens and Mastenbroek provide the most poignant descriptions of women's and children's attempts to account for violence in ways that allow and provide reason to the continuation of the destructive relationships that, nonetheless, they depend on for warmth, support, protection and, in short, affiliation or belongingness.

Baumeister and Leary (1995) noted that in his theory of human development Maslow (1968) placed achievement of love, affiliation, and belongingness needs after fulfilling basic needs such as those for shelter, food, and safety but before those of self-esteem and self-actualization. Accordingly, they proposed that the need to belong is an innate, evolutionary-based drive to form and maintain a minimum quantity of interpersonal relationships. These relationships must be characterized by a minimum of conflict and negative affect wherein the individual believes that the other cares about her or his welfare and feels and expresses to her or him a positive affection. Further, these interpersonal relationships must be marked by stability, continuing unchanged in their nature into the foreseeable future. Baumeister and Leary (1995) hypothesized that a lack of the resulting sense of belongingness " . . . would constitute severe deprivation and cause a variety of ill effects" (p. 497). Belongingness differs from attachment in that the latter is specific to an individual or relationship whereas the need to belong can be directed toward any other person. Consequently, the loss of belongingness subsequent to relationship dissolution can be replaced by a new relationship with any other individual. However, investment in current relationships and the costs (i.e. time) and uncertainty related to establishing new relationships are major deterrents to dissolving discordant and unsatisfying relationships and replacing them with (potentially) more satisfying ones, in part, accounting for the stability of dysfunctional relationships.

Recognition of the need to belong has significant implications for family violence interventions. If individuals have a need to belong, it may not be productive to rely on interventions that threaten the stability or maintenance of relationships (e.g. mandatory arrest and prosecution, separation, divorce, etc.) without facilitating formation of new, substitute relationships. Victims of family violence may need support in the formation of alternative relationships to which they can "belong." Current emphasis on provision of financial and other material resources support is indeed appropriate and necessary. However, we may need to go beyond material support and offer relational support as well. In the absence of a "family," victims of family violence may be reluctant or unlikely to terminate abusive relationships. Likewise, the absence of a "family" may render it likely that victims of family violence return to their abusive relationships or quickly involve themselves in new dysfunctional relationships. Consistent with the application of belongingness theory, Byrne and Arias (1993) found that while battered women's subjective norms about relationships and relationship dissolution did not predict their intention to terminate their abusive relationships, "normative" beliefs did. That is, women's perceptions and expectations of the community's standards and support for leaving their abusive partners were significantly related to their commitment to leave their abusive partners permanently.

While the importance of attention and provision of alternative relationships for victims of family violence is fairly evident, addressing the need to belong may be equally relevant in empowering perpetrators to cease violent conflict resolution as suggested by Cerezo in her chapter. As specified by the social interactionist perspective, aggression and violence are instrumental behaviors functioning to address a perceived injustice or to achieve another's compliance (Felson and Tedeschi 1993). Baumeister and Leary (1995) hypothesize that aggressive, violent and other forms of controlling behaviors may function to maintain a relationship that fulfills the perpetrator's need to belong. While it is important to substitute methods for resolving relationship conflict, effectiveness of these attempts may be influenced by the perpetrator's perception of how alternative methods will maintain the relationship and their sense of belongingness. If the perpetrator perceives alternative methods as loosening relationship bonds and fostering structural or emotional relationship dissolution, there may be a high probability of resistance to change.

Family structure and functioning are determined and influenced by a wide-ranging variety of micro- and macro-system variables. Families are subjectively aware of such multideterminism and struggle to reconcile a multitude of competing demands. We do a disservice to families when we fail to recognize that same level of complexity. Family theory, research and treatment need to be ever cognizant of the different but interrelated levels of family functioning determinants. Most importantly, we have to be mindful of the impact at other levels of change within any one level of determinants. Lack of coordination and consistency across levels of influence, at best, significantly decrease our ability to make fundamental changes in family functioning and, at worst, create another source of conflict for families to accommodate or assimilate.

## BIBLIOGRAPHY

Aguilar, R.J. and Nightingale, N.N. (1994) "The impact of specific battering experiences on the self-esteem of abused women," *Journal of Family Violence* 9: 35–45.

Arias, I. and Pape, K.T. (1994) "Physical abuse," in L. L'Abate (ed.) *Handbook of developmental family psychology and psychopathology*, New York: Wiley.

—— (forthcoming) "Psychological abuse: Implications for adjustment and commitment to leave violent partners," *Violence and Victims*.

Arias, I. and Street, A.E. (1996) "Children of psychologically abused women: Effects of maternal adjustment and parenting on child outcomes," paper presented at the 8th International Conference on Personal Relationships, Banff, Canada.

Arias, I., Street, A.E. and Brody, G.H. (1996) "Depression and alcohol abuse: Women's responses to psychological victimization," paper presented at the American Psychological Association's National Conference on Psychosocial and Behavioral Factors in Women's Health: Research, Prevention, Treatment, and Service Delivery in Clinical and Community Settings, Washington, DC.

Astin, M.C., Lawrence, K.J. and Foy, D.W. (1993) "Posttraumatic stress disorder among battered women: Risk and resiliency factors," *Violence and Victims* 8: 17–28.

Baumeister, R.F. and Leary, M.R. (1995) "The need to belong: Desire for interpersonal attachments as a fundamental human motivation," *Journal of Personality and Social Psychology* 117: 497–529.

Bograd, M. (1988) "Feminist perspectives on wife abuse: An introduction," in K.Yllö and M. Bograd (eds) *Feminist perspectives on wife abuse*, Newbury Park, CA: Sage.

Byrne, C.A. and Arias, I. (1993) "Predicting women's intentions to leave abusive relationships: Applications of interdependence theory and the theory of planned behavior," paper presented at the 27th Annual Convention of the Association for Advancement of Behavior Therapy, Atlanta, GA.

Cascardi, M., O'Leary, K.D., Lawrence, E.E. and Schlee, K.A. (1995) "Characteristics of women physically abused by their spouses and who seek treatment regarding marital conflict," *Journal of Consulting and Clinical Psychology* 63: 616–623.

Coser, L.A. (1956) *The functions of the social conflict*, New York: Free Press.

—— (1967) *Continuities in the study of social conflict*, New York: Free Press.

Dobash, R.E. and Dobash, R.P. (1979) *Violence against wives*, New York: Free Press.

Edleson, J.L. and Tolman, R.M. (1992) *Intervention for men who batter*, Newbury Park, CA: Sage.
Felson, R.B. and Tedeschi, J.T. (1993) "Social interactionist perspectives on aggression and violence: An introduction," in R.B. Felson and J.T. Tedeschi (eds) *Aggression and violence: Social interactionist perspectives*, Washington, DC: American Psychological Association.
Follingstad, D.R., Rutledge, L.L., Berg, B.J., Hause, E.S. and Polek, D.S. (1990) "The role of emotional abuse in physically abusive relationships," *Journal of Family Violence* 5: 107–120.
Kemp, A., Rawlings, E.I. and Green, B.L. (1991) "Post-traumatic stress disorder (PTSD) in battered women," *Journal of Traumatic Stress* 4: 137–148.
Marshall, L.L. (1996) "Psychological abuse of women: Six distinct clusters," *Journal of Family Violence* 11: 379–409.
Maslow, A.H. (1968) *Toward a psychology of being*, New York: Van Nostrand.
Simmel, G. (1955) *Conflict and the web of group affiliations*, New York: Free Press.
Sprey, J. (1969) "The family as a system in conflict," *Journal of Marriage and the Family* 31: 699–706.
—— (1974) "On management of conflict in families," in S.K. Steinmetz and M.A. Straus (eds) *Violence in the family*, New York: Harper & Row.
Straus, M.A. (1979) "Measuring intrafamily conflict and violence: The Conflict Tactics (CT) Scales," *Journal of Marriage and the Family* 41: 75–88.
Vivian, D. and Heyman, R.E. (1996) "Is there a place for conjoint treatment of couple violence?," *In Session: Psychotherapy in Practice* 2: 25–48.

Chapter 13

# The status of family violence research in Europe

*K. Daniel O'Leary*

Daniel O'Leary is a Distinguished Professor of Psychology at The University at Stony Brook. He was president of the American Association for Advancement of Behavior Therapy and received the Distinguished Scientist Award from the Clinical Division of the American Psychological Association. He holds an NIMH Research Training grant for pre- and postdoctoral fellows who study wife abuse. He also has federal support to (1) assess gender specific and couple treatments for decreasing wife abuse and to (2) evaluate a prevention of dating violence program for high schools. He wrote the DSM-IV Diagnosis for Relational Problems with Partner Abuse (O'Leary and Jacobson 1997) and the corresponding Source Book chapter on Partner Abuse.

Family conflict and violence, the two central concepts in this book, are approached by professionals from different disciplines in various countries. The multidisciplinary perspective of this book is refreshing. Multidisciplinary offerings from one country alone would have been a useful contribution, but the combination of having different disciplines as well as different countries represented is a double treat. One might expect that one could read the book and come away with a sense of how prevalent conflict and violence are across countries. Based on the title, one might also expect that the book would provide quite different views of conflict and violence because of the multidisciplinary perspective. Instead, one gets the sense that, regardless of the country or the discipline represented, conflict and violence are very significant problems. Given the nascency of the research on family violence in many countries and the absence of common methodologies used to assess prevalence, correlates, and etiological factors associated with violence, specific common comparisons on these dimensions are impossible. I was struck, however, by the common etiological themes that are raised by the contributors. To some extent, the commonalities that will be discussed later reflect the fact that the disciplines represented are basically social science disciplines, with a preponderance of contributions from sociologists, psychologists, and anthropologists. Some other disciplines that have recently been addressing issues of family violence are evolutionary biology (Ridley 1993), sociobiology (e.g. Daly and Wilson 1988), neuropsychology (Rosenbaum and Hoge 1989; Warnken *et al.* 1994), biochemistry/psychiatry (Markowitz and Coccaro 1995), genetics (Rushton *et al.* 1995; Plomin *et al.* 1994), nursing (Campbell 1989) and emergency medicine (Bell *et al.* 1994). The absence of these disciplines certainly makes common themes more likely and the etiological factors decidedly less divergent, but one should be fully aware that the disciplines represented constitute only one segment of the disciplines that are involved in research on family violence. Nonetheless, the similarity in the social science approaches makes the book much easier to digest and probably more useful to many instructors. Further, the fact that all the contributions come from Europeans increases the likelihood of common features, especially with respect to cultural and anthropological factors.

In providing commentary on this book, I discuss several important, common themes in the chapters, and I then provide brief comments about the specific chapters and raise issues for additional consideration. Finally, when discussing the last chapter, I raise two final issues that bear repetition here. First, there is a need to have less divisiveness and more understanding of differing viewpoints about the causes and methods of preventing and treating family violence, and about how to advocate for individuals caught in the web of family violence. Second, for both political and scientific advances to be fully accomplished, I believe it is time to provide models and conceptualizations that adequately portray the men who do *not* rape and beat their wives, *and* who would not do so even if they could get away with such behavior.

One common theme that is addressed in various chapters is the large-scale denial of family violence as an important issue for the country being discussed (e.g. Greece, Greenland). The ground-breaking work of Straus and Gelles in the United States as well as similar survey work in Canada helped tremendously to bring the issue of violence to the public's attention. The coverage of violence in the public arena internationally, however, was made blatantly clear by the media attention for over a year to the O.J. Simpson case and the murders of Nicole Brown Simpson and Ronald Goldman. Moreover, the international press that it commanded brought more attention to the problem internationally than the United Nations Conference on Women held in China in September 1995 (Fourth World Conference on Women, Beijing, September 4–15, 1995). The media attention to this case was not a minor issue even though it played on sensationalism in many ways. It also helped dispel a myth held by many in the general public and discussed in this book that violence is a phenomenon only among the working classes and/or among alcoholics (e.g. Greenland).

Another theme that one can glean from this book is that there are common threads in child abuse and wife/partner abuse. This was apparent in the work of Cerezo from Spain. There are clear similarities across countries in the depictions of the escalation patterns of child abusers and wife abusers in that nonabusive parents and nonabusive partners do not engage in patterns of escalation that are as long or as intense. The work on children that Cerezo cites (e.g. Lorber *et al.* 1984 and Reid *et al.* 1981) as well as the communication work of Vivian and O'Leary (1987) with partners in abusive relationships all indicated that the chain of negative interactions is longer for those in abusive relationships in comparison to those in nonabusive relationships.

A point noted by Cerezo in her discussion of child abuse is that it also makes perfect sense in the partner abuse area to consider competence on a continuum rather than in a dichotomous fashion, "especially since all parents may resort to what might be considered inappropriate behavior *vis-à-vis* a child on at least a few occasions." The same point can be made regarding wife/partner abuse, especially since approximately 40–50 percent of all young married partners have been in physically aggressive relationships (O'Leary *et al.* 1989; McLaughlin *et al.* 1992). Further, at least 30–40 percent of high school females in six ethnically diverse high schools on Long Island, New York (*N* = 3,300) have been in such relationships (Avery-Leaf *et al.* 1997) and 25 percent of 13-year-olds in junior high school have been in physically aggressive relationships (Foshee *et al.* 1996). The debate about the value of conceptualizing abusive behavior toward children or adults dichotomously or on a continuum is a complex one that is discussed in some detail elsewhere (e.g. O'Leary 1993). However, two points about this issue bear repeating here. First, more severe abusive behaviors are almost always preceded by a systematic progression from the less abusive ones to the more abusive ones. Second, the more severe forms of behavior have different predictors than the less severe ones (e.g. drug use and ethnic variables) even though there are a number of common predictors (e.g. marital discord, verbal or psychological aggression, and wife's threats to leave the relationship; Pan *et al.* 1994). The arguments regarding dimensional versus categorical approaches have raged for years and will continue, especially with the emphasis by public health agencies and insurance companies for prevalence data on various disorders. From both a clinical and a research standpoint, however, it makes perfect sense to me to conceptualize a continuum of aggressive behaviors toward a child or partner as follows: verbally aggressive behaviors, moderately physically aggressive behaviors, severely physically aggressive behaviors and murder of child/partner. The causal variables in partner violence and the differential prediction of violence against men and women was described elsewhere (O'Leary 1993), but it can be assumed that many of the factors that predict partner abuse also predict child abuse. In fact, since 50 percent of parents who report severe partner abuse also report being severely aggressive with their children (Neidig *et al.* 1995; Straus and Gelles 1986), this makes the likelihood of some common correlates and causes even more likely.

The larger macro views of child abuse and partner abuse that emphasize poverty as a causative factor or correlate in child and partner abuse were not discussed by the authors of the chapters. Such macro views place parenting in the broader social context of poverty as one of the most crucial risk factors for abuse along with being a young single mother (e.g. Wolfe 1987). Similarly, little is said about the possible psychopathology of the abusive parents or abusive partners. While empirical research with abusive parents has not provided much evidence that they differ in terms of psychopathology from nonabusive parents, wife abusers do differ from non-wife abusers in terms of personality styles (e.g. impulsivity and defendence: O'Leary *et al.* 1994), Axis II personality disorders (Hamberger and Hastings 1991; Murphy *et al.* 1993) and with respect to borderline personality organization (Dutton 1995).

The way in which we perceive relationships clearly has an impact on our behavior. Croghan and Miell address this relationship in two studies. In the first, they interviewed women who experienced childhood disruption and who were currently experiencing high social stress. In a second study, they interviewed women who had experienced severe childhood disruption and who had been separated from their biological parents and placed in substitute families or in institutional care. Following some feminist theorists who eschew data-based research (Wilkinson 1981) the studies involved interviews of participants, and, in some fashion, the interviewer disclosed her own personal experiences. Unfortunately, the nature of the experiences disclosed and the childhood background of the interviewer were not made explicit. This reviewer welcomes qualitative research, but it becomes especially important in qualitative research to make these biases apparent (Murphy and O'Leary 1994 ).

The first study addressed women's accounts of stress and support following the birth of their first child, and in addition to interviews, time-use diaries were provided by the participants. The researchers said that there were marked inequalities in the division of labor between men and women in terms of parenting and domestic work. This finding alone is not at all unusual in the USA. More specifically, even among men and women working full time, there are major differences in parenting and domestic work. For example, in work at my own university, mothers of hyperactive children report completing about 70 percent of the parenting duties whereas their husbands completed only 30 percent of such duties

(Arnold *et al.* 1996). On average, these women were in heterosexual relationships they rated as satisfying. Domestic work differences also abound across genders, and have existed for decades. What has been surprising to this reviewer is that the gender differences have not lessened significantly across the last decade.

The voices of the mothers in the first study by Croghan and Miell may provide some explanation of why fathers are not more involved and/or why their relative lack of involvement does not cause more marital discord. As they stated, "all these accounts were characterized by high expectations of maternal responsibility and effort and lowered expectations of paternal involvement." They went on to say that "the women's sense of responsibility as mothers limited their expectation of other support, particularly from the male partner, and obviated their sense of grievance at the long hours they worked and their unequal share in the burden of parenthood. Because the women saw themselves as primarily responsible for parenting, paternal involvement was construed as an optional gift rather than a right." The authors suggest that mothers cope with parenting and the relative lack of support by their husbands by "reconstruing the notion of support to exclude practical help and to cover only emotional support." However, as might be expected, the stress was more apparent for mothers who worked full time in relatively low-paid unrewarding occupations. Unfortunately, Kim, in the example provided to illustrate just this kind of stress, was angry with herself, and her way out was to use tranquilizers.

A central theme of the women's voices was to minimize conflict regarding the gender difference in parenting, even among women who felt they were feminists and who considered themselves married to "new men." Of special interest to me were the accounts of women in relationships they described as abusive or exploitative. They did not see the relationship as one of equality and they were at a loss to explain the behavior of their partners. In addition, mothers who walked out on a family, even when physically abused, were blamed by the adult female offspring. Even direct abuse by the father was partly seen as the mother's fault.

The views of mothers presented herein was enlightening but sad. In 1997, it seems sad to find so many women placing such great responsibility on themselves for parenting and domestic work. Further, women in abusive relationships had construals of the relationships that provided excuses for the abuse of their partners and fathers. Coming from feminist researchers, the evidence presented from the women was even more surprising in that the women who were interviewed did not present a point of view that portrayed equality in relationships. As a next step, additional research of this nature would be helpful with a focus on assessing more about why the women did not expect more of their husbands, partners and fathers. I would hope that my daughter would expect more, but one is left with a sense that holding expectations or high hopes that can be readily dashed was simply not practical for the women in these studies.

Like most in the abuse field, Römkens and Mastenbroek view violence against persons as predominantly the work of boys and men, and research in the Netherlands has begun to address partner violence. However, as the authors note, very little is known about abuse and rape by boyfriends. Their qualitative study involved interviews with twenty young women from the Netherlands about the dynamics of their abusive relationships. Representative Dutch research in 1989 revealed that 23 percent of young women (up to 24 years old) experienced unilateral violence from a boyfriend at some time. Unfortunately, no specific data was presented about the particular acts of violence experienced. The authors admit that females also hit males, but they accept a commonly held position that there is underreporting of violence by men and overreporting of violence by women. As a researcher, I have in part promoted such a view (Riggs *et al.* 1989; Jouriles and O'Leary 1985). However, with teens, this issue of over- and underreporting cannot be simply extrapolated from work with adult couples, particularly adult clinical couples, for the reports of high school students ($N = 3{,}200$) indicate that physical aggression toward males is more common than physical aggression toward females, even if one uses only reports from the females. That is, our research using self-reports of high school students has shown that females report engaging in more physical aggression than males. However, based on some research with college females about reasons for their use of physical aggression, I believe that ultimately it will be shown that teenage females often engage in physical aggression because their boyfriends or dates made unwanted sexual advances. More specifically, in approximately one-third of the instances of female physical aggression, they reported that they acted in response to an unwanted sexual advance (Kelly and O'Leary 1996).

The interviews in the Netherlands with the twenty young women in seriously abusive relationships were intriguing and very informative. The depictions of the relationships started on average at age 14, and of special interest, the males were approximately four years older than the females. I found the accounts of the young women especially interesting as they depicted what they like about their dating partners. Two-thirds of the girls were "extremely fascinated by the strength of their boyfriend." They seemed to "projectively identify" with a powerful, protective boyfriend. This was illustrated in the following quotation: "The most attractive thing in my eyes was his macho behavior. It made him stronger than my parents and I had such influence over him that he would stand up for me." Another girl described her feeling of being protected as follows: "I felt safe and protected with him. Because once when someone pinched my bottom he beat him up completely."

The first chapter in the extended family section nicely illustrates how members of an extended family in Greece, as individuals and as a unit, can have very strong influences on members of a nuclear family. A Greek value, philotimo (Love of Honor), is used to conceptualize an intrafamily mediation strategy, in the chapter by Vana Theodossopoulou-Papalois and Mara Theodossopoulou. The conflict is about an economic transaction between family members that was made in the spirit of trust rather than through legal means. The Greek family was described as one in which "the father controls the economic power and is an authoritarian in his relationship with the spouse and the children." No data is provided to justify this claim but it is one that I have often heard. Similar depictions have been made of other family values including those of US citizens, but when we have attempted to document the power differential by looking at power *vis-à-vis* particular topics on which husband and wives might have differential influence, the results were not so clear cut (Rathus 1996). Similarly, research with some Hispanic populations has not borne out a unilateral male dominant family structure. Further, the Theodossopoulous also report literature that suggests that the traditional hierarchical views are gradually being rejected by people, especially the young. Yet, as was apparent from the transcripts, even well-educated people like John, the architect, believed that philotimo is "something you are born with." At the same time, however, John questioned how two people from the same family could differ so much in the extent to which they have philotimo. It may seem far-fetched to think that such a trait could be inherited yet research in the last decade has shown that approximately 50 percent of the variance in a wide range of personality traits is due to genetic influences (Rushton *et al.* 1995), and those influences include altruism. The case study makes clear that the concept of philotimo is very influential in the family life of some people and that it has a strong influence.

The chapter by Le Gall (in the extended family section) documents how strong family values are in France. The recent infatuation with genealogy along with fifty surveys conducted from 1968 to 1988 are said to reflect the strong interest in family values. On the other hand, France has an increase in divorce, drop in birth rate, and an increase in the number of births out of wedlock. Interestingly, Le Gall argues that it is not so much the family that is in crisis in France as it is marriage. "As conjugal disagreements easily bring about separation, matrimony becomes fragile."

Family conflict is used as an explanatory concept to describe how small conflicts can escalate from trivial misunderstandings to arguments that trigger intense hatred. Of special interest to me, because of my research on partner violence, was the characterization of marital violence as being viewed differently in the upper and lower socioeconomic classes. "To a certain extent, slaps on the face would not be perceived by men as an act of violence but rather as a normal end to an increased aggression coming from women." They went on to say, "The men resort quickly to violence when they can no longer contain a verbal attack which is a more feminine technique of contesting." In contrast to the patriarchical view portrayed of Greek families in the next chapter, Le Gall describes a contradiction in family life that was characterized by Schwartz (1990). "Governing of household affairs is feminine and the fiction of authority should rest in the masculine."

The work of Le Gall in France, as well as research by the Theodossopoulous in Greece, utilize narrative accounts of family life. The family novel is used by Le Gall to portray, through teenagers' reports, what happened in a family. The narrative account appears infrequently in journals in the United States (e.g. *Family Psychology*), but it has a richness that is missing in much of laboratory-based research and even in some of our highly structured interviews. What is not made explicit, however, is how the interviewer moved from one topic to another and/or how the interviewer's own theoretical conceptualizations influenced the structure of the interviews and their outcomes. As I have noted earlier, in qualitative research, making explicit one's conceptual biases becomes especially critical (Murphy and O'Leary 1994 ).

Using Klein and Johnson's characterization, violence was described as "one of the conflict strategies or behaviors intended to manage or resolve conflict" in the chapter by Kwiatkowska. According to a 1993 survey, 8 percent of Polish women had been repeatedly battered by their husbands, and another 8 percent of women reported sporadic beatings. Unfortunately, it was not stated whether these were lifetime prevalence rates or not. It was a surprise, however, to learn that a survey of 11- to 13-year-old students revealed that approximately 50 percent of the children reported a number of physically punitive means used against them, including use of an open hand, being punched with a fist and being beaten with a leather belt. Moreover, 50 percent of the children said that they "would beat their own children." Kwiatkowska addressed the difficulty of making comparisons, but what she makes clear is that Poland is denying the existence of family violence. She states that there is no official policy addressing the issue, little professional attention paid to it, and lack of discussion of the problem in the public media. Moreover, she conveys the common stereotype that has long been seen in the USA, namely, that violence only occurs in families with alcohol problems. Gender stereotypes have long been alleged to be associated with family violence, and Kwiatkowska uses the cultural stereotypes in Poland to attempt to understand crucial roles in facilitating aggression toward women, in justifying aggression, and in reacting to aggression. More specifically, she looks at the Virgin Mary cult, the martyr "Mother-Pole," and the communist past with its "fake" egalitarian values. The study showed that some stereotypes are associated with beliefs related to violence, especially "the image of the Father which must be complemented by the image of the Mother." The next step will be to show that the stereotypes are related to actual reports of physical abuse against a partner.

Sørensen, an anthropologist, argues that violence is a strategically and consciously employed resource. He found that there is a great deal of wife blaming in Greenland; 75 percent of men and 88 percent of women believe that the victims bring violence on themselves. As he notes, most people perceive male violence as an unfortunate but understandable way out of certain situations. As portrayed in various chapters throughout this book, wife beating is seen as a problem of the lower classes even though it is fairly well known that high-ranking officials in Nuuk, Greenland, beat their wives. Of special interest, violence is seen as a symptom of structural change, and individual agency is largely ignored. Violence is imagined as "imported"—as originating elsewhere.

The final chapter by Hagemann-White portrays the transition of violence from a radical feminist issue to one of mainstream women's politics in Germany, and progress is well illustrated by the numbers of shelters, crisis centers, and various services for victims. The continued silence of men about violence is apparently due to their "collective guilt." An intriguing issue raised by Hagemann-White is that the conceptualizations of violence by feminists may have the unwitting effect of normalizing violence. She also notes that the "sweeping theories of patriarchical domination by threat of rape and battering" have not survived as a "lasting orientation for practical and political work with women who have been attacked and violated," for these views "implicitly place all women in the role of a victim from birth, and convict all men of collaboration by virtue of their masculinity." This last chapter illustrates a problem that exists in many parts of the world, namely, that men and women have not been working well *together* to address problems of wife abuse, partner violence, and family violence. One reason that this is true is that there is little conceptualization of men in a positive light, even though most men do not beat their partners. Positive male role models are rarely given any prominence. Until such is done, progress will continue to be more an advocacy issue rather than a cooperative venture of both genders. In some men (and some women), physical aggression against a partner can be a very stable phenomenon that is hard to stop or treat, and it is useful for us to be open minded about new conceptualizations of the etiology and treatment of this major social issue. In the United States, applying single-minded solutions such as mandatory arrest and using power-oriented psychoeducational interventions simply do not help all individuals. In fact, we do not have a body of literature to confirm that any single solution, or even combination of solutions, works. Thus, keeping an open mind about promising trends and interventions is the most likely prospect to help move this field forward.

## BIBLIOGRAPHY

Arnold, E.H., O'Leary, S.G. and Edwards, G.H. (1996) "Father involvement and dysfunctional parenting of children with Attention-Deficit/Hyperactivity disorder," *Journal of Consulting and Clinical Psychology* 65: 337–342.

Avery-Leaf, S.N., Cascardi, M., O'Leary, K.D. and Slep, A.M.S. (1997) "Procedural issues, design aspects, and baseline data from the dating violence prevention project," paper presented at the Fifth International Family Violence Research Conference, Durham, N.H.

Bell, C.C., Jenkins, E.J., Kpo, W. and Rhodes, H. (1994) "Response of emergency rooms to victims of interpersonal violence," *Hospital and Community Psychiatry* 45: 142–146.

Campbell, J.C. (1989) "A test of two explanatory models of women's responses to battering," *Nursing Research* 38: 18–24.

Daly, M. and Wilson, M. (1988, October 28) "Evolutionary social psychology and family homicide," *Science* 242: 519–524.

Dutton, D. (1995) *Domestic assault of women: Psychological and criminal justice perspectives*, Vancouver, BC: University of British Columbia Press.

Foshee, V.A., Linder, G.F., Bauman, K.E., Langwick, S.A., Arriage, X.B., Heath, J.L., McMahon, P.M. and Bangdiwala, S. (1996) "The safe dates project: Theoretical basis, evaluation design, and selected baseline findings," *American Journal of Preventive Medicine* 12: 39–47.

Hamberger, L.K. and Hasting, J.E. (1991) "Personality correlates of men who batter and nonviolent men: Some continuities and discontinuities, *Journal of Family Violence* 6: 131–147.

Jouriles, E.N. and O'Leary, K.D. (1985) "Interspousal reliability of reports of marital violence," *Journal of Consulting and Clinical Psychology* 53: 419–421.

Kelly, C. and O'Leary, K.D. (1996) "Conflict in high school dating relationships," unpublished undergraduate honors thesis, University at Stony Brook, Stony Brook, New York.

Lorber, R., Felton, D. and Reid, J.B. (1984) "A social learning approach to the reduction of coercive processes in child abuse families: A molecular analysis," *Advances of Behavior Research and Therapy* 6: 29–45.

Markowitz, P.I. and Coccaro, E.F. (1995) "Biological studies of impulsivity, aggression, and suicidal behavior," in E. Hollander and D.J. Stein (eds) *Impulsivity and aggression*, New York: Wiley.

McLaughlin, I.G., Leonard, K.E. and Senchak, M. (1992) "Prevalence and distribution of premarital aggression among couples applying for a marriage license," *Journal of Family Violence* 7: 309–319.

Murphy, C.M. and O'Leary, K.D. (1994) "Research paradigms, values, and spouse abuse," *Journal of Interpersonal Violence* 9: 207–223.

Murphy, C.M., Meyer, S.L. and O'Leary, K.D. (1993) "Family of origin violence and MCMI-II psychopathology among partner assaultive men," *Violence and Victims* 8: 165–176.

Neidig, P.H., Heyman R.E. and Slep, A.M.S. (1995) *Domestic conflict containment phase II: Parenting; Workbook*, Stony Brook, NY: Behavioral Science Associates.
O'Leary, K.D., Barling, J., Arias, I., Rosenbaum, A., Malone, J. and Tyree, A. (1989) "Prevalence and stability of physical aggression between spouses: A longitudinal analysis," *Journal of Consulting and Clinical Psychology* 57: 263–268.
O'Leary, K.D. and Jacobson, N.S. (1997) "Partner relational problems with physical abuse," in DSM-VI Source Book Volume III, Washington, DC: American Psychiatric Association.
O'Leary, K.D., Malone, J. and Tyree, A. (1994) "Physical aggression in early marriage: Prerelationship and relationship effects," *Journal of Consulting and Clinical Psychology* 62: 594–602.
O'Leary, K.D. (1993) "Through a psychological lens: Personality traits, personality disorders, and levels of violence," in R.J. Gelles and D.R. Loseke (eds) *Current controversies on family violence*, Newbury Park, CA: Sage.
Pan, H., Neidig, P.H. and O'Leary, K.D. (1994) "Predicting mild to severe husband to wife physical aggression," *Journal of Consulting and Clinical Psychology* 62: 975–981.
Plomin, R., Owen, M.J. and McGuffin, P. (1994, June 17) "The genetic basis of complex human behaviors," *Science* 264: 1733–1739.
Rathus, J. H. (1996) Unpublished doctoral dissertation, University at Stony Brook, Stony Brook, New York.
Reid, J.B., Taplin, P.S. and Lorber, R. (1981) "A social interactional approach to the treatment of abusive families," in R.B. Stuart (ed.) *Violent behavior: Social learning approaches to prediction, management, and treatment*, New York: Brunner/Mazel.
Ridley, M. (1993) *The red queen*, New York: Macmillan.
Riggs, D.S., Murphy, C.M. and O'Leary, K.D. (1989) "Intentional falsification in reports of interpartner aggression," *Journal of Interpersonal Violence* 4: 220–232.
Rosenbaum, A. and Hoge, S.K. (1989) "Head injury and marital aggression," *American Journal of Psychiatry* 146: 1048–1051.
Rushton, J.P., Fulker, D.W., Neale, M.C., Nias, D.K.B. and Eysenck, H.J. (1995) "Altruism and aggression: The heritability of individual differences," *Journal of Personality and Social Psychology* 50: 1192–1198.
Schwartz, O. (1990) *Le monde privé des ouvriers: Hommes et femmes du Nord*, Paris: PUF.
Straus, M.A. and Gelles, R.J. (1986) "Societal change and change in family violence from 1975–1985 as revealed by two national surveys," *Journal of Marriage and the Family* 48: 465–479.
Vivian, D. and O'Leary, K.D. (July, 1987) "Communication patterns in physically aggressive engaged couples," paper presented at the Third National Family Violence Research Conference, University of New Hampshire, Durham, N.H.
Warnken, W.J., Rosenbaum, A., Fletcher, K.E., Hoge, S.K. and Adelman, S.A. (1994) "Head-injured males: A population at risk for relationship aggression?" *Violence and Victims* 9: 153–166.
Wilkinson, S. (1981) "Personal constructs and private explanations," in C. Antaki (ed.) *The psychology of ordinary explanations of social behavior*, New York and London: Academic Press.
Wolfe, D. (1987) *Child abuse: Implications for child development and psychopathology*, Beverly Hills, CA: Sage.

# Name index

# Subject index